YESTERDAY'S
Moments...

TODAY'S
Memories

BY
DAVID TURNER

PORTLAND • OREGON
INKWATERPRESS.COM

 *Scan QR Code to learn more about this title*

Copyright © 2016 by David Turner
Interior layout by Masha Shubin; Cover layout by Jayme Vincent
Edited by Andrew Durkin

All rights reserved. Except where explicitly stated, no part of this book may be reproduced or transmitted in any form or by any means whatsoever, including photocopying, recording or by any information storage and retrieval system, without written permission from the publisher and/or author.

Publisher: Inkwater Press

Paperback
ISBN-13 978-1-62901-315-2 | ISBN-10 1-62901-315-3

Kindle
ISBN-13 978-1-62901-316-9 | ISBN-10 1-62901-316-1

All paper is acid free and meets all ANSI standards for archival quality paper.

1 3 5 7 9 10 8 6 4 2

The port-lights glowed in the morning mist that rolled from the waters green.

And over the railing we grasped his fist as the dark tide came between.

We cheered the captain and cheered the crew, and our mates, times out of mind;

We cheered the land he was going to and the land he had left behind.

We roared Lang Syne as a last farewell but my heart seemed out of joint;

I well remember the hush that fell when the steamer had passed the point.

We drifted home through the public bars, we were ten times less by one

Who sailed out under the morning stars, and under the rising sun.

And one by one and two by two, they have sailed from the wharf since then;

I've said good-bye to the last I knew, the last of the careless men.

And I can't but think that the times we had were the best times after all

As I turn aside with a lonely glass and drink to the bar-room wall....

For they marry and go and the world rolls back, they marry and vanish and die;

But their spirit shall live on the Outside Track as long as the years go by.

From "The Outside Track" by Henry Lawson (1867–1922)

Contents

The Carruthers Brothers 1
The Promise and the Dream 9
Oats and Books and Gasoline 19
Hard Work and Hard Living 29
Warm Tubes and Cold Nights 41
The Singhampton-Sudbury Shuttle 54
Rural Escape 63
A Christmas to Remember 73
Victor, Nipper, and I 81
Two Wheels Are All You Need 88
Triple Triangle…Trial and Triumph 97
A Valentine Story 112
A Roll of the Dice 121
Too Much Is Not Enough 129
Ladies and Gentlemen… 136
Battle of the Ballot 142
Water From the Wells of Home 152
What's in a Name 159
Old Cars and Diesels 163
What Could Go Wrong? 174
Midnight at Molly's 183

Highways and Holidays	195
South Wind	202
Jennifer, God, and Me	212
Fair-Weathered Friend	224
Come to the Parade	230
Beans, Tales, and Rusty Nails	237
News Travels Fast	250
Architects of Harvest	255
Mother Nature Has the Final Word	265
The Bard of Thornhill	272
Lesson Learned	281
The House on Hickson	286
Meet Me at the Coffee Shop	293
Beyond the Silver Moon	300
Wedding Bell Blues	312
Lest I Forget	319
World Through a Windshield	325
Treasured Memories	338
Homestead on the Hill	350
Rural Poetry…Final Glance	364
Epilogue	372

YESTERDAY'S MOMENTS...TODAY'S MEMORIES

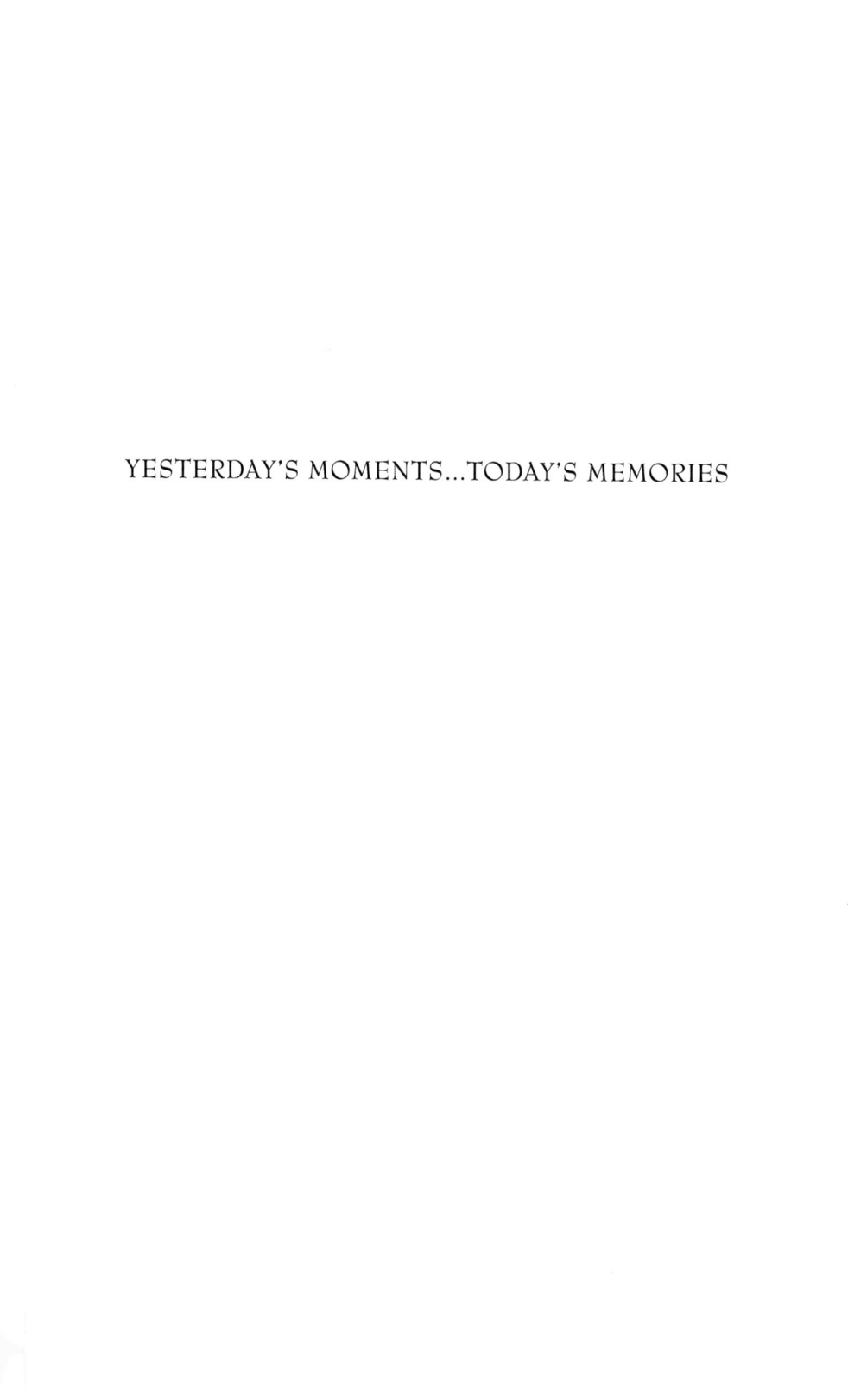

The Carruthers Brothers

SCOTLAND, DEPENDING UPON WHERE ONE RESEARCHES, IS listed either as a country, an autonomous region, or a division of what is known officially as The United Kingdom of Great Britain and Northern Ireland...or, in its common name, simply as the UK.

By whatever label, Scotland claims thirty-three counties, and within one of these, Dumfriesshire, lie hidden the roots of my maternal ancestral heritage—roots I can trace back five generations to James Carruthers, who was born in the early 1790s.

Some of these ancestors I have already written about; others you'll get to know as you read farther into this book. In the meantime, here's a sampling of a few I found interesting for one reason or another.

James Carruthers had eight sons...one son, Robert, emigrated from his homeland in the 1840s and farmed near the village of Beeton in the southern Ontario county of

Simcoe. In 1869, he relocated to Grey County, purchasing land near East Mountain, a tiny community situated in the northeast region of Artemesia Township.

Robert Carruthers' farm was as self-sufficient as an enterprise could be: wheat provided flour for baking while the oat crop produced porridge. Eggs were produced from a docile flock of Barred Rock chickens, and milk was courtesy a mixed herd of Aberdeen Angus and Shorthorn cattle. As with most farms in the area, a diversity of vegetables from a mammoth garden provided the balance of a staple diet.

But Robert's homestead extended far beyond "most farms." Sugar was purchased only during the autumn preserving season. Routine sweetener was honey, courtesy of a small apiary nestled in between two clover fields behind the house; when the honey supply was depleted, molasses, purchased in 45-gallon barrels, sufficed. A generous orchard offered a substantial variety of fruit trees: apples and pears of course, but less routine produce such as cherries, plums and peaches flourished as well within its cedar rail boundary.

Robert Carruthers was a horticultural visionary, even experimenting with grapes. Despite being considered "ungrowable" and "unsustainable" by agricultural research standards of the day because of deficient heat units...the purple fruit provided for an entire generation.

James Carruthers, a grandson of the original "James," emigrated from Scotland while still in his teens and acquired a job as a mechanic in the Toronto shipyards. It was here his fascination with all things nautical took root, propelling a dream that would eventually become a lifelong career: to sail the majestic steamships that plied the Atlantic waters between Britain and New York. Natural mechanical ability coupled with a sustained work ethic functioned in James's favour, eventually securing him the position of Chief Engineer aboard a number of the Cunard Line vessels. As head of engineering he oversaw and was responsible for all aspects of the ship's coal-fired propulsion system.

Throughout his marine career James sailed aboard some of the greatest passenger ocean liners ever launched: the *Carpathia*, which ran between Liverpool, New York, and Boston, as well as Cunard's luxurious trio of steamships: the *Mauretania, Aquitania,* and *Lusitania*. A significant proportion of his marine career was spent aboard the *Mauretania* on its magnificent Mediterranean cruises.

Luxury and speed were the benchmarks of superliners at the beginning of the twentieth century. When launched in 1906, the *Mauretania* was the world's largest passenger ship. But it would also attain the title of fastest, capturing the trans-Atlantic speed record for more than two decades.

The *Carpathia* would gain its footnote of naval notoriety by being the first ship on the scene on that April night in 1912, attempting to retrieve *Titanic* survivors from the icy cold waters of the North Atlantic. The *Carpathia* would have its own meeting with destiny six years later when it was sunk by a German submarine in the North Atlantic.

It wasn't a good time to be on a ship of any kind during the years of the "Great War" of 1914–18. Naval convoys were required for every Atlantic crossing. Despite the protection, disasters happened; fortunately for James, he wasn't aboard the *Lusitania* on May 7, 1915, when it was torpedoed by a German submarine off the coast of Ireland,

and sank quickly to the ocean floor, taking 1200 of its 1900 passengers with it.

George Carruthers, a nephew of James, began his career with the Grand Trunk Railroad, which at that time (1912–15) enjoyed a mainline rail monopoly stretching from Maine to Montreal, then westward across the southern perimeter of Ontario to Sarnia, before linking with its western subsidiaries in Michigan, Indiana, and Illinois.

From this main line, the GTR also owned and maintained thousands of miles of branch lines whose steel arteries spread like fissures of cracked glass throughout the towns and villages that were the soul of Ontario's outreaches in the early part of the twentieth century.

George began his career loading freight at Toronto's Union Station, then graduated from car maintenance to brakeman to engine fireman on one of GTR's branch lines. By the late 1920s he was working for GTR's mainline service.

A fireman's position on a mainline train was viewed with well-deserved respect in the trade. The huge locomotives providing the high-speed freight service of the period consumed vast amounts of coal...as much as a ton every ten miles. Some of the large, long-distance locomotives utilized an automatic delivery system that delivered coal to the firebox via steel auger; for a significant percentage of trains, however, the locomotive's greedy appetite could only be satisfied manually, one shovelful at a time. Headwinds, grades, temperature, barometric pressure, and most importantly, load weight all were contributing factors in how much coal was consumed on a given day.

Besides keeping the firebox stocked with a steady supply of coal, it was also a fireman's responsibility to maintain proper boiler pressure, and most critically, water level. The crown steel sheet—actually the ceiling of the firebox—was to be covered with at least four inches of water at all times. Failure to monitor this function could quickly cause a meltdown under the extreme firebox temperatures (2500 degrees F), leading to an eventual boiler catastrophe. By accident or inattentiveness, a "dry crown" was the major cause of boiler explosions, a condition spelling almost certain death for both fireman and engineer.

George Carruthers' regular route was Toronto to Trenton, an important terminus where freight and passenger cars were decoupled, switched, shunted, and transferred to various sidings. The locomotives were watered and oiled, and the coal tenders refilled. Here the Toronto crew were relieved by a fresh team who continued east to Montreal, while the former piloted the next westbound back to Toronto.

Meals of that era were the same for most blue-collared workers: a thermos of coffee, supplemented by sandwiches and pie carried in a bucket from home. Supplying a steady diet of coal to the firebox left little time for any refreshment other than water and perhaps a sandwich. But on occasion, when fortune found the crew aboard an engine with an automatic feeder, they'd use the free time to advantage and cook a hot meal. A favourite practice was to utilize the burning coal for an oven: at 2500 degrees a pot of potatoes suspended over the fire would boil in no time. The coal shovel—washed, one would imagine—made an ideal frying pan. Just lay bacon or sausages on the shovel and hold it over the fire. In the mood for steak? Just insert the shovel into the inferno until it glowed red, retract, and plop the steak on it. As good as any barbecue!

The automatic auger supplying coal to the firebox was

a huge improvement in working conditions for railroad firemen, especially those on long-distance heavy freights. But it didn't mean the fireman could simply take a nap in the corner of the engineer's cabin. Because steam pressure powered the auger's metering system, boiler temperature and pressure had to be maintained, and the crucial water level on the crown sheet still had to be monitored.

George didn't enjoy a long life, succumbing to cancer at the age of fifty. Whether his nearly thirty years of exposure to coal smoke had any bearing would only be conjecture.

Dave Carruthers, George's older brother, had a harder time settling on an occupation. He spent a number of years working in a variety of Toronto factories—the longest at Swift's Packing, one of the larger meat processing facilities at the time. He even operated his own general store for several years. Variety of employment seemed to be his strength and aptitude.

Since horses were still the dominant transportation at that time, it's noteworthy that according to the Federal Canadian Census of 1910, Dave Carruthers' occupation is listed as "hay dealer."

Dave's favourite avocation was horticulture; on his few acres of property in Longbranch, a village on Toronto's western fringe, he'd erected a greenhouse and nurtured various species of tropical and domestic plant life. He even made a half-hearted effort to turn this venture into a business, but for the most part it was solely for his personal enjoyment.

Another passion was automobiles: a dream born in the closing months of the nineteenth century, on the day he witnessed his first car spluttering and smoking its way down Toronto's main north-south corridor, Yonge Street.

A dozen years would pass before he owned his first car,

but his desire never wavered. The make and model has been lost to history. There's a photograph of my mother at age four or five posing in front of her uncle's car, but all that can be seen clearly is the left front fender and wheel.

Except for special occasions such as funerals or weddings, Sunday was the only day of the week Dave Carruthers ventured out with his prize—and then only in fair weather. He'd spend Saturday tinkering, tuning, and tweaking, assuring all was in order for the trip the following day. Automobile dependency was low in this period. Consequently, the trip would be relatively short—often just to visit his family in the heart of the city.

With its expanse of brass hardware (including acetylene lanterns) polished and gleaming in the Sunday sunshine, and its wooden wheels sporting a fresh coat of varnish, Dave's car would appear, and any family member who wished to risk adventure would climb aboard for the ride.

The ride wouldn't be far, perhaps out to High Park, which in the early twentieth century was considered "out of the city." If it was a particularly hot day, a couple of stops were mandatory to allow time for a boiling radiator to cool; seldom would the expedition conclude without the familiar "pop" on one of the car's four corners. Everyone would disembark and the ordeal of changing the offending tire would commence. The initial task called for removal of the tire from the wooden rim. A little help was always welcomed at this point and passengers would jest how that was the only reason they were invited.

After a strenuous session of prying and pulling, the tire was freed and the tube extracted. The next task was to locate the leak, roughen the region adjacent to the rupture with a rasp provided in the tire changing kit, cement the area, cut a rubber patch of proper dimension and place it over the puncture. This involved maybe a five-minute waiting period while the contact cement adhered to the rubber. Once satisfied the patch was firmly anchored, the tube was reinserted and the tire wrestled back onto the rim. After about 200 strokes with the hand pump, you were ready to proceed: a long way from today, when tires go for years without issue, and most drivers can't recall their last flat.

The Promise and the Dream

IN THE PRECEDING CHAPTER I INTRODUCED YOU TO A FEW OF MY relatives from the Carruthers side of the family. This chapter features my great-grandfather Thomas Carruthers, who in 1882 followed the lead of previous generations, emigrating with his wife Mary from the craggy coves and rolling moors of southern Scotland for Canada.

Like so many before, they'd read with intrigue the government brochures promoting the potential of this "new" land. Canada was an endless expanse of geography promising unlimited opportunity. Motivation and determination were seemingly the only ingredients required to unlock its immeasurable fortunes.

Following a month-long ocean crossing to New York, Tom and Mary eventually made their way to southern Ontario, renting a small acreage west of the city, where they proceeded to raise sheep and cattle. History records a short stay for my great-grandparents, who then relocated to

Toronto and rented a house on Dovercourt Avenue, deep in the city's core.

Although details concerning their farming venture remain shrouded, the selection of vocation is clear. Land tillage and livestock husbandry were the foundation on which generations of Carruthers had built their lives.

In that regard, Toronto's attributes could hardly have been more conflicting. As with most industrial centres of that era, inadequate and overtaxed sanitation systems plagued Ontario's capital. Air quality was impacted by factory chimneys billowing clouds of coal smoke, which combined with the durable essence of horse manure, urine, discarded garbage, and raw sewage.

Other shortcomings included the lack of hard-surfaced streets and sidewalks. Only on main thoroughfares, where horse-drawn streetcars prevailed, were there remnants of a solid surface. Concrete and brick, where it existed, was rife with cavities, cracks, and fractures. Deficient storm drain infrastructure, readily apparent during periods of sustained precipitation, had earned Toronto the nickname of "Muddy York." Although "Toronto" had been its legally registered name since 1834, the derogatory designation would continue for decades.

It seems Toronto had environmental challenges regardless of season; in summer, the muddy avenues were transformed into inches of choking dust mixed with horse manure. During the winter, pedestrians were greeted with a frozen layer of mud, ice, snow, and horse manure.

Commerce was exceedingly class-driven. Instead of striving for the good of all, what existed was no more than a loose collection of self-centred interests. Political affiliation and religious belief set the standard for employment, and success or failure largely depended upon applicant response. Factories in many cases were simply slave houses with barely sustainable wages. No protection of workers' rights existed, employees being at the mercy of management. Nearly impossible production goals thrust upon workers was common practice—if you missed your quota... you got nothing. If you complained, your choices were simple—quit or be fired. Either way, no problem; there was a long waiting line of unemployed.

Recreation was limited, divided by class and governed by resource. Industrial and business entrepreneurs frequently pursued careers in politics, hoping for increased power and wealth, while for the working class—especially the segment who struggled at the low end of the economic trough—there were few diversions from the monotony and stress of ten-hour days labouring in grimy factories. For many, the escape route was booze—relatively cheap and readily available.

Alcohol consumption was a major social issue of the time; the majority of arrests on any given day would be alcohol related. Bootlegging was rampant, profitable, and largely ignored by the authorities. Businessmen, lawyers, local politicians, and police themselves often discreetly participated.

The spectacle of over-inebriated residents sprawled on park benches, slumped against lamp posts, or simply lying on sidewalks was common. During winter, for their own protection, indisposed citizens were either transported to the nearest jail cell or home...if they could recall where that might be. In summer it was more economically prudent to simply let them sleep it off.

Toronto's challenges were not unlike the growing pains of any North American or European city; health and welfare reform moved painfully slowly and social and economic circumstances changed little. This was certainly not the dream promised in the brochures, but whatever the geographical, social, or economic boundaries, the axiom was constant: "Life is what life is, and one does what one can."

Tom Carruthers laboured at a variety of trades as he adjusted to Canadian life. He delivered freight by horse and wagon, from the trains at Union Station to businesses scattered across the expanding city. He drove a bakery wagon. He even owned a bakery for a while—an unprofitable venture lasting less than a year. Several factory jobs of varied description were followed by a stint loading and unloading cargo ships at Toronto's waterfront.

My great-grandfather's turnover of occupations must have made for an entertaining employment resume; the question of such diversity is interesting. Was he unable to secure steady employment? Did he vacate these positions voluntarily? Was he continually fired? Or was he merely searching for the right job? One can only speculate.

The Massey Manufacturing Company was another addition to his lengthy resume. Tom joined the agricultural company in 1887, working in the implement painting department. His apprenticeship preceded by four years the merger of Massey Manufacturing and its lifelong competitor A. Harris & Son of Brantford. The company then became known as Massey-Harris—although from day one my great-grandfather referred to it simply as "the Massey."

Economic conditions that had wavered between severe depression and mild recession for a decade began a decided turnaround as the new century dawned, with the manufacturing sector leading the upturn. Massey-Harris was definitely part of this financial surge, and although facing stiff competition from American rival International Harvester, M-H continued to lead with products second to none, tripling its workforce in the process.

By 1912 my great-grandfather had clocked twenty five years at Massey-Harris—an eternity for one who appeared to be creating a career of occupational instability. Through his tenure at Massey, Tom Carruthers had moved up the pay scale from eight to thirteen dollars a week, and to his credit was able to provide a stable economic environment for his wife and three sons. No doubt convinced that her husband was content to live out the balance of his working years at the M-H plant, Mary was probably surprised if not disappointed when Tom drew her attention to an advertisement for a general store in the Dufferin County hamlet of Marsville.

Noticing the ad a week earlier, my great-grandfather had quietly but methodically considered the position's feasibility. Satisfied the endeavour was workable, he began a prepared speech, promoting the benefits of freedom from paint factory fumes while relishing the open-air freshness of rural Ontario. Mary questioned their ability to operate a store, reminding her husband of the ill-fated bakery enterprise. Tom, expecting resistance, countered that at that juncture the country had been mired in economic stagnation.

"We've saved some money," he argued. "The boys are on their own. I'm fifty years old and have worked half my life at the Massey. If I'm ever to make a change…this is it."

Mary Carruthers had grown rather fond of Toronto, but accepted Tom's invitation to investigate. Living accommodations were located on the second floor and although approaching with limited enthusiasm, she discovered both the store and upstairs apartment to be in a good state of repair. Despite their "discussion," the nature of the times likely dictated Mary had little actual input in the final decision and simply resigned herself to her new role.

As events would dictate, Mary's reticence had merit, the Marsville undertaking being no more successful than their previous attempt at self-sufficiency. After just three years my great-grandparents returned to Toronto, renting a house on Lisgar Street.

Whatever motive or purpose intervened remains unknown...but the result was back to the city, back to Massey-Harris...and back to the painting department for my great-grandfather. With World War One—or the "Great War" as it was then known—in effect, and much of the labour force overseas, re-establishing employment would seem academic, begging the question why Tom would return to an occupation with which he'd obviously grown disenchanted...especially when more agreeable options existed.

One reason for my great-grandparents' return to Toronto may have been Mary Carruthers' health. Soon after their arrival she began to experience medical issues that graduated in severity. Due to the limitations of medical research and x-ray technology being only in its infancy, diagnostic assessment in this period remained cautionary. "Internal complications" was one determination, "catarrh of the stomach" another.

"Catarrh" was an overworked term of the period when physicians were simply unable to explain a certain illness or wished to "soften" a particular diagnosis: "catarrh of the lungs," "catarrh of the liver," "catarrh of the bowel"...all were utilized with frequency and found to be more comforting to a patient than a conclusion of cancer and its inherent connotations. Whatever the medical jargon, it probably meant little to Mary Carruthers, who passed away in her early fifties.

Ever since their return from the Marsville adventure, Tom and Mary, together with their son William and daughter-in-law Reba (my grandparents), and their now three children, had lived in the same rented house on Lisgar Street, an arrangement that continued after Mary died. With little construction during the previous years due to military demands and the upcoming population resurgence of returning soldiers, dwellings were becoming a scarce commodity, prompting discussions of investing in a house. In the spring of 1918, a duplex on Hickson Street just off Brock Avenue south of Dundas Street in the heart of Toronto's downtown became their new home.

Tom Carruthers purchased the house, and the deed was registered in his name. An agreement directed that Will and Reba pay a monthly rent of twenty dollars; a further understanding specified that Tom pay Will and Reba five dollars a week board. Although it appears complicated at first glance, this contract required little actual currency exchange.

Throughout the 1920s, money was never plentiful, but like most, the Carruthers managed. Christmas was spent on a rotating basis between family households. Tom's two brothers and a sister-in-law all lived within city boundaries. Tom purchased a goose every Christmas, regardless of where gatherings were held, and supplied all his family's meat needs year round. Close friends with a butcher who had a shop in the city, Tom was forever bringing home steaks and roasts. Week after week after week, it was the same thing...steaks and roasts. Reba appreciated her father-in-law's generosity, but occasionally would suggest a change...

pork chops perhaps? No problem. Pork chops would then be the feature week after week after week.

In 1927, at the mandatory retirement age of 65, Tom Carruthers bade farewell to the factory on King Street. With the exception of that interval in Marsville, he'd spent nearly forty years at "the Massey." Tom admitted missing the friendship of his fellow workers, some of whom had grown close. Something he didn't miss and hoped would change following retirement were the frequent bouts of stomach nausea endured from paint fumes.

To pass the time while adjusting to his non-working schedule, Tom took a job as bookkeeper for an organization providing funds for people who were enduring difficult times and needed financial assistance. If for instance a breadwinner was taken ill and unable to provide, the agency would attempt to offer relief for his family. Or in cases where a person passed away destitute, the association would extend funds for a decent burial. My great-grandfather spent considerable time keeping the company ledger current: membership dues, transaction amounts, additions and debits, who received what…all were duly recorded, neatly and accurately in his old country script.

Now retired, my great-grandfather was able to devote more time to his favourite pastime…reading. Newspapers never received a more thorough evaluation. No less than three printed news sources arrived at the Carruthers' porch each day: *The Mail and Empire*, *The Globe and Mail*, and *The Daily Star*. As time passed, the *Daily Star* became the main household resource for world happenings…but never the *Telegram*.

"The Tely's too Tory!" Tom would argue. That was true enough, as the *Telegram*'s editorials leaned heavily towards the Conservative viewpoint. However, the *Daily Star* was just as biased towards the Liberals. (Since the Carruthers were stalwart Grits from generations back, this issue was conveniently overlooked.)

Partisan bias was certainly not exclusive to Toronto. In this stage of the late nineteenth century, "objective journalism" failed to exist just about anywhere in the North American print media; practically every daily newspaper was owned, subsidized, or controlled by one of the leading political parties. In many cases editors themselves were sitting members of Parliament, often promoting personal causes within their editorials and attacking rival opinions without mercy...and usually without proof. Truth, unless it favoured your particular agenda, was discouraged, dismissed or simply ignored. Prejudice, gossip, smear tactics, slander, fabrication, larceny, and blatant lies...that's what sold newspapers.

Tom Carruthers didn't enjoy a long retirement, just four years, before succumbing to stomach cancer, adding credence to the theory that his career exposed to lead-based paints was at least partly responsible. (More than thirty years would pass before the true effects of lead poisoning would be brought into focus and guidelines and restrictions on lead content in paints established.)

A few days following the funeral, when the family gathered to read Tom's final testament, it was a surprise to no one that the Hickson Street house had been bequeathed to my grandparents. Ever since Will and Reba's wedding two decades earlier, they'd shared a common roof.

Tom Carruthers was far removed from the stereotypical stigma of his Scottish ancestry. He was a caring and generous man when it came to friends and family, especially his daughter-in-law Reba, whom he regarded very highly. He loved buying Christmas and birthday gifts for his grandchildren and was always the focus of family get-togethers. His legacy would prove to be a study in contradiction...flamboyant yet understated, confident yet cautious, assured yet unpretentious...and his absence would not be recognized without adjustment.

Oats and Books and Gasoline

"Good morning, boys and girls."
"Good morning, Miss Acheson."

For first-year students Harold and Evelyn Turner, who hadn't a clue of their new teacher's name, it was a rather feeble greeting. While introductions and announcements were being dispensed, the two sat quietly analyzing their surroundings.

Occupying the room from side to side in increasing dimension were five rows of maple desks. A series of blackboards blanketed the front and part of the side walls, while portraits of past and present monarchs stood silent vigil from various locations. At the front of the classroom was the teacher's desk, behind which a large wall clock ticked away quietly. A cast iron wood stove situated at the rear of the single-room building completed the scene.

Artemesia Township S.S. #9, the school where my father and his sister received their primary education, was referred to locally as simply the "The 8th Line School." A log structure when built in the 1860s, the schoolhouse had undergone a major rebuilding four years earlier, in 1916. At that time it had been framed and bricked, and whether to save money, time, or heat, the five west windows were bricked in, leaving only the five east windows to provide natural light. This was many years before hydro arrived in the township, so during winter's short days, "gloomy" was the key word by mid-afternoon.

Wood was the daily heat source, and part of every area farmer's job was to provide a portion of the school's yearly supply. That cast iron stove during the season's coldest days was the nucleus of the classroom. Around it you studied, dried your clothes, and ate your lunch. Frequent trips by senior boys to the woodshed kept the stove generating heat throughout the day.

In rural schoolhouses during the 1920s, luxuries were few and subjects basic but detailed. Great stress was placed on reading, spelling, and grammar. No notebooks were provided by the school board, so students made those they had last by erasing and re-using pages. As well, slates were used extensively to save paper. Lunch, generally consisting of pie and sandwiches, was carried in a lard pail, with the pie on top so it wouldn't get squashed. Dad always ate his meal in the order it was removed from the pail...pie first, sandwiches for dessert.

Pupil count was low, so unlike their city counterparts, boys and girls played together at recess. Softball dominated athletic period, starting in September and continuing until the snow fell. The ball consisted simply of a chunk of cork wrapped with an unravelled wool sock and bound with tape. A tree branch sufficed for a bat, while rocks provided the bases.

Home education was basic as well: Harold and Evelyn accomplished their homework at the kitchen table by coal oil lamp, and if by chance their mother needed something from the pantry or cellar, she simply carried the light source with her and they sat in the dark until she returned. So they could concentrate on their studies, the Turners, unlike many rural children of that era, were asked to perform few farm chores during the week.

As an added incentive to good grades, the kids were offered one half cent for each passing mark achieved. Both did well and accumulated a substantial account for the times. However, during a rough financial spell, the elder Turners borrowed what the children had saved. According to my father, they never did repay.

Evelyn was six, and Harold two months short of his fifth birthday, but their parents started them at school together. Although some questioned the decision, my father apparently needed the competitiveness of his sister to keep him motivated. He actually failed "second book" (grade three) but when Oliver Turner argued his son's case, the teacher relented. Figures were juggled and he was pushed through. From that point onward, Evelyn worked doubly hard, assuring Harold lived up to his potential.

No doubt part of the reason for my father's academic stumble at that point stemmed from the fact that his mother was in poor health and had been so for some time. Arriving home one afternoon from school, he and his sister were surprised to see their parents in the kitchen. Mother was wearing the dress she only wore to town, and Father was in a suit—both highly irregular for a weekday. Questioning revealed they'd been to the doctor, where Mother had been diagnosed with "a slight heart problem." What little information the medical field had of internal organs at the time pointed towards heart valve complications, and within a year Janie Turner was gone.

February 28, 1924, was a typical cold and blustery midwinter Grey County day. In the living room of Oliver Turner's house, a number of family members attired in black conversed in hushed tones among the floral tributes that surrounded the open casket. Routinely someone would comment how beautiful Janie looked, and to the children how their mother was now "sleeping with the angels." This "pagan exhibition," as my father called it, was something the nine-year-old would never forget and would haunt him for life.

By June 1927, Harold and Evelyn were counting down their last days at the 8th Line School. There was just one more hurdle: their high school entrance exam—a detailed two-hour cross section of subjects, including history, geography, grammar, literature, general mathematics, memory work, reading, and spelling. Administered at Flesherton High School, the exam cost one dollar per pupil.

Upon completion both students were assured graduation to high school, although Harold had an anxious moment when during the spelling portion he transposed "voracious" for "various." Fortunately there was more room for error than a single spelling goof.

Small in comparison to other educational institutions (105 students), to those recently graduated from a single-room environment, Flesherton Rural High School (its full title) was a major transition. Nowhere was this more apparent than during athletic period. Softball was still the game of choice, but here students were treated to a ball diamond with a wire mesh backstop, "real" bases, wooden bats, and a genuine softball.

As for academic subjects, pretty much the same as elementary school. What also didn't change was my father's love for history and literature. Whether it was modern history depicting the events of Canada's settlement, the exploits of the British monarchy, or all the way back to the Roman Empire made little difference to him. As for literature, high school opened up a brand-new cast of writers. Memory work was an essential force in the learning process, and Harold found it easy to memorize the lines penned by the greats of their day (seventy years later he could easily recall favourite passages from memory).

The trek to Flesherton each winter's day was a frigid ride...and first thing in the morning, the upstairs of the house was little better. Although a large hardwood block was placed in the stove last thing before retiring, by morning it was but an orange glow. When Oliver arose, he'd revive the fire, but little heat seemed to reach the bedrooms above. The ideal location that time of morning was directly in front of the "Happy Thought" kitchen stove—the sooner the better. What a wonderful feeling as the crackling and spitting maple wood generated its warmth throughout the kitchen...but there was still that hour-long, seven-mile cutter ride ahead.

The only heat provided for this daily endurance test was the porridge in your belly and the hot bricks at your feet, heated on the stove then wrapped in a blanket just prior to departure. These bricks, along with a big fur blanket tight around your neck, would keep you warm for about half the trip. But too soon that familiar chill would settle, and on the coldest of days the two children would be nearly numb when they reached town. Their horse, Dolly, was boarded a short distance from the school throughout the day, but this was shelter and water only. My dad would feed her oats and hay at noon, brought from home.

Dolly was a great little mare, according to my father, but high-strung. One morning Harold and Evelyn came up behind a team of horses, pulling a load of lumber up the long grade that led into the village of Flesherton. Dolly was impatiently plodding along behind the encumbrance when suddenly the pin securing the load dislodged, sending the heavy lumber-laden sleigh sliding back down the hill towards her.

The mare reacted instantly, catapulting sideways up the embankment of snow lining the road, overturning the cutter and spilling its contents of blankets, bricks, hay, oats, and human cargo into the deep snow. After determining that neither he nor his sister was hurt, Dad looked around for Dolly, expecting her to be halfway home. But there she was, perhaps fifty feet away, standing alongside a fencepost. Valuable time was consumed righting the cutter, digging everything out of the snow that had been tossed out...and most importantly, persuading Dolly to be re-harnessed.

When spring arrived, Oliver worked out an arrangement with neighbour Alex Cameron whereby Harold and Evelyn would ride to school with their son and daughter in the Cameron family's Chevrolet. A trip more than an hour by horse was now shortened to an amazing ten or fifteen minutes! To my father this was the only way to travel and dreamed of the day he'd be behind the wheel, speeding along the back roads of Artemesia Township.

As recently as five years earlier, an automobile sighting

had been rare, but was now almost a regular feature. One could detect the scent of their internal combustion engines long before they chugged into view. Ford's Model "T" was the mainstay, but Chevrolet's 490 (the model number denoted the price when new) was giving the leader a run. Less common but equally interesting were the Star, Hudson, Grey Dort, Durant, Rickenbacker, Studebaker, Whippet, Essex...

An event about this time (1927) that captured local attention was the marriage of Oliver Turner to Mamie Magee, his late wife Janie's sister.

At this point it would be titillating to imagine how this romance had been simmering in the wings for years, waiting for opportunity. Sorry...this marriage had "arrangement" stamped on it from the beginning, Janie's mother in fact vowing to her daughter on her deathbed that she would "keep the family together" and "no outsider" would ever come between her and her two grandchildren, Harold and Evelyn.

It had been three years since Janie Turner's passing, and while confusing at first that Aunt Mamie was now considered their mother, the fact she was living with them was certainly no issue. For as long as both Harold and Evelyn could recall, Mamie and her unmarried sister Isla had appeared at Oliver and Janie's door any time a squabble had developed at their own home. (This happened frequently.)

Although enjoying an amicable relationship for the most part, unlike his sister, my father would never be comfortable calling Mamie "mother." When pressed, his comment was simply, "Why would I call her mother when she wasn't?"

Transportation to school undertook a new twist a couple of years later when my dad received his driver's license...even though he was just fourteen. An obscure rule in the Department of Transport legislation stated that an underage person could apply for a license under special circumstances. As six students within a concession block were in need of a ride, Oliver foresaw a chauffeur service that would satisfy their needs and generate a little cash as well. Being a close friend of the examiner probably had some bearing on the ruling.

A year earlier, Oliver had traded his 1923 Ford Model T for a new model. The most welcome change between the two Fords was the fact the new one was fully enclosed with real doors—a definite advantage over the previous car, where side curtains had to be unsnapped and re-buttoned each time one entered or exited.

Harold's passengers were his sister Evelyn, as well as neighbours Christena and Rowena Magee, Dorothy Jamieson, and Muriel Cameron. Six made for a snug squeeze—plus Oliver routinely sent along a couple of bags of oats to be chopped at the mill in Flesherton. Often two or three departed groundhogs shared floor space as well. Dad was an excellent marksman, and a man in Flesherton paid a dime per carcass. He operated a fox farm where rodents were the preferred diet. For all this luxury, each passenger except Evelyn paid one dollar a week. A dollar bill would buy a week's gas. No thought was given to insurance.

By his own admission, my father gave little concern for his passengers. "Christena and Rowena walked up the hill to our place each morning. Even in the pouring rain I never considered picking them up. Same at night, I just dumped them at our gate."

On one occasion a neighbour girl approached my father concerning a ride home from school.

"It was probably a couple of miles out of my way. I told her gas cost money but she said she only had a dime. I answered I guess it was better than nothing, took her dime and grudgingly drove her home."

Throughout my father's three-year chauffeur service, only one accident marred an otherwise perfect driving record, and he was alone when it happened—sideswiping another vehicle on Flesherton's main street. The impact caught the left front fender of the Ford, folding it back towards the running board. The shopkeeper in front of whose store the incident happened stormed out of the doorway: "When two people can't meet on a street this wide without running into each other, neither should have a license!"

Harold was more concerned about the car and how he'd tell his father than the shopkeeper's lecture. A quick decision to take the car to McTavish's garage paid off, for when he returned after school to pick it up, the fender had been straightened and his dad never knew the difference.

A tragedy deeper than any mangled metal struck while in their third year of high school. It had started as such an exciting and important day: the annual field day trials, when township students pitted their athletic abilities against each other. All cheered and applauded as Muriel Cameron, one of the best athletes at Flesherton High, took honours in the high jump, broad jump, and running broad jump. A few days later Muriel took ill. Two days later she was diagnosed with polio. A week later she died. Just sixteen, her death was a crushing blow to the tight-knit community...especially her five co-riders.

1930 would mark the final year of the original gang. Another neighbour, Lucy MacDonald, replaced Muriel, but at the end of the school year, all four girls were headed for "normal school" (teacher's college), with aspirations to teach. Harold was still waffling on his own career choices...

teaching or accounting or maybe veterinary school. Whatever direction chosen, he reasoned a fifth-year "senior matriculation" diploma would be a definite asset.

The only subject really needed was chemistry, but to keep the year interesting, he also chose Latin, history, and algebra. He passed history easily, flunked Latin, and just barely survived algebra. Certain my father would post a failing grade in algebra, the teacher asked that he not write the exam for fear of pulling her class average down.

Chemistry, the very credit needed, was a disaster for everyone. The teacher was simply incompetent, with only one student of a class of fifteen managing a passing grade. For my father, who no longer had his sister for competition, it was truly a wasted year. So while Evelyn was successfully completing her year at college, my father went home to ponder his future, dejected that he was no farther ahead than a year before.

By this time, the worsening economic environment was tightening its grip, as the country gradually but steadily slid towards that abyss known as "The Great Depression." But it was still early in this "temporary economic slowdown," as the political leaders of the day referred to it. Prosperity, according to them, was "just around the corner."

...if only it could have been.

Hard Work and Hard Living

It had been a long hot season that summer of 1936, and career-wise Harold Turner was no further ahead than two years earlier when he left to make his fortune in Ontario's capital. Toronto was a heartless host in the centre of the country's greatest economic disintegration. Thus my father's business career lasted mere months, when bankruptcy and subsequent unemployment forced his return to the family's Grey County farm, to sweat through a continuous repetition of planting, haying, and harvest—the cycle broken only by long, cold, monotonous winters.

Hard work and long days never bothered my father... if there was some reward. While working in Toronto, he'd become accustomed to having spare cash in his pocket, but now it was back to simply "room and board," as economically the family farm was barely existing.

One Saturday evening, Harold and best friend Lester were parked on Eugenia's main street, discussing jobs and money and the scarcity of both. Although Harold's father had given permission to take the family car into town, neither had a quarter to contribute a gallon of gasoline to the Ford's nearly arid tank, so both were just basically watching the world pass by.

But this was Eugenia, where even on a summer Saturday night little of anything passed by: life merely strolled by in Eugenia with only the occasional burst of excitement to ignite a dormant populace. Perhaps a building catching fire or a cow detached from its local pasture, wandering aimlessly down the main street. This evening's high point had been the brand-new Pontiac coupe that had stopped at Cairns General store; both young men tried to imagine the feeling of owning such a fine car.

Between them they'd scrounged five cents for a chocolate bar, and while enjoying the rare treat, talked of what they might do to earn a few dollars. Harold checked each bite carefully as the conversation continued. The previous month, when he had broken a chocolate bar in half, a healthy white worm had crawled out. The remaining half had seemed unaffected, however, and there was no sense wasting it. A nickel was a nickel...especially in these challenging economic times.

Lester had a job prospect with the Markdale Creamery, accompanying their truck driver on his route. The position entailed opening gates, loading and unloading cream cans, and some driving. Lester could also supplement the job by helping on the driver's own farm when work was scarce. If he could secure a dollar a day plus board, Lester figured he'd go for it.

The conversation then turned to Harold's predicament.

"What about taking Evelyn's boy-friend's advice about raising mink?" Lester ventured.

Harold admitted giving thought to the suggestion. The boyfriend to whom Lester referred was Aubrey MacDonald. Although his family lived a few miles east of the Turners on the Grey-Simcoe County Line, Aubrey himself had worked for several years at the copper mines in Sudbury. In conjunction with the mining job, he also operated a mink ranch.

Over the years, while Aubrey and his sister dated, he and my father had become close friends. Through him, Harold gained extensive insight into the mink species: their breeding and feeding habits, how to construct an escape-proof cage, and most importantly, how to respect those knife-like teeth, which were capable of removing a human finger in an instant.

The more my father learned, the more he was convinced that a business opportunity awaited. Any financial venture during the 1930s involved creativity; by my father's calculation, the two leading principals of this endeavour would be the cost of breeding stock…and feed.

Start-up capital was paramount; about all Harold had going for him was good character and an honest reputation. Over the next few months my father pitched and promoted his business plan to anyone who'd listen…a dollar here, two dollars there, and if really lucky, maybe five. Aubrey himself pledged a significant portion of my father's initial costs, believing he had what was needed to operate and sustain an enterprise.

"Working with animals demands a special aptitude and commitment," coached Aubrey, "and you have that."

Cages were a significant expenditure. However, the owner of the Eugenia general store donated butter boxes, which worked well, being of sufficient dimensions to allow a good-sized runway for the animals to exercise—plus a sheltered segment, where the mink nested and weaned their young. The runway portion was fitted with wire mesh top and bottom. The mesh bottom facilitated cleaning and the open top was necessary for feeding.

Mink would devour almost any variety of meat, entertaining a special desire for poultry products. Dairy derivatives such as eggs and cheese were also popular. Although expensive, a commercial gruel containing variations of the above mixed with horsemeat made a fine mink menu. During summer, when groundhogs were plentiful, Harold substituted them for the equine portion of the minks' diet, to save costs.

At its peak, my father's mink ranch boasted seventy animals. With their sleek brown coats, white chin patches, spotted white chests and diminutive size, mink were classified by first-time observers as "kind of cute" and "gentle"; they were totally surprised at the ferocity of which mink were capable. Initial impressions were quickly dispelled at feeding time, when their intensity became clear. When the gruel was placed on the wire mesh those terrible teeth attacked with a vicious savagery unimagined.

One important aspect of mink-raising, Aubrey had repeatedly reminded his student, was keeping them in as good a humour as possible, especially when the females were weaning their young. The least sign of danger would send them into an absolute frenzy: a dog walking innocently by, a car starting in the yard, or any sudden unexpected noise.

Anyone in close proximity could easily tell when there was an issue, especially if they were downwind: an unmistakably strong, acrid odour, almost on a par with skunk, would saturate the air. Although unable to actually spray like a skunk, mink managed to release an equally nauseating scent through their glands. At times the females grew so fanatical they would protect their young against the unknown danger...by killing them. Seems rather pointless, doesn't it?

My father sold most of his mink pelts to furriers in downtown Toronto. Aubrey had been instrumental in locating buyers and negotiating contracts, mostly with Jewish merchants who paid between seven and twelve dollars a pelt. Through Aubrey, Dad learned that merchants preferred the darker pelts, as opposed to the lighter shades—and would pay accordingly.

While in the city, Aubrey would take care of other business my father found interesting...such as visiting the giant Canadian Tire store on Yonge Street in downtown Toronto: maybe to buy a pair of premium line snow tires for Sudbury's snow-clogged roads or an extra-strength battery to start a car on a minus-fifty-degree morning. Whatever one was looking for, this very first Canadian Tire store had it. Dad found it entertaining how the clerks rode up and down the warehouse aisles with a roller skate on one foot, to aid in efficiency.

My father had always been somewhat captivated by his brother-in-law. Through his eyes, Aubrey's life represented adventure, intrigue, and excitement, compared to the seemingly uninteresting and characterless qualities of his own.

This was not the reality, however. In the early 1930s, when the Depression was exerting severe hardship on the employment market, a nineteen-year-old Aubrey, along with lifelong friend Orton Neil, headed by train for the copper and nickel mines in Northern Ontario. With no money between them, they travelled the entire journey "hobo style," atop the roof of a boxcar, exposed to the scorching sun and the chilly nights. Rolling into Sudbury after two days of being constantly subjected to coal smoke from the locomotive engine, their faces were as black as the fuel itself.

Fifty years earlier, Sudbury was in the middle of what was considered a "worthless wilderness." That's what surveyors clambering over the endless miles of rock while mapping out a route for the Canadian Pacific Railway had continually posted in their journals. Then someone noticed some interesting bronze-tinted rock and jumped to the conclusion they'd discovered gold. The individual who'd located the specimen was informed by the local assessment office that it was iron pyrite, better known as "fool's gold."

A worker cutting ties for the railroad also noticed the bronze-coloured landscape and, not convinced of the former evaluation, sent a sample to a geologist in Toronto, and was assured it contained high-grade copper. The site where the CPR employee located the sample turned out to be not only a significant copper reserve, but also one of the largest nickel deposits the world would ever discover.

This mineral strike assured Sudbury a place of honour on the geology maps for the next century. As the Great Depression decimated the job market in southern Ontario, the unemployed turned their sights on the copper and nickel mines of this northern Ontario community, where supposedly good-paying jobs were abundant.

At the mining office in Copper Cliff on the outskirts of Sudbury, a surprise awaited Aubrey and Orton: a line of over 400 men extending down the street...all with equal intention. The two wouldn't have stood a chance, except Orton knew someone in management who owed him some kind of debt and had promised employment if and when needed.

The job Aubrey and Orton secured entailed working in the crusher mill, an indescribably harsh environment where copper dust was a constant enemy. Aubrey recalled times when visibility was often reduced to less than six feet. Only when conditions bordered on the extreme did workers wear masks; otherwise they were simply too hot and uncomfortable. For the privilege of labouring under these conditions, the two men received an hourly wage of thirty-seven cents.

Part of these initial wages went towards the purchase of a pair of motorcycles, a relatively inexpensive way to get around. However, on the way home from the mines one night, Orton lost control of his motorcycle on a curve and crashed into a wall of rock lining the roadway. He was killed instantly. Aubrey was devastated, and shortly after, traded his bike for a car—a decision no doubt influenced by the death of his friend.

Aubrey had his own encounter with fate while in the north. He and two mining co-workers, Harvey and Tilden, set out on a moose-hunting expedition in late November. In tow behind Aubrey's old Dodge was a boat Tilden had borrowed from his uncle...a boat Aubrey later realized they should have given a closer inspection.

The strategy was to drive to where the main road ended, then by water to a prearranged point near White River, where the trio planned to rendezvous with three fellow hunters. How does that old axiom go: "the best laid plans..."?

Torrential rains the previous week had completely washed out the road short of their destination. No problem: familiar with the area lakes and rivers from other adventures, and given that the party had an assortment of Northern Ontario maps and plenty of fuel in the boat's tank, they'd simply extend the nautical leg of their trip and meet their companions as planned.

Their only concern was November's short duration of daylight: according to their calculations, a good two hours would be needed to reach the rendezvous point. Backtracking to find a suitable place to launch the boat, thoroughly rechecking maps to establish their position, trying to start a stubborn boat engine...all had stolen valuable time.

Those best laid plans again...no sooner were the three under way when a thick fog descended on the lake, and within minutes visibility was reduced to zero. Relying totally on their compass for guidance, they cautiously made their way in the direction indicated.

Apparently it was Harvey who noticed it first: three or four inches of water had accumulated in the bottom of the boat. Not a good sign. A few minutes more and the depth doubled. No provision had been created for a bucket of any sort, so quickly all three emptied the contents of their lunch pails and began a frenzied bailing exercise. Despite their best efforts, within ten minutes it was readily apparent this was more than just a leak...an entire seam had split from bow to stern. The expedition was over.

Submerged to the neck, the trio clung to the overturned craft: their thick heavy clothes welcome in the chilly water but at the same time seeming to triple their weight. A half hour passed; surrounded by emptiness, all calls for help went unanswered and unheeded. They'd not only lost their compass when the boat capsized, but more alarmingly, all comprehension of direction.

Darkness had settled fully on the fog-bound lake by this time, but Tilden claimed he had an "internal compass" as accurate as any precision instrument, and was "pretty sure" in what direction lay the nearest shoreline. Aubrey and Harvey had their doubts, reminding their friend he'd been "pretty sure" the boat was in good shape as well! It had become apparent, however, that remaining with the boat in the frigid water was no longer an option. Their only chance for survival was to make for shore…praying Tilden's "internal compass" would be their salvation.

Despite his visionary premonition, when actually faced with leaving the "safety" of the overturned craft, Tilden refused, trying to climb up on top of it, but managing only to threaten the precarious position of the other two. Whether it was hallucination or delirium, Tilden began swimming continuously around the boat, spinning it in circles, all the while ranting incoherently. At this point he was knocked unconscious: "We had no choice," Aubrey recalled, "or he would've taken all of us to the bottom of the lake."

Dragging Tilden's unconscious weight while trying to keep afloat, Aubrey and Harvey struck off in the blackness in the direction Tilden had indicated. There was no compromise; if wrong and heading for open water, they would be doomed.

"We just kept swimming, one stroke at a time, maybe a half hour, maybe an hour…I have no idea," Aubrey recalled.

Facing complete exhaustion, seemingly not an ounce of strength remaining, legs almost completely paralysed from the cold, the two vaguely sensed what appeared as solid footing and hauled themselves and their comatose friend onto the lake's rocky shore.

Sometime later, still submerged deeply in his subconscious, Aubrey sensed the comforting crackle and warmth of an open fire; in conjunction with hickory smoke, a variety of other less defining scents invaded his nostrils. Upon forcing himself from this intense slumber, Aubrey realized he was wrapped within a layer of woolen blankets inside a tent. As his eyes became more focused, he realized it was not a tent, but a teepee. Lying next to him and also swathed in heavy blankets was Harvey. It took several minutes to gather their thoughts and determine what had transpired in those previous hours, but both clearly recall their initial reaction when wakening was a sense of simply being "wonderfully warm and dry."

A pale late autumn sun was slowly making its ascent above the evergreen forest that engulfed the large clearing in which they sat. Through the shafts of light filtering through the tall pines, the duo discovered they were guests in one of the numerous Indian settlements that dotted Ontario's northern lake region at that time.

While several curious children stared intently, an elderly woman systematically stirred the contents of a huge iron kettle simmering over a fire contained within a foundation of stones. From this cauldron sprang the diversity of aromas that had initially penetrated their senses. Through a combination of English and the universal language of pantomime they learned that two of the village men had found Aubrey and his friend early that morning, while hunting.

When requesting of their hosts the whereabouts of their third member—and I guess operating under the theory there's no good time for bad news—they were frankly informed that Tilden was dead on the shore where they found him.

For the entire day and practically without a word, the old Indian woman regularly and precisely nourished her two patients with her kettle concoction of herbs, berries, tree roots, bark, and other mysteries of nature.

"If those Indian scouts hadn't found us, Harvey and I would have ended our days on that shoreline as well, as the temperature dropped well below freezing that night. And that medicine—talk about bitter! The worst mixture I ever tasted in my entire life...but neither of us even caught so much as a cold. They could certainly teach us something about medicine!"

Of course there were the legal ramifications needing immediate attention; a report had to be filed with local authorities concerning their deceased party member, resulting in an autopsy and subsequent official proceedings. Aubrey confessed they said as little as possible and certainly didn't complicate matters by mentioning the fact they were forced to knock Tilden unconscious, in case the police concluded "we hit him too hard." In the end, however, the coroner's final report merely stated hypothermia as the cause of death.

Reflecting on the ordeal sixty years later, Aubrey couldn't explain how he survived in the first place. "I guess it was a case of being young and strong and healthy...in a similar situation today, I probably wouldn't last ten minutes."

My father continued his mink-raising business for another five years at the home farm in Artemesia Township before being offered a co-partner/managerial position with Aubrey's continually expanding enterprise in Sudbury. Here it seems Harold's friend Lester played another key role when it came to career decisions. Lester had secured a posting at a large dairy farm in Peel Township on the outskirts of Brampton, Ontario, and because a majority of Canada's labour force was overseas helping Britain in its fight against Adolf Hitler, the operation was suffering a severe shortage of capable employees. Dad was married by this time...and for my mother, Brampton and its close proximity to her family in Toronto simply appeared more appealing than the isolation of Northern Ontario.

Convincing himself he was ready for a new challenge, Dad chose the fork in the road leading to Brampton, exchanging raising mink for milking cows: a career choice that would effectively span three decades, involving four relocations.

Warm Tubes and Cold Nights

WHEN ONE RECALLS SOME OF THE TRULY GREAT SCIENTIFIC developments of the last century or so, certain discoveries far outdistance their competition: not necessarily due to extraordinary inventiveness or originality but merely because of the consequences of their invention. Electricity would definitely fall into this specialized category—as would the telegraph, telephone, and radio.

Guglielmo Marconi's 1901 trans-Atlantic message between Cornwall, England, and Glace Bay, Nova Scotia, utilizing a 500-foot-high aerial held aloft by a kite, is generally considered the beginning of what would become known as "wireless radio." By 1920, Marconi was broadcasting a marine weather report four times a day from his "radio station" VAS—"Voice of the Atlantic Shoreline"—to the settlement's several hundred residents. That was the extent of local programming.

Although mind-boggling in their own right, at least

hydro-electrics, telegraphs, and telephones had an actual medium—a wire to pass through. But transporting sound through the air was beyond both imagination and comprehension. In the days before airspace was cluttered with microwaves and satellites, radio aficionados would sit for hours huddled over their "receivers," as they were known, listening for an audible signal. To actually hear an announcement from New York, intercept a message from a ship in the North Atlantic, or catch a few moments from a symphony in Vienna would be the topic of conversation for days.

Factory-made radios, although commercially available, were expensive and often unattainable for the average family's budget. A small two-tube unit could cost in the $150–200 range, while a top-of-the-line six-tube mahogany console, made to resemble fine furniture, could cost three times that much. Radios in this high-end price range equalled the cost of a new Ford or Chevrolet.

If a monetary commitment on that scale was prohibitive, magazines such as *Radio News* and *Popular Mechanics* offered detailed instruction in assembling a receiver using off-the-shelf parts, as dozens of companies at the time specialized in components for do-it-yourself builders.

Students with scientific inclination could construct a workable radio receiver utilizing whatever was available: any wooden or cardboard container tightly wound with fine wire and coated with varnish or shellac could serve as an adequate conductor. Abandoned automobiles provided a great source of parts for the industrious; ignition coils, generators, and magnetos could all be found. Windshield glass was popular as a grid to increase current flow between the vacuum tubes, and to aid in sound amplification. Discarded microphones, telephones, phonographs, speakers...all proved helpful in donating parts for the cause.

For many, radio was not just a part of life but practically their entire life. Enthusiasts would authoritatively discuss such terms as diodes, vacuum tubes, condensers, capacitors, transmitters, filaments, resistors, and grids—though most had little knowledge of how a radio receiver actually functioned. Batteries and aerials were the only components commonly understood to any degree. Batteries provided the current flow through the vacuum tubes. They were furnished in "A," "B," and "C" categories, and varied in capacity, longevity, and price.

A cost-effective and power-saving alternative was the use of an automotive battery in conjunction with "regular" batteries. In winter a car battery residing on the parlour floor was common practice, especially in rural regions when the family car was in storage.

Aerials, on the other hand, were pretty straightforward: string a piece of telephone wire from a house window and attach it to the highest point. Chimneys were popular installation settings, as were windmills and telephone poles. Aerial installation instructions stressed the importance of a positive ground: a galvanized water pipe was recommended for best results.

It's interesting to observe that in its infancy, radio was considered mostly winter entertainment; programs offering a far-ranging field of comedy, drama, variety and mystery provided rural audiences in particular with unparalleled escapism on a frigid February evening.

But summer was different, not only on farms but in towns and cities too; by choice or circumstance, people were outdoors and simply less interested in the airwaves.

Program sponsors often cancelled their advertising accounts during summer months, realizing listenership simply wasn't there. Similarly, reception was compromised in summer; lightning, humid air, even tree foliage interfered with airwave response. Randomly strung telephone wires were seemingly no match for Mother Nature's summer network of obstacles.

In the late 1930s this seasonal vacancy of radio listeners made a dramatic turnaround. Improved and more dependable components in conjunction with built-in aerials were certainly a major influence in addressing the problem of broadcast interference, but the most profound reason for this change was broadcasting itself.

In 1936, a national public broadcasting system was born in Canada: the Canadian Broadcasting Corporation. It quickly became the prime motivator in this shift of public attitude. This new communication network united the country as never before; so whether you resided in the highly populated areas of southern Ontario or Quebec, on Vancouver Island, on the rocky wind-swept shores of Newfoundland, or within the vast isolationism of the Arctic, the CBC brought world news to your door.

By the end of the decade, German Chancellor Adolf Hitler's exploits were gaining world-wide attention and people were listening to the news with increased intensity. From Hitler's invasion of Poland—officially signalling the beginning of World War Two—through his conquests in Holland, Luxembourg, the Baltic States and finally France, listeners remained glued to their radios. Whether reporting on the London Blitz, the Dieppe disaster, or the Japanese attack on Pearl Harbour and subsequent South Pacific conquests, radio made listeners feel that they were on the front line. In view of that era's political climate, little wonder CBC announcer Lorne Greene's nightly national news broadcasts, delivered in his passionate baritone, earned him a reputation as the "voice of doom."

My earliest recollection of radio is much less intense: a New Year's Eve in the early 1950s with the strains of Guy Lombardo's orchestra transmitting "the sweetest music this side of heaven" through the speaker of our RCA Victor console all the way from New York. This was our living room machine; purchased in 1946, it featured both standard broadcast and shortwave radio bands as well as a turntable designed for 78 rpm records.

As well as the RCA, we had a Stromberg-Carlson "mantle" or "table" radio. Whereas the RCA was constructed of rich walnut and mahogany, the Stromberg-Carlson was finished in a cream-coloured Bakelite coating. Although a fine unit in its own right, this was our everyday kitchen radio and main communication link to the outside world.

This link began each weekday morning with our Stromberg-Carlson tuned to Toronto's CJBC "Toast and Jamboree" breakfast program. Bruce Smith was the announcer of the CBC affiliate and Walter Bowles, a veteran of the broadcast business, read the news. Smith would introduce the eight o'clock news package with the tagline, "Here's Walter Bowles to tell us what's in the news!"

Sports were handled by Ed Fitken, my brother's hero. Bill saw him at some event in Toronto back in the 1950s, and procured an autographed picture which I believe he still has.

Each morning around 8:15 a.m., Bruce Smith would play a march (a still-popular musical genre at the time). Hoping I suppose to stimulate both the minds and bodies of his radio audience, Smith would announce: "Everybody up and march around the breakfast table!"

We kids would comply by scraping our chairs back on the linoleum-covered floor and making a couple of quick dashes around the wooden table while Mom yelled at us to finish our breakfast or we'd be late for school. Each day began with that same ritual: Mom yelling as we ignored her. I don't know why she bothered!

We left at 8:30 a.m. for school each day. A musical ditty would signal the moment. Its short, blunt message is sealed in memory:

> When you cross the street in the day or the night,
> Beware of the dangers that loom in sight
> Look to the left and look to the right
> And you'll never ever get run over.

We had a third radio as well; it belonged to Bill, who received it as a Christmas present when he was eleven or twelve. My brother received little encouragement from Mom and Dad where interests outside the farm were involved, so through the magic of the airwaves and this miraculous little box he could effectively rise beyond the seemingly endless dreariness of milking cows and cleaning stables.

The presentation of this radio gift, strangely, was due to Bill's poor eyesight. Bill had relied on glasses since the age of seven, and our parents reasoned that if their son had a radio he'd be less likely to read, thereby saving his eyes.

In an earlier story I recounted their refusal to purchase Bill a pair of rubber boots, crediting rubber as detrimental to eye health. I'm not judging their obsession with ophthalmology...merely reporting it!

But I digress...

Radio was the beloved medium of our parents (we did not own our first television set until 1957). I recall the programs they enjoyed most: "The Jack Benny Show," "Amos 'n' Andy," "Our Miss Brooks," and "Fibber Magee and Molly." During these presentations we were told to sit and be quiet—or else to go upstairs or outside.

For more general musical offerings like the Toronto Symphony or New York Metropolitan Orchestra, our parents were more lax in their "be quiet" curriculum. And Saturday night hockey was hardly an issue as Dad spent half the time asleep in his favourite chair—waking only when Foster Hewitt would holler "He shoots...he scores!"

Daytime radio was Mom's personal time and she had her favourites. "The Happy Gang" began with the sound of a knock on a door—in actuality one of the band members rapping his knuckles on his violin. "Who's there?" someone would answer. A whole chorus of voices would respond, "It's the Happy Gang!"

Six or eight musicians provided a well-rounded upbeat half hour of entertainment. The show had a loyal following, running 22 years before being replaced in 1959 by the "Tommy Hunter Radio Show".

Kate Aitkin was a Canadian institution; born "just next door" in our neighbouring town of Beeton Ontario, "Mrs. A." had been a long-time radio personality, and under her direction, thousands of women (and probably men as well) were shown new heights in the art of homemaking and cooking. Bright, practical, and witty, Kate Aitkin's daily programs of interviews, ongoing and upcoming social events, household hints, cooking tips, and recipes inspired a generation of listeners. She claimed no formal training in the culinary arts—"practical experience" was her motto, the result of being the eldest and only girl in a family of boys. Aitkin also ran a successful preserving and canning operation from their Beeton family farm, producing upwards of 12,000 jars and cans yearly. Her cookbooks were famous; Mom probably had hers for forty years before it simply fell apart from use.

One couldn't comment on 1950s radio without mentioning Arthur Godfrey, whose wit, warmth and laid-back persona endeared him to fans everywhere. His weekly morning program was filled with music from a wide spectrum of fields, casual conversations with the great and the unknown and folksy monologues on affairs in his country and around the world.

Most radio hosts of that era read their sponsor's commercials...as did Godfrey. Unlike his peers however, Godfrey spurned scripted material as too impersonal and chose instead to inject his own quips and witticisms into commercials, poking good-natured fun at program advertisers. His show's major sponsors (Frigidaire, Lipton, Chesterfield, and Pillsbury) weren't amused—until sales improved dramatically. Apparently Godfrey's entertaining ad libs were highly regarded by consumer audiences, who answered with their wallets.

A musician and recording artist himself, Godfrey was always searching for new talent. Two notable quartets of the 1950s—the Mariners and Chordettes—auditioned for Godfrey and became featured regulars. Steve Lawrence, Eddie Fisher, Patsy Cline, Tony Bennett, Pat Boone, Tommy Hunter, and Roy Clark all received their start on his morning show. But Godfrey's auditions were tough and many failed. Surprising notables in the "flush" department included Buddy Holly and Elvis Presley.

At the beginning of this commentary I referred to Arthur Godfrey's compelling and informal on-air personality. As evidence of his media influence, consider that then-current US President Dwight Eisenhower confided in Godfrey about recording a number of public service announcements to be played in the event of a nuclear catastrophe...a graphic reminder of that era's precarious political environment and the president's perception of imminent danger.

Eisenhower believed Godfrey's soothing grandfatherly manner would re-assure listeners and provide a calming voice amid the expected disorder, chaos and panic. The question of whether the announcements were actually recorded provided media speculation for decades. Not until 2004—some five decades later—did Columbia Broadcasting confirm that the messages were indeed recorded.

Another personality favourite of Mom's was Gordon Sinclair, a veteran of newspaper and radio. Sinclair's daily "Let's be Personal" editorial, preceding his noonday newscast on CFRB Toronto, was a "never miss" in our mother's radio listening catalogue.

"Warm up the radio!" she'd command every weekday around 11:45, to whoever happened to be closest to the set. If one was in a hurry to hear something in particular, that interval to activate the vacuum tube filaments seemed an eternity (in reality it was probably no more than thirty seconds).

Sinclair's commentaries were basically whatever caught his attention that particular day. He'd spend the morning gleaning items from Canadian and American newspapers, before blending them with his personal often prejudiced views and comments.

The phrase "slow news day" never existed for Gordon Sinclair. He could always discover something in which to alienate at least part of his listening audience. Sex and religion were always good ice breakers. He particularly enjoyed unearthing stories about so-called proper people...especially if they were highly regarded in the religious hierarchy. He specialized in asking tough questions.

"If there's a God," he'd begin, "where was he when six million Jews were processed? How is it that anywhere a war develops, God is always on the side of everybody?"

Sinclair on charities: "Of all the money raised, only a small percentage ever gets near those who need it. Most is gobbled up through administration and organization."

On fluoridation: "Simply adding rat poison to the public water supply."

On the Block Parent Program: "It's structured to make children trust nobody and be afraid of everyone."

Mom herself often disagreed with Sinclair's philosophies, sometimes quite vocally...but she never dared miss his program! And she wasn't alone; Gordon Sinclair's "Let's be Personal," and the news package that followed, captured fully 50 percent of the station's total listening audience; an unheard-of figure that has since never been even closely duplicated by an individual broadcaster.

Beginning in the early 1950s, a new medium, television, began its ascent into the nation's living rooms. Some communication analysts at the time predicted the absolute demise of radio. That forecast didn't occur; radio instead changed direction, focusing less on drama, variety and comedy—its mainstays for decades—and concentrating on recorded music, talk shows, and more regional interests.

This new direction might have failed but for some significant factors. First was the invention of the transistor, which effectively replaced the bulky and power-consuming vacuum tubes of current radios. The greatest advantage of this new power source was that components could be reduced in size to produce a radio of much smaller dimensions.

As a result of this downsizing, radios suddenly became both portable and affordable. Texas Instruments introduced the first practical transistor unit in 1955. Subsequently, other manufacturers joined the ranks: Raytheon, Zenith, RCA, DeWald and Crosley. In 1956, Chrysler Motors, in conjunction with Philco Electronics, introduced the first transistor car radio, available on all their new models as a $150 option.

Intrigued with this electronic wonder, Japanese electronic engineers and associated executive personnel from Tokyo Telecommunications visited numerous US companies during the 1950s, gleaning knowledge not only of product, but solutions in manufacturing and distribution capabilities as well. Utilizing this information, Tokyo Telecommunications—now known as Sony Corporation—introduced its own transistor radio to the world...and you know the rest.

Even the most captivating or technically advanced product requires customers—so how about sixty-million potential consumers? Enter the baby boomers, the most educated, prosperous and mobile generation in history. Whether blasting from the large dash-mounted speaker of your parents' Plymouth, or the tiny four-inch speaker of a Sony or a Sanyo, and whether at the beach or simply the back yard, a transistor radio was the ultimate connection to what was "hip"—and that basically meant one thing in this era: music. Rock and roll, the "Folk Boom," Top 40, protest music, the British Invasion, Woodstock, and other musical mega-happenings of the 1950s and 60s solidified an entire generation in almost cult-like fashion.

To most of our parents it was a phenomenon they found both bewildering and baffling, and never did figure out. Radio as they knew it had seemingly changed overnight. It was actually easier to accept television as many of their familiar radio artists and programs had transferred to this new audio-visual medium. Jack Benny, Steve Allen, Dinah Shore, Perry Como, Bing Crosby, and Arthur Godfrey were now all available on the TV screen; so who needed the infernal racket that this new generation referred to as "music" anyway?

For those who'd grown up with radio, television was an amazing transformation. "So-and-so doesn't look anything like I imagined!" was a collectively overheard comment from former listeners, since one of the most rewarding aspects of radio was the individual imagery that only that medium could command. Six people in a room could picture six different visuals of the personality they were hearing. So however new, exciting or electrifying, television couldn't begin to captivate the magic that had been radio's domain. Radio was like a good book, a favourite sweater, a comfortable pair of slippers...an old friend.

"Some of my fondest memories involve radio..."

It was 1994. My father had just celebrated his eightieth birthday, and was reflecting on that long ago pre-hydro era, and in particular the role radio had played.

> "...the sound and smell of a crackling wood fire on a cold winter's night, with all the family sitting in our parlour, listening to radio. The

only light came from the flames from the fireplace, which created the strangest shadows and shapes on the walls and floor. The sound and smell of burning wood, the flickering fire, the soft orange glow of the vacuum tubes reflecting off the wall behind the radio: the memory is as clear as yesterday!"

The Singhampton-Sudbury Shuttle

ON SEPTEMBER 8, 1931, EVELYN MARGARET TURNER WAS no doubt apprehensive and anxious, facing her first day of trying to instill knowledge to the roughly two dozen students seated before her, ranging from age five to fifteen. It seemed like only yesterday that she herself was a student in an almost identical context.

When Miss Turner graduated from secondary school in 1929, Teacher's College (or "Normal School," as it was then called) was the ultimate goal of many young women. My aunt was no exception. Five hundred dollars was the salary offered by the Osprey Township school board for the new grad, and for that $500 figure, certain academic qualifications were expected:

- To be able to read intelligently and correctly, any passage from any common reading book.

- To be able to spell correctly the words of a common sentence, dictated by the examiners.
- To be able to write in a plain hand.
- To be able to solve problems in the simple and compound rules of arithmetic, and to be familiar with the principles on which these rules depend.
- To know the elements of English grammar and to be able to parse any easy sentence in prose.
- To be familiar with the basic elements of geography, and the general outlines of the globe.
- To have some knowledge of school organization.

Teachers of this period supplied their own materials for day-to-day operation. This included a daily register book, a regulation strap, chalk, pencils, fountain pen, blackboard brushes, a couple of erasers, yardsticks and rulers, a pointer, thumb tacks, blotters, glue, carbon paper—and on went the list.

With the exception of books, student supplies were courtesy of the Education Board. The basic reader of the period was aptly named *The Ontario Reader*, and was filled with stories and poetry whose focus projected sentiment and nobility. All school books were published in two volumes, junior and senior, and a student's grade determined the book used; junior third, senior third, junior fourth, senior fourth, etc.

Completely lost on today's educational instructors is the monumental challenge one-room school teachers faced in keeping eight grades working in unison, while at the same time assuring each individual grade could function independently. Added to this balancing act was the organization of Christmas concerts, graduation exercises, Bible study, Red Cross meetings, Arbour Day activities, sports tournaments, and field trips.

Miss Turner's teaching base, S.S. # 5 Osprey, located between the 8th and 10th concession of Osprey Township in Grey County, was arguably the most isolated institution in the township; situated on a lonely side road, it was literally in the middle of nowhere, more than a mile from the nearest farmhouse. Educational doctrine of the day decreed that individual schoolhouses be situated in the centre of a certain square mile area; the central intersection was where the school was built, regardless of student proximity.

My aunt taught at the Osprey school for three years, until a school board trustee with a newly-graduated niece came looking for a teaching position and...well you get the idea. Evelyn knew she was history, but not wishing to create a scene with the local school board, resigned her post and began a search for a new school. My dad chauffeured his sister throughout the surrounding countryside, burning countless gallons of 25-cent gasoline, until a prospect surfaced at a school on the Grey-Simcoe County line, just north of the hamlet of Singhampton.

Next to the school, on the Simcoe side of the county line, lived the MacDonalds, who offered to provide board. Well-respected in the community, Dan MacDonald was a renowned stone mason whose wife had boarded teachers for years. With all signs pointing towards a family of good character, my father came away satisfied his sister was in good hands.

The MacDonalds had four children, and one, Aubrey, gradually developed a crush for the new school teacher. It was sort of a slow-burning romance, as Aubrey was only home every three or four weeks. As noted in a previous chapter, working at the copper mines in Sudbury and being the proprietor of a successful mink ranch left little time for social activity.

However, Aubrey and Evelyn's relationship ambled along, eventually culminating in matrimony. The click of cameras, and congratulatory messages (and tears) from friends and family members, pronounced the conclusion of the ceremony on that June Saturday in 1937.

"I'll never see her again!" Evelyn's step-mother lamented to anyone who'd listen.

"She's going to Sudbury, not around the world," someone commented. To Mamie Turner, it may as well have been the far side of the globe.

Aubrey had built a cabin near the mines at the Sudbury borough of Copper Cliff, and the house was now ready to receive his new bride. Hooked onto the back of Aubrey's Ford was a small homemade wooden trailer he'd manufactured strictly for this purpose. What wouldn't fit in the car had been stashed in the trailer. Settled in the narrow front seat, the two offered their last good-byes. Mamie took one final look at the trailer and moaned that it looked just like "a little black coffin." On that cheery note, the couple departed.

Moving the calendar ahead fourteen months to August 1938, we find Aubrey and Evelyn settled into their new home with a two-month-old baby, and the Turners planning a trip to Sudbury to meet their newest family member. No one had known until recently that Evelyn had even been pregnant. She wrote regularly but made no mention. Her family learned only by accident, when Aubrey's brother, who helped with the mink operation, mentioned Evelyn's condition in the course of regular conversation.

Mamie agonized over her stepdaughter in the period

following—and her concern was justified. Evelyn had witnessed gradually but steadily-developing rheumatoid arthritis during the previous decade, reaching a point where she'd been warned by her own doctor that a strong possibility existed that she would be unable to carry a baby to term.

Evelyn's condition had been a worry to everyone. When no one in the local medical field had any definitive conclusions on how to treat or at least curb the disease's advancement, Evelyn sought help through a doctor who practised from his home near Hamilton Ontario. While undergoing treatment—a period of six weeks—she stayed with her aunt and uncle in Toronto.

Family positions varied widely on the character of this so-called doctor. Some dismissed him as a quack, while others believed he was much lower on the character scale, bilking innocent, desperate people out of hard-earned money.

This "doctor" entertained weird hours, picking Evelyn up at 11:00 p.m. sometimes, and bringing her back at around 2 or 3:00 a.m. He'd randomly pick up other patients on route as well, always courtesy of a chauffeur-driven Packard limousine...all in all, a strange affair.

Evelyn said little about the treatment, and so family members, despite their anxieties, generally remained silent. Worries notwithstanding, a healthy baby boy was born. For Mamie in particular, this trip to Sudbury would be a chance to dispel any lingering doubts.

The Sudbury excursion proved to be a real family affair. Saturday morning's departure witnessed my father at the wheel of the family Chevrolet, and his dad in the passenger seat. Squeezed in the narrow front seat, straddling the floor-mounted gearshift, was Dad's fiancée...my mother. In the rear seat were Mamie; Dad's two step-brothers, Doug and

Eldon (aged ten and four, respectively); and four female mink in a wooden cage on the floor beneath Mamie's feet, to be delivered to Aubrey's mink-raising enterprise.

No paved roads existed to Sudbury in 1938. Despite the 35 mph speed limit, the travellers maintained a rigid schedule, stopping only for gas, a couple of bathroom breaks and time to consume the sandwiches they'd packed. Time was allowed as well to offer the mink an occasional breath of fresh air and a drink.

Aubrey and Evelyn welcomed everyone to their humble home, and once an appropriate fuss was made over the baby, the three men transferred the mink from the car to the rows of cages out behind the house. Aubrey's mink ranch was a major operation; he had even commissioned his own abattoir, slaughtering horses for mink meat. The meat was kept in coolers packed with ice, sawdust, and newspaper. Aubrey mentioned how the horsemeat was for human consumption as well. "Last year, we ate it throughout the winter. It's just as good as beef."

The MacDonalds lived frugally, but that evening, as a special treat, Aubrey drove the entire contingent into downtown Sudbury to see the movie *Dodge City*. Once back home they chatted for a while, then retired for the night. Although the MacDonald home was basically a two-bedroom cottage, by utilizing the woodshed, couches, chairs, and blankets, space was somehow located for everyone. It had been a long and tiring day for the guests, so whatever or wherever the bed, no one had any trouble falling asleep.

Except nobody could have slept through the pandemonium that surfaced a short time later. Evelyn and my mother were assigned a room adjoining the woodshed—basically a lean-to designed to offset winter's chill from invading the main house. In this woodshed, tied beside a chair, was a dog...a very large dog.

The German shepherd was one of several Aubrey retained to guard the mink from predators. My mom elected to visit the outhouse just outside the woodshed door, but was wary of walking past the dog. "Just hurry by and he won't bother you," Evelyn whispered.

The dog probably wouldn't have paid a great deal of attention, except Mom in her haste tripped on the steps directly in front of him. A bloodcurdling growl from the dog was matched by a scream from my mother as the monster lunged at her. In the inky blackness she had no accurate gauge of how long that chain was!

The commotion certainly brought the household to life, as the barking, growling, snarling, teeth snapping, and chain rattling summoned everyone to witness the carnage. Aubrey retrieved a flashlight and managed to settle the dog while my mom tried to resume breathing. Then the fun was over, everyone returning to their beds and to sleep. I imagine it may have taken my mother just a little longer.

The MacDonalds spent three more years in Sudbury. In the intervening period, Evelyn's arthritis continued its deliberate course, and a decision was reached to return to Singhampton, where medical treatment and assistance might be more readily available. More importantly, Aubrey, an extremely compassionate man, understood the isolation his wife had endured, and the psychological benefits of being close to family.

By now, Evelyn's health had deteriorated to the point where many family members lamented that she probably wouldn't be around much longer.

That was 1943—in 1993 I attended her eightieth birthday with my parents. No, there was no medical miracle, cure, or even significant breakthrough in rheumatoid research. My aunt simply endured with cortisone injections, Celebrex and Aspirin. Still in her 40s, I recall how her hands and fingers were twisted and distorted. Two decades later, she would be confined to a wheelchair. I still remember and admire her positive attitude...despite the predictions of medical and non-medical intellectuals.

And what I remember about Aubrey is the untiring sensitivity displayed towards Evelyn's ever-increasing medical and emotional needs.

Aubrey was an outdoorsman in every sense of the word. His passion for hunting, trapping, and fishing was unparalleled. Several inches over six feet, broad-shouldered and muscular, he was the epitome of the active but challenging life he'd lived. Yet the hours spent and the gentleness and patience shown to his wife were truly admirable. I don't ever recall him uttering a word of profanity or even raising his voice. Aubrey was in fact extremely soft-spoken—yet when he talked, his audience listened and learned. A recollection of the MacDonalds that remains clear in my mind is Aubrey in his signature three-piece black suit and matching fedora, standing next to Evelyn, who appears a diminutive figure beside her husband.

Throughout this period, Aubrey continued to farm the original family homestead on the Grey-Simcoe County Line. From the beginning, he was well ahead of his peers when it came to land stewardship. Realizing that every area has growth limitations, he discovered the means to adapt the agricultural environment to suit the particular crop.

Aubrey was the first person I knew to experiment with

trefoil, a legume comfortable in an environment of less-than-ideal nutrients and excess moisture...the exact opposite of alfalfa and clover. He grew trefoil for years, harvesting some as hay for his cattle, and some for seed.

As the years advanced, Aubrey knew he could no longer provide the care his wife needed; subsequently Evelyn moved into a retirement lodge in Collingwood, about a twenty minute drive from the farm.

Until his 80th birthday, Aubrey knew only excellent health, but a year later he was forced to undergo hip surgery. His recovery was slow, and his biggest frustration during his recuperation was the fact he was unable to drive the new Ford pickup he'd recently purchased. As long as I knew Aubrey—more than 40 years—he never drove anything but a pickup. In his words, it was "the only vehicle worth owning, and all anybody needs."

Aubrey was a prolific reader, especially business and news magazines. *Maclean's* remained his favourite; he called it "the best magazine printed!"

An hour in the company of Aubrey MacDonald acquainted you with the absurdities of municipal, provincial, and federal politics; modern agricultural practices; the education system; the Canadian constitutional fiasco; immigration policies; welfare and unemployment systems; unions; modern medicine; environmental issues; and a myriad of other topics. His comments and opinions were well-analysed, and once stated, seldom retracted. However, I can think of few others of his generation with whom I would rather have spent that hour.

Rural Escape

Thinking back to when I was a kid, I'm continually reminded of the seemingly never-ending stream of friends and relatives our parents entertained over the years. More often it's the city relatives I recall, for the simple reason that their stays were of longer duration.

As most of our rural relatives had livestock to tend morning and night, their visits would be restricted to four or five hours. A typical visit would witness them landing in time for a pre-arranged midday meal, after which Dad would say; "We'll get out of the way and let the women do the dishes."

That would be the signal for a tour of the farm, comprising a close look at the years' crops, both in the barn and in the field. Also included would be a detailed inspection of any new machinery or vehicles that might have appeared since the last social call. This would allow sufficient time for the women to have "their" work completed. All would then continue their visit over a cup of tea until it was time to go.

Mom's sisters—all Toronto habitants—enjoyed escaping to the country, provided they didn't have to stay too long. They were like their mother in that regard. (Back in 1953, when my Grandmother Carruthers first set eyes on our new farm—which lacked running water, a bathroom, and a furnace—she turned to my mother: "Evelyn, you gave up the city for this?")

Grandpa Will Carruthers was nearing 70 by this time, but no doubt due to his 40 year association with Massey-Harris, his enthusiasm for agriculture remained. Whatever was going on, Grandpa was there, complete with fedora and cane, asking questions and offering comment.

The Valentines—Mom's youngest sister's family—never failed to bring a stockpile of cereal with them, usually Kellogg's variety packs. Our cereals, although wholesome, tended to run on the unexciting side: oatmeal porridge, shredded wheat, or corn flakes. It was always somewhat of a mystery why mom's sister Lillian, who was meticulous concerning diet and nutrition, purchased these pre-sweetened cereals. Frosted Flakes, Sugar Pops, Fruit Loops, Cocoa Crispies...who eats chocolate for breakfast? They brought their own milk—only skim would suffice—and they'd dump it on those horrible sugar-coated cereals. It never made sense.

Our city relatives were always overwhelmed by our big breakfasts. We'd have porridge or cold cereal, depending on the season, and fried eggs and bacon—the good, thick, fat, greasy stuff you sliced right off the slab. There'd be jam, cheese, or peanut butter for "dessert," and a couple of glasses of orange juice or unpasteurized milk to wash the whole works down.

The Watts—another sister's family—spent their first

week of vacation at a lakeside cottage somewhere in the Muskoka region, then like clockwork on Tuesday of the second week, the familiar Plymouth would appear in our driveway. Their son Doug, a couple years older than I, never could get used to our expansive garden—compared to the handkerchief-sized plot they had at home.

"There's no use keeping part of a package of seeds," Dad would announce every year.

"But I can't handle it all at once when it's ready!" Mom would likewise protest every year.

"Oh, we'll help you when the time comes." Dad made that promise every year as well.

As far back as memory would take her, Mom dreamed of a beautiful country garden, abundant with vegetables and flowers. But no matter how pleasant the delusions in February, when the Dominion Seed Catalogue arrived, reality often stated otherwise. There was the year the severe thunderstorm washed most of it downhill to the creek, or the summer it shrivelled away in drought. Or the time the cattle broke in. Or the aphids took over. Or it overgrew with pigweed. Or the hailstorm ruined it. There seemed no end to crop failure possibilities.

Then there was the year Dad planted over an acre of peas in the furthest reach of the farm. The seed drill had apparently missed a swath—rather than waste it, Dad figured it a convenient setting for peas.

"Don't worry," he promised. "We'll be there to help when the time comes."

Mother could have shot Dad several times over the course of that particular season. Walking nearly a mile to weed a pea patch in the broiling mid-summer sun was loads of fun. When picking time arrived, Dad of course was nowhere in sight.

The Watt family found our breakfast choices overwhelming as well. Since their holiday usually followed the Valentines, there would inevitably be a few variety pack leftovers. Try as we might, we could never convince Doug to eat the Cocoa Crispies either.

Our "flystickers" never failed to garner interest for all our city cousins. Perhaps you remember these? They may have gone the way of black-and-white TV and homemade buttermilk, but when I was growing up, flystickers were at the forefront of the never-ending battle to keep flies from the kitchen.

They came in a compact package, measuring three or four inches long. One end of the sticker was carefully pulled from the cylindrical carton. Heat was needed to help it unroll, so this task was usually accomplished over a stove element. When extended to its maximum, the sticker measured about three feet long. Whatever was on it was more adhesive than any glue and also attractive to flies. It simply hung from the ceiling, and when a fly had the misfortune of landing, it was stuck fast. It wasn't very humane, as the flies just buzzed away until they expired from exhaustion or starvation—not that we really cared.

We generally had three flystickers in the house: one somewhere in the food preparation area of the kitchen, one over the table, and one hung outside the screen door. Once the sticker became clogged with flies, it was replaced. I recall an occasion when a loaded fly sticker dropped directly onto my brother Don's head as he entered the kitchen. He had a real thick crop of hair and I remember it was a real bear dislodging the sticky mess!

Our cousins were constantly in awe of our cats. At one point we had seventeen. All had to be named—although some of the names were pretty vague, like "grandmother cat." Just about every other feline on our farm could trace their lineage to her. There was Hal—black as midnight and probably the best rat catcher we had. Boris was a big solid tomcat, built like a cement block. Then there was "Bruce"—whose name we changed to "Bernice" when she had kittens.

Because we had an abundance of feline offspring, we were regularly searching for adoptive homes. One spring day, we packed two kittens in a feed bag and delivered them to some friends near Berkeley, in Grey County. By autumn, one of the cats had come back (to paraphrase a popular Lee Moore song from the 1940s). Whether two had begun the trek homeward, who knows? That one made it was remarkable enough: a 50-mile ride inside a burlap bag, in the trunk of a car, and yet it found its way home! Not surprisingly, it appeared a trifle thin—but what an incredible example of homing instinct.

Probably the most interesting of our relatives were the McIsaacs. One never knew from one visit to the next where Mom's brother-in-law might be working. Since he'd come back from the war, Mac had driven trucks, taxis, and busses; worked at a lumber yard; did carpentry work; sold cars... Mac never stayed long at any particular place. Usually, he had a "falling out" with management.

During one particular visit, Mac was holding down a job at a tobacconist shop. Somehow—and sometimes it was just better not to ask—Mac had procured a case of Crispy Crunch chocolate bars. There must have been at least three dozen. We kids seldom got chocolate of any description, so ate like pigs. Mom then instigated a quota system of one bar a day, ending most of the fun. I have to admit, though—by the end of that holiday, I didn't care if I saw another Crispy Crunch bar for years!

As with his varied occupations, one never knew from one visit to the next what vehicle Mac might be driving. Mac always drove a nice car—often one that was more expensive than he could afford. Guys like Mac—who spent the first half of the 1940s in Europe, fighting Hitler's Nazi regime—learned to live one day at a time. They saw war's horrendous consequences first-hand, and knew only too well how quickly and horribly a life could be lost. Many returning veterans claimed that four or five years of battle exacted double or even triple that from the soldier's lifetime. Each prayed that, if they survived to get back home, they be given the opportunity to make up for what had been lost, in whatever venue that might be.

For Mac, that void was filled with cars. One was a Packard—*the* luxury car of his generation, until it was overtaken by Cadillac. He also owned a Buick with the ultra-modern Dynaflow transmission, which needed no shifting ("just one uninterrupted smooth flow of power," claimed the ads). But my favourite was a 1957 Monarch Lucerne. It was black and white, with red and black interior and upholstery. I recall Mom commenting on their "beautiful car," and her sister Lois merely answering that "I would rather have had a new dining room rug!"

The McIsaac kids, roughly our ages, were always up-to-date on the latest jokes and information to impress their rural cousins.

"I hear they're stopping all the buses in Toronto today… to let the people on and off."

"What goes ninety-nine, clomp, ninety-nine, clomp? A centipede with a wooden leg."

"Do you know how many people are dead in that cemetery? All of them."

"Did you hear about the guy who got electrocuted? He stepped on a bun and the currant went up his leg."

"You see the exhaust coming from that jet?" my cousin Randy asked. "Know what it is?"

"Some type of airplane gas," was my answer.

"Nope, it's used oil."

"I thought it was some special gas."

"Nope, it's used oil."

Well, then—used oil it was.

Randy's brother Tim then took up the challenge. "Know what those jets are carrying?"

"People, of course."

"Nope, nuclear warheads."

"Nuclear warheads?!" I exclaimed. "I thought it was people!"

"That's what they want us to think—but it's nuclear warheads."

I couldn't sleep for days.

For some reason we tended to get into more trouble when the McIsaacs were around—especially when Tim, their oldest, was in the equation. Tim once stayed an extra week while the rest of his family had gone back to the city. For a variety of reasons, Tim and his father had a strained relationship, and Uncle Mac thought perhaps the change of scenery would do them both good.

"If Tim gives you any trouble," said Mac, "don't be afraid to knock him back into line. He's used to that!"

The very first day, Tim sent a picture crashing to the

floor, breaking its glass pane. Then there was the broken window incident. Another time, a chocolate bar was left to melt on the car seat. And once, while washing dishes, Tim broke a casserole dish.

One evening Tim confronted me. "Why don't we go meet Uncle Harold?" (Dad was working with a neighbour who lived a little ways down the road.)

"Well," I hesitated, "I don't know if we should or not."

"Oh, come on," prodded Tim. "Uncle Harold will be real surprised to see us!"

I was about six at that point, and fully aware that we weren't to walk on the road except when going to school. The idea did have a certain sense of adventure however, and since Tim was practically an adult (twelve or thirteen) I agreed. "I'll just tell Mom."

"I already asked," Tim lied. "She says okay."

The sun had sunk to the horizon by the time we reached the end of the lane. Since the cows were pasturing in the two fields either side of the laneway, the gate was closed. Tim unlocked the chain and we started up the road. We'd travelled about a half mile when we met Dad with the tractor and wagon. He wasn't nearly as excited to see us as Tim had led me to believe.

"What are you doing walking on the road when it's almost dark?"

There seemed no good reason anymore, so we said nothing.

"Does Mom know where you are?" Dad continued. I answered that Tim had asked and she said we could. Dad turned his gaze to Tim. "Well, get up on the wagon!"

If we thought Dad was a little upset when he first saw us, you should have seen him when we reached the entranceway and discovered the gate wide open! Luckily, the cows hadn't noticed, but that didn't stop Dad from launching into a tirade about the consequences that might have evolved. "Even you should have known better than that, Dave," he ended by saying. "And for you, Tim, there's simply no excuse!"

"I'm sorry, Uncle Harold, I thought the gate would automatically swing shut when we passed through."

Tim was always so polite that one almost felt guilty bawling him out. Dad must have had been on a real guilt trip that week. The episodes continued. There was the spilled milk incident. Then there was the day that Tim dropped a bale of hay from the hayloft onto someone's head. Another time he was helping Dad and Bill load manure into the spreader when he threw a full forkful at Dad. And you should have seen Dad's reaction the time Tim was forking straw and jammed a prong of the pitchfork through Dad's hat...while he was wearing it!

The major encounter of the week came when Tim, after being informed several times that he was not allowed to drive the Allis-Chalmers tractor, went ahead and did it anyway. He got it started and in gear, and was making a circuit of the barnyard—but in the confusion that followed, Tim forgot where the clutch was located, and Dad had to jump onto the moving tractor in order to stop it. With some solid encouragement from Dad's boot, Tim was ushered toward the house.

When Tim's parents returned that weekend, Mac immediately asked, "Did Tim give you any trouble, Harold?"

I thought, oh boy, Dad's been waiting all week for this moment. The reaction from Uncle Mac should be interesting!

"Well," Dad began, "we had to discipline him a time or two...but all in all he was pretty good."

I couldn't believe what I was hearing. That was it? And that *was* it. No more on the subject was mentioned.

It was years before I understood and appreciated what my father had done for Tim McIsaac that day.

A Christmas to Remember

WHEN I THINK BACK OVER THE YEARS—BACK TO THE 1950s in particular—I'm reminded how simple Christmas was. Before inflatable Christmas creatures and banks of outdoor coloured lights illuminated our neighbourhoods, strings of tinsel, a can of spray-on snow, and a couple of candle wreaths in the window were as good as it got.

November's short, cold days and scattered snowfalls were the initial indicators of what lay ahead. Significant signs of winter and the upcoming Christmas season abounded: the neatly stacked cords of seasoned wood already generating cozy warmth via fireplaces and kitchen stoves; chevrons of geese racing southward, ahead of winter's frigid blast; the first truckload of Christmas trees passing by on their journey to Toronto; early renditions of "Silver Bells" and "I'll Be Home for Christmas" radiating from the speaker of our Stromberg-Carlson kitchen radio.

Each new holiday season seems only to remind us of

days past. Like the Christmas we shivered in a cold house all day without hydro, or the equally frigid Christmas morning our old furnace broke down and Dad spent the entire day trying to revive it.

I remember 1971...the beginning of my "against everything" campaign, when I decided to add the commercialism of Christmas to my protest list. For some reason, Mom and Dad decided we should open our presents on Christmas Eve—something we'd never done before. That didn't suit me, so I simply went to bed early and refused to take part. The following year I stayed out in the barn Christmas morning, performing extra chores that didn't need to be done, just so I could delay everyone from opening their presents as long as possible.

I also refused to purchase any gifts for the family, and made it clear I expected the same. Nevertheless, I received three or four nice gifts from various family members. If their point was to make me feel like a jerk...they were relatively successful.

For my family in the 1950s, the festive season really got into gear with the arrival of the Christmas catalogue from the T. Eaton Co., Canada's leading department store. By the time our mother got around to ordering from it, the catalogue was nearly unrecognizable from five children leafing through the magical world within its pages.

Another sure sign of the season was when Mom gathered her ingredients together for the annual Christmas fruitcake. She would make about six, in a variety of sizes. A couple were routinely given away and we had no trouble devouring the rest. Home-made bread was baked year-round, but Mom always baked extra around Christmas. Slathered with butter while still hot from the oven, the taste and aroma were overwhelming, especially during those dark days of December. Mom would also dig out her fancy cookie-cutting artillery, moulding the pastry into Santas, gingerbread men, reindeer, stars, snowmen, and Christmas trees.

A few days before the big event, Dad and my oldest brother, Bill, would trek to the furthest edge of the farm for the annual tree-cutting ceremony. The roughly three-acre, mostly maple and ash woodlot had little going for it when it came to coniferous trees. Because of this deficiency, you had to take what you could get—hence the chosen tree always appeared a little ratty when first dragged into the house. But it was surprising how much a few decorations, several feet of tinsel, and a couple strings of lights added. Our Christmas trees were always too tall even for our high-ceilinged living room, and we were forced to bend them at the top. As a result, we never could finish them off with a star or angel.

"Why do you always cut such a large one?" Mom would scold every year. And every year Dad would answer, "They never look that big when they're in the bush."

A grand highlight of the festive season was the annual journey to Toronto to witness the wonderful displays Eaton's and Simpson's had constructed for their department store windows. Simpsons, on the south side of Queen Street, and Eaton's, directly across, competed with each other every year. Mom usually shopped Eaton's, so I recall it best. The store occupied a full city block. I have fond memories of standing with thousands of others, just staring at the grandeur of the storefront. Then it was out of the frosty air and through the revolving doors, until the elevator delivered us to the 6th floor…Eaton's "Toyland." To a four- or five-year-old, it was without a doubt the most magical place on the face of the earth.

Toys covered what seemed like a hundred acres! There were tow trucks, milk trucks, bread trucks, beer trucks, friction cars, silent cars, wind-up cars, racing cars, pedal cars, and kiddie cars. There were drums, flutes, bells, whistles, bicycles, tricycles, sleighs, and toboggans. There were dolls that laughed, cried, stood, sat, and slept. Some dolls had curly hair, some had long hair, and some had no hair. Some had complete sets of clothes, and some had no clothes. Some walked and talked and even wet themselves. There were games, crayons, paints, building blocks, books, blackboards, trains, airplanes, children's records, music boxes, spinning tops, six-guns, holsters, caps, rifles that fired corks, bows that fired arrows, pistols that fired darts...

And riding high above this fantasy world was Punkinhead, Eaton's toyland mascot. Back and forth on his unicycle Punkinhead rode across a tightly-stretched wire, while below, uncountable numbers of children drooled over the toys, or joined the long line for a chance to sit on Santa's knee.

On Christmas Eve, I and my brothers Richard and Brian dutifully draped our stockings over a chair—we had no fireplace—left some cookies for Santa, reminded Dad to leave a few slices of hay beside the barn for the reindeer, and went to bed. Although it was difficult to sleep with sugarplums dancing in our heads, we realized Santa would be a no-show otherwise.

Early the next morning, while it was still dark, we'd creep quietly down the stairs in our bare feet, and then quickly back to bed with our stuffed stockings under our arms. By the glow of the bedroom lamp, we'd begin unloading our treasures. A few comic books were generally the first items extracted. Perhaps we'd find a harmonica, some gum, chocolate bars, small games or puzzles, a variety of candy, a couple of toy cars, and maybe some building blocks. In the toe was the obligatory orange or apple. One year I discovered a large chunk missing from my apple. A mouse had obviously enjoyed a Christmas Eve snack, chewing right through the stocking.

By breakfast we were—surprisingly—no longer hungry, and uninterested in anything but what lay within those wrapped parcels beneath the tree. As soon as the breakfast chores were finished, sometime around ten, the coloured lights would be switched on and the excitement would begin. First the soft presents—shirts, socks, underwear—unexciting but necessary. Then the good stuff: trucks, machinery, guns, games, etc. These gifts would keep us occupied for the duration of the holiday season—or until they broke.

Just when our festive spirit was beginning to flag, we'd celebrate another Christmas with our grandparents in Toronto. With only the occasional exception, their gifts would all be categorized under the "soft" label. A sweater, perhaps—and always mittens. Grandma Carruthers knitted for all her grandchildren, each child receiving their own design and colour. Maybe it was just me, but Grandma's mittens always seemed just a bit warmer than the ordinary kind.

Grandpa doled out the gifts—a role no one questioned. His training as an army drill sergeant was strongly evident as he called out each recipient's name. "Harold! Vivien! Bill!" He'd sit in his favourite chair beside the tree, hauling in anything out of reach with the crook of his cane.

With well more than sixty Decembers under my belt, the one that stands out most clearly was in 1955. Christmas fell on a Sunday that year. To a six-year-old, the wait to open gifts on Christmas morning can seem an eternity. It would

Yesterday's Moments...Today's Memories

be even longer this particular day, as church and Sunday school took precedence.

"Oh, do we have to go today?" we whined.

"Of course you do!" snapped Mom. "Especially today. What do you think Christmas is all about? Have we taught you nothing? You ought to be ashamed to even ask such a question!"

She was right. Mom looked forward to church anytime, but today there would be not only a special service, but special music as well. Scotch Settlement Presbyterian Church was blessed with a choir only on special occasions, usually just Christmas and Easter.

Following the usual scramble to get washed and dressed, we were finally ready to go. This was despite my last-minute "I've lost my shoes" routine. This routine had met with success in the past, as I'd discovered some clever hiding places. But Mom was in no mood for shenanigans this morning—if I didn't find them, she threatened, my other option was slippers. Almost by magic they surfaced. So with the errant shoes polished and bow-tie straight, out the door we went.

I guess it was Dad who noticed it first. Our Pontiac's right rear tire was as flat as the proverbial pancake. "Dash!" was Dad's comment. "Oh Harold!" was all Mom could say. Both realized that by the time Dad changed his clothes, wrestled with the tire, and dressed again, the service would be half over. Mom was practically in tears, but we younger kids couldn't have cared less. The only thought running through our minds was that now we could open our presents!

Ever since daybreak, we had wondered, discussed, and imagined what might be inside that large parcel beneath the tree. It measured nearly three feet square. "To Richard, David, and Brian," it read, in bold print, "from Santa

Claus." Confusion ensued as to who should be involved in the unwrapping, but Richard ended the debate by pointing out that he was the oldest. Once the coloured paper was stripped away, large block letters appeared underneath:

MARX STREAMLINE STEAM TYPE
ELECTRICAL TRAIN

Inside the box awaited a black shiny engine, a coal car with "New York Central" printed on the side, a hopper car, a baggage car, flat cars, a couple of passenger cars, plus a caboose. There were also some cardboard buildings, some signs, and numerous sections of track to complete the set. Finally there was the heavy black box that Richard informed us was something called a "transformer."

Richard voted himself engineer and took charge of track assembly. Brian and I tried to assist, with little luck. In no time, Richard had the transformer wired and the engine and cars circling the steel track. As with all Marx train sets, a middle rail transferred power to the train's engine via the transformer. Richard warned us that any contact with that middle rail would mean instant electrocution. I never questioned his warning for a second...even today you'd never catch me near that middle rail!

Except to eat and listen to the Queen's radio message from Buckingham Palace, I doubt we let that train rest the entire day. It gave us probably more enjoyment than any toy has since. I still have it, plus the box in which it arrived.

But there's one recurring cloud that darkens my memory of that otherwise joyful day from long ago—the absolute lack of compassion and utter insensitivity we displayed toward our mother's feelings. In our youthful selfishness, the only thing that mattered that Christmas morning was opening our presents. All Mom had requested was one solitary hour enjoying the message and music of this holy day, in the sanctuary of the church she loved. It really wasn't much to ask.

Victor, Nipper, and I

I WAS RUNNING THE NEEDLE THROUGH SOME OLD RECORDS OF mine today and was reminded how certain songs trigger special memories.

A few of the earliest songs I recall hearing on our old RCA Victor floor console—I was probably five or six—included "Shrimp Boats" by Jo Stafford, Tennessee Ernie Ford's "Sixteen Tons," and "Cool Water," by the Sons of the Pioneers. I guess I always had a passion for recorded music, because even at that tender age I remember asking Mom what a shrimp boat was, and also about the reference to "the company store" in the Ernie Ford song.

My parents had purchased that RCA Victor record player in 1946, at a cost of $260. A fair bit of comparison shopping was undertaken prior to this purchase, but the tonal quality had far surpassed the competition, in my parents' opinion. Included in this purchase price was a ten dollar shortwave option, which Mom claimed was simply a waste of money. I guess the salesman's pitch—how one could capture programs from across the globe—captivated Dad, but reality stated otherwise. Apparently if one tuned in after midnight and could stay awake for three or four hours, one might decipher intelligence from somewhere.

"I guess it might be alright for city people with nothing to do," Dad eventually acknowledged. That was as close as Mom would get to a "you were right."

I remember experimenting with the SW when I tired of regular records. All I recall was a loud continuous droning that my brother Richard insisted was an airplane flying over the Atlantic.

That statement was both impressive and intriguing, since at that time trans-ocean air travel was relatively novel. My active five-year-old imagination easily and naturally transformed the drone emitted from the single speaker into the powerful engines gliding the giant aircraft through the cloud-scattered heavens towards Europe. Sitting comfortably in front of that old RCA Victor, volume control up loud, I could easily envision myself in the cockpit, my mind alive with youthful adventure.

Mom didn't share my enthusiasm. "Turn off that dreadful racket!" she yelled.

Although it was the early part of the twentieth century before the phonograph could be regularly found in typical Canadian homes, the device had been around since the late 1870s, when Thomas Edison first devised his "talking machine," as he called it. The initial recordings made on tin foil cylinders were of extremely poor quality, and it was only after Alexander Graham Bell patented an improved wax cylinder that the phonograph's popularity was truly realized. This became especially true when the cylinder evolved to the more familiar flat wax record.

As with television today, radio and records characterized our lives 50 or 60 years ago. Radio may have dominated daylight hours, but with the exception of the regular Saturday winter night hockey game from Toronto, our vast selection of recorded music was our family's prime evening entertainment.

Like today, musical tastes within the family differed. Mom and Dad enjoyed Broadway musicals. Often my brothers and sister and I had to patiently sit through countless renditions of *Oklahoma!* or *South Pacific* before we could play our favourites. This was before the days of "extended play" recordings, better known as LP's or 33s—thus Broadway musicals were recorded on several numbered 78 rpm records and played in a particular order.

I have trouble visualizing my childhood without that record player. The machine fascinated me as far back as I can remember. The cabinet was manufactured in Owen Sound, Ontario, and constructed entirely of wood except for a large grille section in its face, behind which a twelve-inch speaker amplified that wonderful sound.

As for electronic components, the RCA contained a changer that would stack and automatically dispense one 78 at time, from a stack of up to ten. A good half hour's entertainment could be had without interruption. When the set was complete, I'd immediately yell for Mom to "turn them over!" I didn't care what she chose, as long as it wasn't more of those Broadway musicals!

I guess Mom quickly tired of running back and forth from the kitchen to the living room; by the time I was six she taught me to operate the controls myself. Apparently there was ample discussion between my parents on this subject, due to my tender age. But my absolute care and commitment toward the machine—a passion almost bordering on fanaticism—swayed the vote.

After all, I knew what to do, as I'd watched Mom hundreds of times: I'd pick out a bunch of records (I hadn't yet learned to read, so label content mattered little), lift the lid on the small copper-coloured box contained within the changer system, place the centre hole of the record over the spindle, and set the first record on the turntable For the balance of the chosen recordings, the outer rim of the record would rest on the lip of this copper box. Once all the records were stacked, one would close the box lid—gently—on the edge of the topmost recording, and slide the start switch to the "on" position—again, gently. The rest was automatic.

The tone arm would scoot smartly out onto the first recording. Once the song was completed, the arm would race back to its original position, and an egg-shaped disc beneath the lid of the copper-coloured box would rotate, pushing the edge of the next record on the spindle just far enough to release it onto the turntable.

With those 78 rpm machines, everything happened fast! The records dropped fast, the tone arm arced back and forth fast, and the record itself spun fast. I sometimes worried that the mechanics would get out of sync and the entire machine would self-destruct before my eyes.

As I couldn't read, it was always a surprise to hear what song I'd actually selected. I often ended up with "Frosty the Snowman" or "Rudolph the Red-Nosed Reindeer" in the middle of summer.

Probably two-thirds of our record collection came from three main record labels. Columbia featured artists such as Guy Mitchell, Lefty Frizzell, Doris Day, and Gene Autry.

Decca included such greats as Guy Lombardo, Bing Crosby, the Weavers, and Evelyn Knight. RCA Victor stuck to more traditional country and gospel singers, like Hank Snow, Wilf Carter, the Sons of the Pioneers, and the Carter Family.

I was especially fond of the Sons of the Pioneers. "Cool Water," a classic, was my favourite song when I was a kid. I recall one day my public school music teacher asking our first grade class their preferred song. Answers ran along the lines of "Yankee Doodle," "Jimmy Crack Corn," and "I'm a Little Teapot." When I announced "Cool Water," everyone laughed. I was devastated, but what did those idiots know about good music anyway?

On hot summer afternoons that song would remind me of the old water pump outside the door of our Simcoe County farmhouse. I'd often sing it on the way home from school. My rendition sounded particularly good, I thought, when it resonated from the concrete walls of the highway overpass.

We probably had over 200 records in our collection. There was only one I was not allowed to play…a recording by Sir Harry Lauder. It was much larger than the standard ten-inch 78, resembling instead the dimensions of later LPs. If I wanted to hear Harry, I had to ask Mom, and she would play his record for me.

Sir Harry was a Scottish singer who became renowned for his sojourns to the battlefields of World War One, where he entertained the soldiers. For some reason, all Lauder's recordings were oversized. The one we owned was always stored in the safety of Mom's dining room linen drawer. When we moved to a new farm in 1957, only two records from our vast collection failed to make the seventy-five mile trip; sadly, one of them was that Sir Harry Lauder recording, which Mom had taken such care to protect for so long.

Yesterday's Moments...Today's Memories

As a kid, all I ever wanted for my birthday were records. I think it was my fifth when I was given two dollars from Mom and Dad...a windfall. From Kilkenny's Music Shop in Bradford I chose three records. The first was by the Mariners—musicians of note in the late 1940s and early 1950s, who broke ground by establishing a racially-mixed pop music quartet. They were part of Arthur Godfrey's morning radio program for several years.

My second choice was a Charlie Chamberlain recording. Chamberlain was the featured Irish vocalist for the Don Messer band. Finally, there was "Sound Off," a number by the comedian and musician Spike Jones and his wacky band, the City Slickers...an eclectic choice to be sure.

Although the first two records were played for years, "Sound Off" did not last long in my house. It was not lost or broken, but banned—not by Canadian Standards, but by my Mom. It was an army song of which I now have only a vague recollection. But I recall marching around the house with my brother Richard, making vulgar sound effects while it played. Mom soon sent "Sound Off" unceremoniously to the dump.

Another birthday witnessed me in the music department of Toronto's downtown Eaton store, trying to decide between "Teddy Bear's Picnic" and "The Silly Song" (the latter from the Walt Disney's *Snow White*). After plenty of deliberation on my part, and unreserved frustration on Mom's, I chose the latter.

When listening to records as a kid, I didn't lounge on some comfortable chair on the opposite side of the room. Instead, I sat on a straight-back pulled tight against the record player, with the cabinet lid open so I could observe the spinning records. Hour upon hour I could be found tucked up close to that grand old RCA Victor, my cheek resting on the cabinet's felt-lined ledge, watching the revolving 78s and occasionally glancing at Nipper, the RCA Victor dog.

Nipper the terrier had been an RCA Victor trademark icon since 1910, sitting with his head cocked slightly to one side, supposedly listening to the sound emitting from the horn-type speaker. Printed underneath this delightful image was a caption: "His Master's Voice." I would pretend that Nipper was my dog, and that I was playing just for him.

By 1960, 78s were but a memory, so we either had to buy a new record player or update the one we had. Finances dictated the latter, so Jack's TV, our neighbourhood electronics outlet, removed the old changer and installed a unit that would accept the new 45 and 33 rpm discs.

The development of these modern records actually began during the 1940s, when the shellac imported from the Far East and used for coating 78 rpm records became scarce because of the war. It was substituted with a low-cost vinyl resin, which was easily handled and virtually unbreakable, thus counteracting the fragility of 78s.

The last two 78 rpm records my family owned were purchased in 1956. The first was Johnny Cash's "I Walk the Line," a record my sister Vivien practically wore out that summer. The other was a Bing Crosby and Grace Kelly duet, "True Love." That was the same year the well-known American actress married Prince Rainier of Monaco and became Princess Grace of Monaco. That 1956 recording was the only record she ever made.

That's 60 years ago, as of this writing. But even now, it doesn't take much for me to recall those days, when the melodies of the old RCA Victor delighted an appreciative audience...and in particular a fair-haired, blue-eyed Simcoe County youngster.

Two Wheels Are All You Need

IF YOU STOP TO THINK ABOUT IT, THE WORLD HAS BEEN RIDING on two wheels for nearly 200 years. The familiar appearance of today's two-wheeled, human-powered bike is merely the evolution of a form that began in the 1800s with the "boneshaker"—aptly named because of its unmerciful riding qualities. In those days, the combination of a hardwood or iron frame and solid rubber tires in conjunction with inferior roads made for a stimulating riding experience.

Following the boneshaker was the "Penny Farthing," with a pedal-operated front wheel that measured up to 60 inches in diameter, and a much smaller wheel of about 18 inches to provide some semblance of balance at the rear. The diameter of the front wheel was determined by the length of the rider's leg. Generally, the taller the rider, the faster the speed—meaning that this bike could be a lively mover, depending upon the operator's height (or, more accurately, his or her nerve). Because of the precarious riding position, retaining balance was crucial, and when—not if—you took a header after hitting some pathway obstruction, it was a long way to the ground.

The modern bicycle, with its equal-sized wheels, chain drive, and pneumatic tires, was popularized in the final two decades of the nineteenth century. More than likely due to the shortcomings of its predecessor, it became known as the "safety bicycle." Except for the fact that modern bicycles are constructed of super light materials such as aluminum and even titanium, and feature enough gear ratios to rival an eighteen wheeler, the basic configuration hasn't really changed.

My father got his first two-wheeled bicycle when he was about ten. Fred Wilkinson, a long-time employee of my grandfather's, had bought it for forty dollars...a lot of money in the 1920s, when the going wage was a dollar a day. Fred later sold the bike for thirty dollars to my grandfather, who in turn gave it to his son.

For a decade, my father travelled the length and breadth of Artemesia Township on the seat of that bicycle. During the early years of the 1930s, when the country was mired in the depths of the Great Depression, it was the only vehicle he could afford to drive. When Dad went off to Orangeville Business College in 1934, his father figured it was time to exchange the bicycle for some much-needed cash, and sold it to a neighbour for eight dollars.

The next two-wheeler to enter the scene was for Dad's brother, Doug. This would be in the late 1930s, and when Doug outgrew it, the bike was passed down to his brother Eldon, who rode it until the early 1950s.

There were no younger siblings, so when Eldon became more interested in four wheels, the bike was given to my oldest brother Bill. By this time, Bill had long outgrown the little two-wheeled "Sunshine" bike he'd ridden for years, with its solid rubber tires and belt drive. Because Eldon's bike featured a 28-inch frame, for my brother it was a big step up, literally, from the diminutive Sunshine model.

About this time, Richard, the next-youngest brother down the age ladder, received a brand-new bicycle. With its two-tone maroon and white paint, colour-blended rubber handle grips, and contrasting mud flaps, the two-wheeler struck an impressive pose. A colour-accented parcel carrier added further style as well as practicality. Rich was fanatical about that bike. No one was allowed to touch it. Any transgression to this rule was taken as an invitation to get clobbered.

Meanwhile the original generations-old two-wheeler became my "push bike" (since I couldn't ride yet). In our backyard, imagination allowed me to be in any field of our farm, plowing sod, planting and cultivating crops, cutting and baling hay, swathing and combining grain…even spreading manure.

One hot summer day I discovered that the front tire needed an infusion of air. I retrieved the hand pump from the garage, screwed the hose fitting to the valve stem, and proceeded to inject about fifty shots of fresh air into the ancient tire. That was probably about forty-five too many, especially since the inner tube was protruding through the sidewall.

Upon inflating the tire, my next project was to loosen a seized pedal. I don't know why I cared, as I didn't ride it anyway. This was before WD-40 became the accepted means of both lubrication and rust removal. To my knowledge at the time, the only product with similar properties was gasoline.

I borrowed one of the quart glass sealers my Mom used for preserving fruit and vegetables, and filled it to capacity from the supply tank in the implement shed. Adding a small amount of engine oil to the gasoline made it the perfect lubricant. I poured a liberal amount over the offending pedal, its mate, the chain, the steering mechanism, and anything else that moved (or should have). About this time, Mom hollered from the kitchen door, so I replaced the lid on the jar and left the partially-filled container beside the bike and went for lunch.

Perhaps an hour later, a loud explosion erupted from the vicinity of the garden. I was cutting grass with our push mower, and glanced up just in time to see the aforementioned bicycle returning to earth, followed closely by what appeared to be the front wheel.

In hindsight, it's obvious that the overinflated tire, the sealed jar of gasoline, and the midday sun had combined to render the front wheel unrecognizable. All that remained were a few shreds of rubber dangling from a mangled rim. Needless to say...a rather inglorious ending to that two-wheeled fragment of family history!

Now there was just one two-wheeler left on the place—Richard's—but as mentioned, he wasn't overly receptive to letting anyone use it. However, things change. For whatever reason, Richard eventually softened his stand, and his bicycle became my new push bike.

I don't know why it didn't occur to me to actually learn to ride. I was quite content with this system of travel until one day that autumn some old neighbours from Bradford paid a visit. Jimmy Hughes, a year younger than I, spied Richard's bicycle and asked if he could ride it.

"I guess so," I answered, with some trepidation. I wasn't completely at ease with my brother's supposed personality change.

"Do you have a bike?" Jimmy asked.

"No, I can't ride a two-wheeler."

"It's easy!" he said, hopping on and taking a few circuits around the yard. Well if he could...I could!

When dedicated to a specific purpose, it's surprising the effort one will expend. No sooner had they left when I began my quest—although to this day I don't know how I was able to convince Richard to let me use his bike for practice. Pushing was one thing, but the inevitable spills courtesy of an amateur rider were quite another.

My sister Vivien volunteered for basic training. Beginning on the lawn, where minimum damage could be done to both bike and rider, she held onto the seat while I wobbled around in circles. Maybe an hour passed when she announced it was time to graduate to the laneway, reasoning that the gentle slope would afford an ideal means to improve my balance without having to concern myself with pedalling.

I timidly settled my behind on the seat, and with a mild send-off courtesy Viv's hand, was underway. If I could maintain my balance, theoretically I should roll all the way to the hollow some 300 feet away. I probably went about a third that distance before falling off, but Vivien was there to prevent a total wipe-out.

Back on the horse and off again. On the third attempt I sailed right past the site of the previous spill and on down the driveway. What a glorious feeling! And then I approached the hollow and felt the bike slow, and begin leaning left. There was no one to grab it this time, but Vivien had warned of such an event.

"If the bike starts to lean...shift your weight the opposite way," she had said. I did exactly as instructed and promptly took a header off the right side of the bike.

I practised all afternoon...riding and falling...but soon learned to get my leg out before tumbling into the thistles and burdocks that bordered our laneway. By suppertime I could ride all the way from the barn to the hollow and up the grade to the road. Despite my parent's insistence on moderation, I spent an entire Sunday travelling up and down our side road.

Monday, I was in bed...sick as a dog. I guess Mom and Dad were correct; all that pedal-pushing had been too much for unconditioned stomach muscles.

Confined to bed and vomiting every half hour was a terrible letdown from the weekend's high. Bill poked his head into my room at one point during the morning and began singing a line from a Four Preps song that was popular at that time.

I was a big man yesterday but boy you ought to see me now...

For the rest of that autumn I rode Richard's bicycle anytime he'd allow, waiting for the day I'd get my own. The dream came true during the Easter break the following spring, when I received a red-and-white CCM from McPhail's Cycle in Waterloo, reconditioned and ready to ride for thirty dollars.

("Just as good as a new one, and ten dollars less," the salesman said.)

Once home I wasn't long getting it on the road. Up at the railway crossing I met my school chum, Larry. "So, you got a new bike, eh?"

"It's not new...it's reconditioned!" I replied, proudly recalling the term.

"You wanna race?" Larry asked.

"Naw...I guess not."

"Why, ya scared?"

"No, I'm not scared."

"Well then let's see who's fastest."

"Just because a bike is fast doesn't mean it's the best!"

"So you're chicken…"

"I'm not chicken!" I argued. However, I was becoming irritated.

"Okay then…we'll race to my gateway," said Larry, mounting his bike.

His bike was light years from new, with the old 28-inch wheels like the one that exploded in our yard the previous summer. "One, two, three…go!" hollered Larry.

Not expecting such a quick count, I got a poor start, but in a short distance had nearly caught him. However, the tall gearing of the old bike came into effect at that point, and he pulled away.

"I won!" yelled Larry as he passed the imaginary finishing line, two or three lengths ahead.

"Yeah, well I'm not real used to this bike yet."

"Maybe these old buggers of bikes don't look like much," boasted Larry, "but I guess they can beat a brand new one when they have to!"

"It's not new," I repeated. "It's reconditioned!"

As he turned to go, Larry hollered back, "You bringin' it to school Monday?"

"Sure am!"

On that point, however, I collided with some opposition.

"You haven't had enough experience," Dad began.

"You've never been across the highway," added Mom.

"Well I guess I know how to ride a bike!" I answered, not hiding my frustration. "I've been riding Rich's bike since last year!"

"You haven't ridden all winter," Dad countered. "I think you should practice a little more."

It took a while, but following a lot of arguing and a bit

of sulking, I was able to convince them that neither knew what they were talking about. Consequently Richard and I headed out Monday morning for school.

We generally came home for lunch, and as we crossed the highway, Richard accelerated ahead of me. I accelerated too, and was doing fine until I hit those potholes at the bridge. At the time I recall blaming the township. I remember thinking, "They have a goddam grader, why don't they use it?"

I felt the rear end of the bicycle rise off the ground while the front wheel bounced along in the succession of holes. Suddenly the bike and I were heading for the ditch, in roughly that order.

I felt a stab of pain as my chest slammed into the handlebars. Panic gripped me as I realized I couldn't breathe. A ten-year-old knows little of anatomy, but I was pretty sure I'd punctured a lung. Richard came back to survey the damage and see if I was alright.

"I'm fine...I'm just lying here in a ditch unable to breathe, and I'll be dead in a minute you stupid idiot!" At least that's what I wanted to say, but I couldn't talk...and still couldn't breathe.

It seemed an eternity but finally my lungs inflated with a jolt as the air came rushing back. It was then I truly felt the chest pain. Then I noticed my cut knee through my torn trousers. And my scraped elbow. And my cut lip. I believe it was at this point that I began to bawl.

Richard helped me retrieve my bike from the ditch. It was in much better shape than I. Tearfully and painfully, I made my way home. It's to my parents' credit they never said "I told you so." I was such a wreck, both physically and emotionally, that I didn't even return to school that afternoon.

"Everybody saw you fall off your bike and crash into the ditch," Richard said to me that evening. "The entire school was laughing at you all afternoon."

Thanks, Rich. I really needed that.

Despite that near disaster, I spent many hours on the seat of that CCM. I purchased a cyclometer for it that summer, and sometime before I graduated from public school three years later, I'd clocked over a thousand miles. I still recall what a milestone that figure was to me at the time.

I even rode it one winter, though there was even more opposition from my parents after the aforementioned calamity. "Stupid," "idiotic," "retarded," "brainless"—these were some of the adjectives I recall.

Larry and I were trying to see who could ride their bike to school the longest during the upcoming winter. As a gesture of good sportsmanship, and since Larry had twice the distance to travel, I spotted him a few "free" days. The marathon lasted until sometime in February, when even Larry realized my idea was a masterpiece of stupidity, and withdrew from the competition.

My win proved to be a two-edged sword, as bucking snowdrifts for three months destroyed the drive gears on my bike. When spring arrived, I was without wheels. Dad, not usually one to say "I told you so," didn't mince words this time. I don't recall his exact wording, but it was something to the effect of "What did you expect for being an idiot?"

Just to make sure I didn't miss the point, Dad took his time in getting the bike repaired. In fact, three weeks went by (an eternity to a ten-year-old) while everyone else enjoyed two-wheeling in the beautiful April weather. Okay, Dad…point taken!

Triple Triangle...
Trial and Triumph

At precisely 7:20 a.m., a giant locomotive eased its string of railway cars into the crowded station, generating a last-minute scramble for suitcases and shopping bags from the waiting room. At that moment a latecomer sprinted into the ticket office, nearly toppling a thin, middle-aged man in a brown fedora, who was rising from the bench on the platform in front of the building. The victim of the encounter glared at the offending party, having no tolerance for anyone with such disregard for punctuality.

He'd been here for some 40 minutes, enjoying from his vantage point on the station bench the resonance of a city awakening: the familiar rhythm of streetcars clattering along the concrete and brick arteries, and the faint but steady sound of horse hooves returning an empty milk wagon from its morning route. The echo of a steamer's horn on Lake

Ontario was obscured by the whining gears of a passing truck on its way to a downtown department store.

As the train shuddered to a standstill, the gentleman in the brown fedora joined the rapidly expanding crowd on the platform. A conductor attired in dark blue greeted each passenger as they entered the train.

"Good morning, Will," said the conductor, acknowledging the man in the brown felt hat. My grandfather returned the greeting, choosing a seat third from the rear on the right side of the coach and placing his briefcase on the vacant seat beside him. Will Carruthers was well-known to railroad personnel. For two decades he'd been making these trips into the rural reaches of western Ontario in his capacity as a service advisor for his employer, the Massey-Harris Company.

"All aboard!" Will Carruthers checked his watch and noted the time with approval. The engine gave a mighty heave as pressurized steam rushed to fill its cylinders. As momentum increased, Will settled comfortably into the soft leather while the city slowly faded from view.

The huge locomotive was soon gliding its cargo of passengers through the rolling hills of Acton and Georgetown towards Guelph. Here my grandfather would transfer to the Hamilton-Owen Sound passenger train. A twenty- to thirty-minute delay was common at this important junction, where passengers could observe the never-ending ritual of freight cars being shunted around the rail yard, coupling and uncoupling to join different trains to a variety of destinations.

From Guelph, the train threaded northwesterly toward the picturesque village of Elora, whose unique buildings were made from solid stone mined from the quarry on which the village was built. Then Fergus, home of Beatty Bros., a company whose line of livestock equipment and household appliances were renowned in North America, and Canadian National Railroad's largest customer north of Guelph. Without fail, Beatty Bros. generated a full rail car of freight every day.

Through Drayton, Goldstone, and Moorefield, the train traveled to the most important centre on the Guelph to Owen Sound line, Palmerston—the hub of all railroad activity in southwestern Ontario during the 1920s. Spreading outward like wheel spokes from Palmerston's rail yards were lines to scores of communities.

The first stop north of Palmerston was the town of Harriston. Here, flat cars of lumber, oil and gasoline tankers, coal, grain and fertilizer hoppers, and refrigerated boxcars from Canada-Packers together contributed to make an important link in the CNR freight chain.

From there the train passed the hamlet of Drew, site of no less than four brickyards, and then the busy mill town of Ayton, and the village of Neustadt. Several industries—including lumber, furniture, and beer—made Neustadt an important stop for the rail lines.

North of Neustadt the terrain changed from picturesque rolling hills to the lowlands of the Saugeen River basin. When Will Carruthers had visited this area in the spring, water had completely immersed the tracks for a considerable distance.

There were no such distractions this September day, and soon the northbound train was negotiating the several-mile incline between Hanover and Elmwood, its black smoke pouring past the coach windows. At 12:30 p.m., train #173 passed beneath the long wooden overpass, angling across the railroad tracks just south of the Chesley station. Few travellers were more familiar with the train stations in western Ontario than my grandfather, and the tall, pointed twin roofs of Chesley were among his favourites.

Practically every town and village of that era was home to a machinery dealership of some description—sometimes two or three, depending upon population and area. Almost without exception, these were family-owned and family-run operations; often no larger than modern day two-car garages. Husband and wife would handle all facets of business...equipment sales, parts ordering, bookkeeping, and warranty issues. The employment roster generally consisted of one, possibly two mechanics. All ordered machinery, parts, etc., arrived by train and were stored in the railway's freight sheds for pickup by the local dealer.

Dealerships followed a pattern dictated by the times, and whether you were in the counties of Bruce, Grey, Wellington, Huron, or Perth, the layout was prescribed. There was always a section where welding and other repair work was undertaken, while shelves and cubbyholes behind the counter abounded with the most frequently-stocked machinery parts. A cluttered collection of cream separators, fanning mills, feed grinders, etc., jostled for position amongst an assortment of mower knives and guards, binder twine, canvas, chain of varying lengths, lubricants, and hardware of every description. Invariably a haphazard arrangement of the larger machinery the company manufactured would be stationed in a nearby yard.

Will Carruthers' service trips involved an agenda set by Massey's head office in Toronto; a central "jumping off" point, where the area Massey dealer would meet my grandfather and drive him to customers who were experiencing problems that for one reason or another he was unable to address.

My grandfather's specialty was cream separators...a division that had been a profit-maker for the company from its inception two decades earlier.

Prior to the invention of this amazing machine, cream separation was performed by simply allowing a pail of milk to sit while the cream floated to the surface in its own good time—at which point it was manually skimmed.

The heart of an automatic cream separator was the series of discs which used centrifugal force to bring the lighter cream in one direction while the heavier butterfat was brought another. Each would then drain into a separate container. A hand-operated crank had to be turned at about sixty revolutions a minute (a timing bell on the crank alerted the operator when the correct rpm was reached). If a problem arose—for instance, not enough cream being removed—the culprit would invariably be an imbalance in the aforementioned discs.

Will Carruthers seldom wore coveralls for the numerous service calls he'd undertake in a day. Casual observers found it compelling that he was able to formulate his duties on often grimy, greasy machines, clad in dress shirt and tie, and never seem to suffer sartorial consequences. The fedora was part of my grandfather's attire as well. It was worn partly as a shield from the sun, but mostly because of sensitivity to his baldness...a condition he'd endured since his twenties.

Noted for impatience in many aspects of his life, Will Carruthers was a study in meticulousness when it came to the time-consuming job of balancing a cream separator. Crank the handle, stop, add weight to one side of the separator bowl; crank, stop, add more weight; crank, perhaps subtract a little weight from the opposite side. His chalk was always in hand so he could mark various places on the bowl.

Although separator service was his bread and butter, my grandfather would often be asked to investigate problems on other Massey equipment a farmer might own. Perhaps an oat roller wasn't cracking the grain to suit a customer's wishes, or a fanning mill was failing to sufficiently remove the desired amount of wild oats or weed seeds. Maybe the gasoline engine so prevalent in a variety of machines in that pre-hydro era wouldn't start. Maybe a milking machine pump was suffering from low vacuum.

Warranted or not, farmers placed a lot of faith in Will Carruthers, who'd been around the Toronto factory long enough to garner a keen insight into many activities deemed outside his realm of expertise. Even if he couldn't actually remedy the situation onsite, he'd gained enough knowledge through the years to at least direct the area dealer to the course needed to rectify the complaint.

My grandfather would sometimes work in this capacity for two or three days, covering a large portion of the county. These excursions into the wild countryside—breaks from factory life and the hurried atmosphere of the city—were among his greatest enjoyments. For twenty years, "riding the rails" had been his station with the company, and he sincerely hoped it would always be.

But then came the financial disaster an entire generation would refer to simply as "the Depression." Beginning with the economic collapse in late 1929, manufacturers of most any product were reduced to a fraction of what they'd known. It would be no different for Massey-Harris, who experienced eight uninterrupted years of losses totalling nearly twenty million...probably three hundred million in today's inflated dollars...and were pushed to the financial brink.

A new general-manager was installed at Massey-Harris in a desperate attempt to stop the economic hemorrhaging. Bert Burtsell knew nothing of selling farm machinery, nor did he care; profit and loss statements, cost projections, and production goals were of little importance to him. His philosophy centred on the premise that people, not figures, were the key ingredient in running a business. If they were worth their wage...fine...if not, firing was the simple solution. The very things that Massey-Harris shareholders wanted proved to be Burtsell's speciality and priority: mop up the mess by slashing costs, trimming excess fat, and weeding out the deadwood.

Canadian workers in one European factory learned the new general-manager's technique the hard way. Those Burtsell considered expendable were issued a prepared speech. "Get yourself and your family on a boat back to Canada, my friend," it began. "You're finished here. Good luck somewhere else. That's all, thank you."

Although Burtsell's "house cleaning" tactics were in many instances unfair and unwarranted, Massey-Harris did manage to survive the Depression. But only a complete reversal of fortune would offset the financial pummelling the company had endured.

Massey got exactly what it needed...not in agricultural sales, but in war contracts. By early 1940, Massey's Toronto and Woodstock factories were both producing 40 millimetre anti-aircraft shells and military truck bodies. Wings for fighter bombers were built at the Weston plant and army tank treads at Brantford. Beginning in 1942, M-H signed a contract with the US government to manufacture

1200 tanks a year, to be assembled at the recently vacated Nash-Kelvinator plant in Racine, Wisconsin. This lucrative contract would account for 60 percent of the value of all war-related products for the company.

Massey-Harris never had what might be known as "average" years. From its inception in 1847, when it was known as the Massey Manufacturing Co., the company experienced a constant succession of extreme highs and lows. It had stumbled in the late 1800s, learning the hard way that business wasn't sustainable in the Canadian market alone. The company then embarked on an extensive and expensive multinational undertaking that over several decades would witness factories operating in North and South America, Europe, Britain, Asia, Australia and Africa. If an economic or political crisis upset local sales somewhere, it was management's belief that because of their global empire, the effect would be minimal.

Following World War Two, an expected recession materialized, but the company had seemingly regained its footing by the 1950s with two major accomplishments: acquiring Perkins Diesel in Britain, and partnering with Irish inventor Harry Ferguson in order to gain access to the brilliant hydraulic system he'd developed...a hydraulic system that would revolutionize the agricultural industry.

Although it was the leader in combines, Massey-Harris had lagged far behind its competitors when it came to tractor development. Ferguson's "three point hitch" was the ticket needed to ignite this stalled segment of their industry. But even that achievement proved to be a managerial headache. The company tried to operate Ferguson and Massey-Harris as separate entities under the awkward and cumbersome title Massey-Harris-Ferguson. Both were basically selling the same size tractors, putting them in direct competition with one another. Five years passed before this unwieldy management structure was able to forge a single distribution and dealer network—Massey-Ferguson—but not before dragging the machinery company to the brink of economic disaster again…seemingly a once-a-decade occurrence.

What would prove to be Massey-Ferguson's most profitable and successful period was during the 1960s and early 1970s, when worldwide sales of tractors and self-propelled combines reached a zenith. Nearly 50 percent of all tractors sold in the world at that time had the Massey-Ferguson triple-triangle logo emblazoned on their hoods; and M-F combines had an 80 percent market share…unheard of for a single agricultural unit from any company before or since.

This utopia lasted until the latter 1970s when the roller-coaster ride disguised as the farm machinery business began another downward plunge. Ballooning interest rates increased the cost of servicing debts, and the nation's agricultural community faced a financial crunch due to rising borrowing costs and declining commodity prices, which in turn made it difficult for farmers to purchase new machinery.

South American markets had gone into a precipitous economic slump of their own, and European farmers had suffered poor crops two years in succession, which also affected sales. Massey-Ferguson's global operation seemed a sound concept when things were going well, but quickly became a disaster when the financial tide turned.

The weak link in Massey's chosen path seemed to be its sheer size and complexity. With a multitude of operations in as many countries, controlled by vice-presidents and general-managers preferring to do things their own way, the economic fallout from global calamities took weeks or even months to trickle back to the head office in Toronto.

If ever a company needed strong leadership and guidance it was now. Interest rates were 20 percent or more and the agricultural industry was on the verge of total collapse. Massey-Ferguson's losses were staggering: $100 million in 1976, $200 million by 1978, $400 million by 1980. When tough decisions on how to reverse company fortunes should have been paramount, M-F executives were preoccupied with finding a new president to guide the company into the future...if indeed there was one. The organization now controlled by politicians, lawyers, accountants, lumber magnates, and brewery tycoons had seemingly lost touch with the grass roots.

During its two-decade heyday beginning in the late 1950s, company meetings centred on building a better combine or tractor. Twenty years later, the company was preoccupied with personality conflicts, self-interest disputes, shareholder dividend issues, and other political wrangling, while issues such as new product development or improved dealer relations were overlooked or underestimated.

Finally, in 1981, facing a staggering debt load of nearly $700 million, Massey-Ferguson was rescued in one of the most complicated bailouts in industrial history, one that involved governments, banks, and other financial institutions worldwide. But the cost was enormous: 5,000 workers from Massey-Ferguson's Toronto and Brantford factories faced instant unemployment, as well as nearly 2,000 in the United States. A similar story affected Massey's company offices and factories across the globe.

Despite continuing high interest rates on borrowed money and low returns on farm commodities, Massey-Ferguson carried on, although just a shadow of itself in some areas. In 1985,

M-F, once a leader in the self-propelled combine market, shuttered the Brantford factory that it had spent 13.5 million to build two decades earlier. It was the end of another era when, after a century and a half in Toronto, corporate headquarters was transferred to New York.

Massey wasn't alone in the agricultural freefall of the 1980s, as industry giants Allis-Chalmers and International Harvester succumbed to insurmountable debt. IH was absorbed by Case and A-C by German farm equipment leader, Deutz.

The following decade would witness Massey-Ferguson itself purchased by US-based AGCO corporation—at that time the only company left in the world totally dedicated to sale of agricultural equipment. With this new organizational boost, M-F combines once again returned to fields throughout the world. Although far outdistanced by industry leaders John Deere and Case-IH, today's Massey harvesters are making a valiant resurgence, with machines in many respects more technically advanced than their competitors'.

Despite all the challenges, Massey-Ferguson continued to maintain its enviable position in tractor production as the century drew to a close, celebrating nearly 40 consecutive years with the top-selling tractor in the western world.

While production came to an end in 2002 at the Coventry factory in Great Britain—a site that had built more than 3,000,000 tractors—2011 witnessed AGCO shift production of large Massey-Ferguson tractors from France to a brand-new American factory in Jackson MN. The goal was to be closer to, and thus more competitive in, the strong US market, with established competitors Case IH and John Deere. Today, with engineering technology second to none, the company wearing the venerable triple-triangle logo appears full of promise. But as history's economic lessons have so often demonstrated, perhaps the most fitting reaction should simply be cautious optimism.

The clock on the Tara post office was striking 2:00 p.m. as Will Carruthers stood at the village railroad station ticket counter. Following three days of providing service and information to area Massey-Harris dealerships and farmers, he was heading back to Toronto's head office. Departure time for the southbound train was a half hour away...barely sufficient for a man of such passionate schedule.

Settled comfortably in the third seat from the rear on the right side, southbound passenger #174 eased away from the tiny Tara station. Whether simple superstition or compulsive disorder, this "always sit in the same seat" syndrome was practised with regularity by my grandfather, and was as important as his obsession with schedule.

The first station south of Tara was the hamlet of Dobbington, which was no more than a "flag stop" for mail and an occasional passenger ten months of the year. The exception was in autumn, when western Canadian cattle arrived by the carload at Dobbington's livestock holding pens, for delivery to area farms.

Next, Chesley, where my grandfather had disembarked 72 hours before. Like its southern sister, Hanover, Chesley thrived on the craftsmanship of furniture manufacturers, and their exports provided the rail lines with decades of steady income.

Elmwood...Hanover...Neustadt...Ayton...Drew... Harriston...Palmerston. With a 20 minute respite, many passengers took advantage of this stop for a quick lunch at the Queen's Hotel, which adjoined the Palmerston station.

But not my grandfather: he might get delayed by some unforeseen force at the lunch counter, and miss his train... or, almost as traumatic, lose his designated seat! Will Carruthers instead retrieved a chocolate bar from his vest pocket, purchased with foresight earlier in the day for this very occasion.

Moorefield...Gladstone...Drayton...Alma...Fergus...Elora...Guelph. Large or small, major freight customers or simple flag stops, Will Carruthers knew the individual communities by heart. And not just the Owen Sound line but equally the railway subdivisions to Southampton, Wiarton, Kincardine and Stratford.

My grandfather loved train travel, whatever the season. He found winter especially calming, half-sleeping as the train wound its way through the darkness, soothed by the rhythmic clicking of the steel wheels on the coupling joints beneath his feet, and the far-off chant of the whistle echoing through the hushed snow-covered countryside.

But this life to which my grandfather had grown accustomed was fast disappearing. As the aforementioned Great Depression gradually and steadily strangled North American and European industries in the 1930s, Massey, like everyone else, did what they could to stem the frightening tide of financial loss. Compared to Massey's major cost-slashing practices during this time, curtailing employee expense accounts may have seemed inconsequential. But train tickets, hotel lodging, food allowances, and other service specialist perks added up. For now, at least, franchise dealers could look after their issues themselves.

Because of his seniority, Will Carruthers retained employment throughout the 1930s, although in the depths of the financial paralysis, his regular 45-hour week was cut to less than half. He'd gained a keen insight into all facets of the company's manufacturing process, and so offered his assistance wherever needed.

It was full employment and more during the 1940s... sometimes 60 hours a week, as the company fought to fulfil large government military contracts and at the same time keep some semblance of continuity in their agricultural line. While the government had banned automobile production, agricultural machinery was considered essential, though it was severely curtailed because of limited time and resources. A farmer could order a new piece of machinery, but would have to prove, through endless provincial and federal government forms, that the need was justified. The wait might be 18 months— if the request was approved at all.

My grandfather reached the mandatory retirement age of 65 in May 1950, but continued until August, thereby fulfilling 40 uninterrupted years of service. When he began his tenure in 1910, tractors were little more than an experimental exercise. Several of the huge steamers, which were closer in appearance to locomotives, existed back then, but were used strictly for threshing purposes. An everyday all-crop logically-sized tractor was still years away.

For his 40 year tenure, my grandfather received the customary gold watch that companies issued in those days, as well as a personal thank-you letter written on official Massey-Harris stationery and signed by company president James Duncan.

Although my grandfather had witnessed a significant evolution in the manufacturing of machinery during his 40-year tenure, in the grand scheme of things it would be but a moment in time. At Will Carruthers' farewell party, he and an associate were reminiscing about the transformations that had taken place during his four decades of Massey employment. Will nodded in agreement and answered, "Yes...I've seen it all!"

But compared to the seemingly insurmountable trials and challenges the company would encounter in the future, in actuality, my grandfather had seen very little!

A Valentine Story

My maternal grandparents, Will and Reba Carruthers, raised a family of five girls: Evelyn (my mother), Jean, Alma, Lois, and Lillian.

From an early age, music generated a common interest throughout the family. My mother took violin lessons throughout elementary school, and in her opinion was "pretty good." Providing just the necessities of life was a challenge during the 1930s, but despite the difficult economic times, my grandparents scraped together the dollars needed to purchase a used piano, reasoning that any flare for music among their children should be explored.

My grandfather's brother, George, didn't share this vision, only consenting to music lessons for his daughter after a long argument. Inquiring after a few sessions when this would be "all over," he was informed by the teacher that "the study of music is never over!" Well, it was over as far as George was concerned, and the lessons ceased.

Will and Reba, in contrast, provided as much encouragement as possible for their daughters. As a result, Jean took lessons for years, becoming a beautiful pianist. Then she became a teacher herself, at twenty-five cents a lesson. It was through Jean that Lillian too became an accomplished artist.

Another collective thread among the five sisters was their aptitude for business. After high school, all but Jean attended Western Commerce and Technical, an educational institute whose curriculum featured typing, shorthand, and bookkeeping skills. Lillian excelled in this environment, as a newspaper item in 1940 boldly stated:

Lillian Carruthers Winner of Western Tech Awards

> Lillian Carruthers will be the star of the evening when Western Comm. & Tech. holds its commencement tomorrow night. She is the winner of the wristwatch donated by W.H. Spence, teacher, for top student in fourth year Stenography; the Sir Isaac Pitman Shield for General Stenography and the Pitman Gold Medal, which means the winner made a speed of more than 150 words a minute in shorthand.

Following graduation, Lillian associated her commercial talents with the British-American Petroleum Company's Toronto office. Here she met her future husband.

Don Valentine was one of several salesmen regularly travelling the Toronto-Windsor corridor (Highway 2 in those pre-401 days) distributing B-A products to gas stations and automotive stores. Don had grown up in the neighbouring town of Oshawa, where his first taste of salesmanship was in menswear.

It was a tough task selling anything during the most crippling economic collapse the world had known. It was even tougher that Oshawa's major employer was automobile manufacturing, one of the hardest-hit industries of the Depression. The Valentine family certainly weren't immune; Don's father operated a bakery, but was unable to keep the venture afloat, and, following years of economic adversity, was forced into bankruptcy.

To keep the store operating, the senior Mr. Valentine had mortgaged his home and consequently lost everything. Don had been working long enough by this time to have gained considerable trust within the financial world and was successful in securing a mortgage to buy back the house, which he in turn rented to his parents.

Following a variety of sales-related positions, Don graduated to the B-A company in the mid-1940s. His outgoing personality and natural ability consistently placed him in the top category of monthly sales totals. Each Friday, upon submitting his order book, Don would linger at Lillian Carruthers' desk, making conversation. Finally he asked for a date.

Although her office co-workers were quite taken with the young salesman, Lillian perceived him to be rather struck on himself. But she accepted his offer nevertheless. She must have sensed some relationship potential, for she spent thirty dollars on a new dress. "I hope he's worth it," her mother remarked.

The two were married in October, 1951, at Royce Presbyterian Church in Toronto. The ceremony was followed by a supper and reception in Mimico. A half century ago,

Mimico was just one of a series of little towns that dotted Highway 2 along the north shore of Lake Ontario west of Toronto. Lillian's aunt, Ada Genoe, known throughout her life for her poetic endeavours, penned a few lines to commemorate the day. I include an excerpt:

> ...It was nice to meet our many friends, who had assembled there
> Reverend Whitely heard the marriage vows, confetti filled the air.
> There were aunts and uncles, sisters four, and in-laws, cousins too,
> With ushers to escort the ladies to their proper pews;
> The bride's Mom wore a grey dress, the groom's Mom wore blue,
> They both looked extremely nice, as good mothers always do.
> The bridesmaid was a princess in her peachy satin gown,
> As handsome as our "Princess E," who comes from London town.
> The "Pickfair" is at Mimico, they served the supper there,
> To sixty-eight, the place was filled, every table held two pair.
> I met my brother from the country and my sister from the states,
> And they served us turkey supper heaped up on dinner plates...

A few months following the wedding, Don Valentine, to the surprise of many, left B-A. Believing he'd extended his salesman's role as far as possible with the company, Don was searching for a new challenge when he spotted a newspaper advertisement. The ad described a small but growing Montreal-based wholesale company that needed an aggressive and industrious salesperson to spearhead activities for their new Toronto office. Through the owner and president, Gerald Wyant, Don learned that the company provided cleaning supplies and paper products—towels, tissue, cups, plates, towel and soap dispensers—to businesses, schools, factories, hospitals, and other institutions.

This appeared to be the opportunity Don had been looking for. All he had to do was convince his new wife... and her father. Lillian was naturally hesitant about a career change at this juncture, and Will Carruthers cautioned his new son-in-law to give the decision serious thought, reminding him of the risks involved with new ventures. "You have an excellent job with a well-respected company," he said.

My uncle was a cautious man, so I'm certain he gave the matter the consideration it deserved—but in effect a decision had been already reached.

After driving Plymouth vehicles (both company and personal cars) for several years, Don bought a new Ford in 1956. Two years later, he traded it in for a Pontiac. I recall Dad asking his reasoning. According to my uncle he had nothing against the Ford...he thought it was a great car. However, he'd recently scored a coup by capturing a large portion of General Motor's Oshawa account, and in his words, "when you pull up in front of General Motors headquarters, it's just good business to be driving a General Motors vehicle." Hard work and long hours would garner many lucrative accounts and contracts, not to mention many more Pontiacs in the years ahead.

Aunt Lillian paid her dues as well. Over the years she'd dutifully sacrificed family and social life for the company. Just arriving home from the hospital following their second child, Don received an urgent call from his partner. He was needed in Chicago that night.

"Gerry...I can't right now!" argued Don.

"You've got to!" Wyant maintained, just as strongly, and making clear the subject wasn't negotiable. Don was gone for five days. Wyant sent Lillian flowers as compensation.

For as far back as I can recall, Mom's sisters—all Toronto inhabitants—made a habit of spending a portion of their summer holidays at our farm. The Valentines were part of that annual ritual. They usually stayed for five days. For Don, those few days in the fresh air and open spaces, away from the pressure of business, were idyllic.

My uncle loved home cooking, and Mom enjoyed having Don for a guest, as he was full of praise for whatever was on the menu. She made every variety of fruit pie imaginable, and fruit preserves were always complimented by her famous tea biscuits.

Don and Lillian had two boys: David, who was five years younger than me, and Randy, who was three years younger than that. Randy was fascinated with rural culture. "Take me out to the farm, Uncle David!" he would say when just three or four years old. (Despite being first cousins, he always referred to me as "uncle.")

The "farm" was actually the barn...and Randy loved every facet, whether cows, calves, or cats. He'd gladly spent his entire vacation in or around the barn if possible. David, on the other hand, had little interest in farming, and was generally bewildered as to what inspired his brother.

It always seemed David was trying to figure everyone

else out as well. "Why do you ask so many questions?" he inquired of me on one occasion.

"That's the only way you learn things."

David pondered my response. "I think people ask questions because they feel it's easier than figuring the answer themselves."

Questioning *him* on a particular subject, however, merely invited more questions. "So what do *you* think the answer is?" he would ask.

The Valentine kids were well-equipped with toys and games, and were never hesitant to share. We'd spend hours marvelling at the Etch-a-Sketch, or playing one of a half-dozen board games they'd bring with them...and usually losing if David was your partner.

Even at the age of seven or eight, David had perfected the art of imbalanced play. After several rounds of a particular game we'd finally reach the conclusion David was utilizing his own rules. When confronted, there was never any look of shock, denial or even repentance...just a shrug of the shoulders that seemed to indicate, "So, what's the problem?"

I don't ever recall Uncle Don having to discipline Randy, but David was a different story. Any transgression on David's part would culminate in "a talk." I well remember the day David told his father to "shut up."

"What did you say, young man?"

David was brave, but he wasn't stupid, and he didn't repeat the statement.

"I think we'd better have a talk!" Don then led his eldest son behind the implement shed for what I guess was "a talk."

Personally, the thing I liked best about a Valentine visit

was the opportunity to fawn over their latest car. Don used his car for business and traded it in every other year. In 1960 he'd just purchased a new Pontiac while we were still driving our 1950 model.

"A lot of changes in ten years," commented our father, comparing the two cars. After they'd walked away, David asked me which car I liked best. This was hardly worth a dignified answer, so I merely shrugged my shoulders. "Well, yours, of course!"

"Why?" inquired David.

It was then I realized my cousin had asked the question in all sincerity. To him, a car was a car; old or new, rusty or showroom perfect...just a car. Both vehicles got their passengers to where they wished to go. No one could accuse David Valentine of bragging about material possessions!

David and Randy's initial steps in the business world began at Wyant and Co. but both chose to go their own way as time passed. David pursued the legal field, becoming a corporate lawyer, while Randy chose a career with Canada Post.

Wyant and Co. continued to thrive despite stiff pressure from local competitor GH Wood, whose main office was on Wellington Street in downtown Toronto.

Geoffrey Wood had made his mark early in the twentieth century with the development of the disposable paper cup. Promoting sanitation and disease prevention as much as convenience, his paper cup became an institutional phenomenon and his "Sanitation for the Nation" slogan a household phrase.

Wyant and Company scored a business coup by acquiring the GH Wood Company in the 1980s, becoming known as Wood-Wyant. Some thought the reason "Wood" was placed first was that it had a longer history and its name was more recognizable to consumers. Actually, the new company's marketing managers simply figured Wood-Wyant sounded a better tone than the reverse.

Being a major player in the highly-charged business world for so many years, Don Valentine realized he simply couldn't retire "cold turkey." He chose instead to taper off over a period of two or three years. But things had changed. Gerald Wyant had retired and his son was now head of operations in Montreal.

Wyant and Valentine had known a great relationship; from their initial meeting they had enjoyed a seemingly natural pairing of personality and purpose. Sales meant everything—whether a grand scale order to General Motors, or a carton of toilet paper and a tub of detergent to their next-door neighbour, each sale generated the same enthusiasm. Someone once commented that both men "would rather sell than eat."

But it was a different world now. A new generation of management who relied on others to promote new ideas, launch new products, and stimulate sales...tasks both founders had relished in their "hands-on," personal approach to business.

Although there was nothing wrong with this new approach (Don had always maintained that "new ideas stimulate new business"), it wasn't his way. Without his partner, Don quickly realized there was little room for him within this changed business environment.

Nothing proved that point with more clarity then the young Wyant's assertion that "I'll certainly never work my ass off like you and Dad did!"

A Roll of the Dice

A FARM IS A GREAT ENVIRONMENT FOR RAISING CHILDREN, BUT constantly working and playing around vehicles, machinery, and animals invites many potential dangers. One of my mother's earliest memories is of being at her grandparents' Grey County farm. Her grandfather was cutting oats with the binder and saw something pink in the tall grain. Bringing the three horse team to an abrupt halt, he discovered the "something pink" was a ribbon in his granddaughter's hair. Mom, no more than three or four at the time, had waded out into the uncut grain for a closer look at the operation.

When my sister Vivien was eight or nine she tumbled head first out of a hayloft, falling several feet onto the wooden plank floor. She heard a crack when she hit the hard surface and had a very sore neck for several days. She could have broken her neck and probably should have undergone

Yesterday's Moments...Today's Memories

x-rays, but since she had been warned by Mom just the day before about playing in the hayloft, never mentioned it.

Still, when one considers the variety of ways six kids could get into trouble, I guess we fared above average. There were the usual things, of course...a cow standing on your foot or kicking your shins, or perhaps someone dropping a bale of hay onto your head as you were walking under the feed chute. These were normal everyday occurrences, and were given little thought.

Some incidents were more memorable. When Don was still preschool age, a group of heifers surrounded him in the pasture. When he tried to run, one took up the chase, butting him in the backside and knocking him to the ground. Each time he rose he was walloped again. Although one heifer was the ringleader, the rest of the herd followed along, enjoying the fun. After a few more somersaults, Don reached the safety of the electric fence, and crawled under. The herd was running full speed now, and he was afraid that the cattle might simply crash through the wire barrier. They stopped short, however, and Don walked home relatively intact. He never told Mom or Dad, but later confided in me. I dismissed it at the time as an active imagination, informing him that "only bulls chase people."

Machinery provided plenty of possibilities for trouble. It's not a good idea for kids to ride on tractors, but that's the way we grew up. However, if a wagon was being pulled behind a tractor, Dad insisted that's where we should ride. There was always the chance of toppling off the back of the loaded wagon onto the road, but I guess Dad considered that better than falling off the tractor in front of the wagon.

"Now you kids be careful up there; remember to duck when we pass under those hydro wires!"

Our father had instigated a lengthy list of "never" rules:

Never let your foot off the clutch when there is anyone around the tractor, unless you're absolutely certain the transmission is in neutral.

Never take a tractor out of gear when going downhill.

For the older children, who might be driving cars and trucks, there were guidelines as well:

Never get into a vehicle without first checking underneath for kids and pets.

Never work on a machine unless the PTO (power-take-off) is disengaged—and be careful around any moving belt, chain, sprocket, or pulley.

At some point we managed to break or bend most of these policies. Brian recalled giving Don and a couple of city cousins a fast-paced ride in the grain wagon, when he tried unsuccessfully to downshift on a steep slope and the transmission went into neutral. "I was about ten years old," he said, "and of course our tractors never had any brakes. I remember racing down the long grade and the kids bouncing around like beach balls in the empty wagon and the relief when it finally slowed and stopped. If I'd attempted to slow the momentum by turning or some other evasive manoeuvre, the wagon would've flipped for sure!"

My oldest brother, Bill, made the same mistake—while towing a wagonload of hay, he tried to downshift on the notorious Wallaceville Hill some five miles from our place. While it may have proved frightening for him, spectators witnessed an impressive sight; the runaway tractor and wagon racing downhill at triple speed, engine revving wildly, with twelve inches of flame shooting from the exhaust pipe!

Bill had a few anxious moments while backing the car from the garage one day. He heard a tapping noise on the outside of the front passenger door, and believing that he'd scraped something, hit the brake. Leaning across the passenger seat, he spied his two-year-old brother's curly head just below the window. Don had apparently noticed Bill get into the car and had run towards the vehicle in hopes of a ride. He had some toy in his hand and he was banging it against the door while trying to open it.

Any time Dad warned about excessive speed he was usually referring to Richard. Richard believed a tractor should travel at full velocity. He was spreading manure one afternoon, and when he didn't return on schedule, a look back through the fields revealed the manure spreader up on high ground, but the tractor down in the creek.

If I remember correctly, Richard's excuse went something like this: "As I was turning out of the gateway, Old Dixie"—one of the foundations of our Holstein herd—"wandered in front of me. It was either run over the cow or slide down the bank."

Another time, Richard suffered a close call through no fault of his own. I was operating the tractor that day. I had hitched onto the mower and was about to exit the implement shed when Richard motioned for me to stop, noticing something incorrect about the draw pin. While he and Dad muddled around behind the tractor, I sat patiently waiting, with my foot on the clutch. Not locating what was needed in the tractor toolbox, Richard began rummaging through an assortment of hardware scattered on a shelf directly in front of the tractor.

By now, my leg was beginning to cramp, and I realized I was still depressing the clutch. Upon release I was immediately reminded I'd failed to put the tractor out of gear. The Allis-Chalmers lurched forward, pinning the back of Richard's ankle beneath the front tire. Fortunately, the engine was just idling, and it stalled. Dad shot us a horrified glance as he desperately tried to roll the tractor rearward. He succeeded, and Richard pulled his foot free.

All I recall of the next few moments was Dad repeatedly asking Richard if he was alright. I just sat there, numb. I was sure I had broken his leg or at least his foot. It was an unparalleled sense of relief when he convinced us he was okay.

For me, what happened next was equally memorable. My Uncle John, who was visiting from Toronto, walked by the shed at that moment and noticed me on the tractor seat.

"Well, I didn't know you drove the tractor, Dave! It seems last year you were just this high...and now look at you!" I was wishing for the world he'd just shut up and move on, but no such luck.

"I can't get over you driving the tractor!" John repeated. "The boys sure grow up, don't they, Harold?" Dad never answered, but that didn't bother my uncle. He seldom heard what you had to say, anyway—what with his bad ear and all.

"Yes, they sure grow up. I guess they're quite a help, eh, Harold?"

"Sometimes," was Dad's curt answer. Mercifully, something caught my uncle's attention at that point, and he left to investigate. He couldn't have appeared at a more inopportune time, and I was never so glad to see anyone leave. As for the event itself, Dad said nothing more. But later that day, when no one was looking, Richard took the opportunity to administer me a thorough pounding.

An injury concerning Brian occurred because one of the most important rules governing machine safety was broken: all moving parts must have a guard at all times. We tried to adhere to that rule, but there were often exceptions. The drive chain on the bale elevator, for instance: we realized this guard should be in place, but it had such an annoying rattle.

I was in the hayloft while Brian was feeding bales onto the elevator from the wagon. One fell to the floor, and while Brian was repositioning the bale back on the conveyor, he leaned against it for support. With the swiftness of a rattlesnake, the chain grabbed his leg, pulling him onto the drive sprocket. I heard Brian cry out and, peering over the edge of the loft, witnessed him trying to disconnect the power cord. Just as he succeeded, Dad rushed in. The knee of Brian's pant leg was ripped, and blood was pouring from a nasty gash. Dad bound the wound with his big red polka dot handkerchief and rushed him to hospital.

Following the accident, I spent a fitful period awaiting the outcome. I was worried, of course. I'd heard about tendons being severed, and envisioned Brian crippled, or at least condemned to a lifetime limp. But I was bothered by more than that. For whatever reason, I'd been mean to Brian that morning...taunting and calling him names from the haymow, right up until the moment of the accident. Now, as I waited, I was overcome with shame and guilt.

It didn't help my anxiety when Richard noted that there was a good chance Brian could develop tetanus. I was under the impression the bacteria could only be transferred via earth-encrusted objects, such as rusty nails, etc. But according to Richard, a rusty chain in the atmosphere of a dusty hayloft could be rampant with moulds and bacteria. Time was crucial.

"Once your jaw clamps shut, it's game over! I heard about a guy whose mouth locked shut within two minutes!"

"Two minutes!" I replied, almost afraid to ask the next question. "What happened to him?"

"He died...he couldn't open his mouth so he simply starved to death."

Realizing I was about to break into tears, Rich added reassuringly, "Dad probably put something in Brian's mouth to keep it from closing until he gets the shot...most anything will work...I heard about a guy whose mouth they stuffed with a wool sock."

Waiting for the verdict on Brian seemed the longest period of time I'd ever encountered; I don't recall if I prayed, but I certainly vowed that if Brian escaped this encounter, I'd be a lot nicer to him in the future.

Whatever power I had summoned on Brian's behalf was generous—but my relief was short-lived when Richard explained Brian wasn't out of the woods yet. "There's always the threat of gangrene."

Several stitches were in order, along with some follow-up therapy, but other than that, he was fine. No lockjaw, no gangrene, and no debilitating aftereffects. I later asked Brian what Dad put in his mouth on the way to the hospital, and I recall him looking at me like I was some kind of idiot.

But one thing was certain. True to my word, I became the best brother Brian could have ever imagined...for almost a week.

We kids were often warned about fire and gasoline, and their inherent potential for disaster. I still remember the initial thrill upon witnessing what a little gasoline would do to ignite a stubborn bonfire! I also remember Dad explaining such terms as "flash fire" and "back flash." "So you kids remember...when throwing gasoline on a bonfire, throw the entire container!"

One day Dad was about to transfer gasoline from the 200-gallon gravity flow supply tank to the tractor, and discovered the shut-off valve open. His initial reaction and first suspicion was that someone was pilfering gas. A second possible scenario was standing directly in front of him; I honestly knew nothing, and Dad must've believed me, for he turned to Richard.

"Do you know anything about it?"

"No," Richard replied at first. Unconvinced, Dad asked again.

"Were you fooling around with gas?" Richard began to blubber.

"What were you doing with gas?" Dad repeated.

"I put it in there," Richard motioned, pointing towards a shelf a few feet from the supply tank.

Dad's pulse must surely have quickened when he saw his son pointing at a kerosene lamp. Most likely he was afraid to pose the next question, as there was a lengthy pause.

"And what were you going to do with it?"

"I tried to light it," Richard answered momentarily, "but I couldn't get it to go."

After seemingly endless silence, Dad administered a stern lesson on the property differentials of kerosene and gasoline. Then he lowered his voice. "There will be no more said on the matter...just don't ever forget what I told you!"

Even at the tender age of eight or nine, I was fully aware of the seriousness of the situation, if only by Dad's tone of voice. I was surprised how Rich escaped reprimand so easily.

Thinking back now, I wonder if the thought of what might have happened cooled any zeal our father may have had for punishment?

Too Much Is Not Enough

Earlier in these ramblings I mentioned how during my early teens I spent a week or two in Toronto each summer with my cousin Doug Watt. Our vacation time would be filled with various venues...visiting the downtown department stores, visiting relatives, experiencing the excitement of the stock car races at the Canadian National Exhibition Grounds, and so on.

An added bonus was the Exhibition itself. Plenty of buildings made up the CNE complex, but the best, in our opinion, was the Automotive Building. Every August this huge arena was jammed with new cars. That they were nine or ten months old was of no consequence; it was the closest we ever got to such an array of new metal in one place, and we took full advantage of the opportunity. Most of these cars were from Detroit, although there were several European models. Japanese cars simply didn't exist in the North American market at this point.

The 1950s and 60s were a great time and place for automobile enthusiasts. Styling ran rampant and every year saw a major restyle. Longer, wider, lower, more power, more chrome, and vivid paint schemes...that's what sold cars.

Over the years, and for a variety of reasons, some automobiles far outdistanced their competitors when they debuted. Others never came close to fulfilling the colourful ad campaigns that were designed to sell them, and simply became another in a series of good ideas gone awry. The Tucker is one that comes to mind. Another contender for this dubious title would certainly be the Edsel.

I vividly remember when the Ford Motor Company introduced the Edsel in the fall of 1957. We had just gotten our first television set. "One look will tell you this is no ordinary car!" blared the commercials.

True enough. The car's heavily-sculptured metal sides and combination of curves and angles made it a curiosity even amid 1950s stylistic excesses. Probably because vertical grilles had disappeared from the automotive styling scene twenty years earlier, the Edsel's tall chrome structure became a favourite target among its detractors. Most kindly, it was referred to as the "horse collar" grille, but there were other descriptions: "an Oldsmobile sucking a lemon," "a yawning hippopotamus," "a toilet seat," "a part of the female anatomy"—the interpretations becoming progressively more tasteless as the months passed.

During its initial year, Ford Motor Company planned on selling as many cars in this hot medium range sector as the factories could build; and this sector was hot in 1955, when the Edsel was conceived. However, by 1958, largely due to a severe economic recession, this particular market had tanked. An independent network of exclusive dealers pushed the programme total to 350 million dollars. At today's dollar you'd be talking nearly three billion!

Several factors conspired against the Edsel, but the separate dealership organization proved to be the major flaw. All their models were in the same general market...the market that suffered most during the 1958 recession.

The Edsel was surrounded by controversy even before its introduction, particularly when it came to selecting a suitable name. Six thousand entries were submitted for consideration. Among them: Venus, Fairlane, Fairlawn, Fairweather, Fairmount, Henrietta, Henry, Henford, Clara, Dorf—the longer the list the worse it got.

A marketing executive got the idea of hiring Pulitzer Prize poetry winner Marianne Moore for some professional input. Her poetry had always been a little "over the top" and her suggestions for the new car mirrored her style. "Mongoose Civique," "Turcotinga," and "Utopian Turtletop" were but three of her proposals.

She was politely thanked and the search continued; not surprisingly, Ford Chairman Ernie Breech by now had lost patience with the name fiasco and decided to call the car what he wanted all along—Edsel—after founder Henry Ford's late son.

Sales began slow and never improved. Ford estimated 200,000 Edsels were needed to break even, and the year-end total was a dismal 67,000. A slight facelift for 1959, including different taillights and a softening of the controversial grille, failed to help. Only 47,000 went out the factory door that year.

Personally, I thought the 1959 Edsel was one of the best-looking cars on the road that year, and wondered whether things would have been different if that model had debuted first. It wouldn't have changed the economic climate of the times or the public's shift in direction to more practical automobiles, but at the very least it might have cooled the media's obsession with the car's unorthodox styling.

After a 1960 restyling offered nothing more than a regular Ford with a different grille and taillights, and only 2800 sold, Ford pulled the plug.

Except for some problems with the steering wheel-mounted push button automatic transmission in the first year, the Edsel was a well-built car. It just had the unfortunate timing to be introduced during a severe downturn in the economy, and a growing public rejection of the flamboyant style and high horsepower that had been so popular a few years previous.

The new direction of consumer taste was toward simpler compact designs, a path which all North American auto makers would be following within the next year or so. The Edsel was simply on the wrong side of this new vision. As a Ford company executive later put it, "The aim was right but the target moved."

A sad aspect of the entire experience was the fact such a colossal flop had to be named after Henry Ford's only son. Edsel Ford was an engineering and design genius, but never could convince his father as to the changing ways of the automobile world. Although he became president of Ford Motor Company in 1919, it was in title only, as Henry vetoed his every decision and treated him like a child. The frustration and humiliation he endured gradually took its toll. Serious stomach ulcers progressed to cancer, which took Edsel's life in 1943, just short of his fiftieth birthday.

We are approaching six decades since the Edsel debacle and unfortunately the name Edsel is still used to describe some major project that has bombed in grand style. Not a very complimentary or fitting epitaph for such a remarkable man.

Despite all the problems and challenges behind the scenes, flashy cars such as the Edsel and its competitors were the perfect ingredient for "car nuts" like Doug and I, and the city of Toronto the perfect setting to indulge in this passion.

As the 1950s rolled on, the cars got bigger, heavier, and more chrome-laden. Tailfins sprouted from practically every fender and in every possible direction, particularly on Chrysler products. Cadillac provided perhaps the most grotesque example with its 1959 model, whose fins were nearly as high as the roof itself.

Following this period of excess came the economy or "compact" cars. First was the Rambler American, followed by the Studebaker Lark. The bestseller proved to be the Ford Falcon. Ford Motor Company may have missed the mark with the Edsel but made up for it with the Falcon. Initial year sales reached half a million, and by the end of the second year, more than a million Falcons had found their way into North American driveways.

A batch of similar-sized competitors clamoured for a chunk of this new market. Plymouth Valiant, Dodge Dart, Oldsmobile F-85, Buick Special, Pontiac Tempest, and Mercury Comet; Chevrolet fielded two contenders: the Chevy II and its Volkswagen challenger, Corvair.

With the exception of the German Volkswagen, there was a large contingent of imported cars we rarely saw in the country, but which flourished in varying degrees on city streets.

Toronto's traffic arteries were alive with Vauxhall, Austin, Morris, MG, Triumph, Morgan, Jaguar, Alfa-Romeo, BMW, Fiat, and Renault automobiles. Then there was that odd little Italian car that sported a single front-opening door and sounded similar to a lawnmower: the Isetta. Volkswagen was in another league when it came to import sales. We'd never heard of a Datsun or Toyota, and Honda was only beginning to make inroads into North American culture, but with motorcycles.

The enthusiasm and excitement of that era's automotive scene now seems so distant. Back in the 1950s and 60s, new car introductions were a big deal, occurring without exception in late September and early October. Depending upon how much room was available, cars, wrapped in tarpaulins, would be dumped off at dealer's lots, or placed in some deserted field. The evening preceding the big event, the cars would then be spirited under cover of darkness to the designated dealers for the grand showing the following day. This would be the first opportunity for the general public to view the new metal. Among balloons and banners, coffee and doughnuts, souvenirs and door prizes, sales personnel would mingle with the crowds, ready to answer questions and hopefully ring up a sale.

If we didn't happen to make it to the grand event, in the following days a cross-section of new models would be lined up on the front row of every dealership in town. We kids would crane our necks as we passed, hollering out, "That must be either the new Chevy or Oldsmobile!" (With the major yearly design changes of that era, it was sometimes difficult to tell.)

My Toronto vacations ended in 1962. A year later would witness Doug heading north to work at a tourist lodge for a series of summers. In my teens now, I was expected to take on a more important role on our farm. The "kid" vacations I'd known became a thing of the past.

Although neither Doug nor I could have foreseen it, the automotive world was changing too. It sounds almost unbelievable now, but almost every third car sold in the 1960s would come from General Motors' Chevrolet division. Who could have guessed that GM itself, which sold more than 27 million cars in the 1950s, and sustained an overall 50 percent market share in the 1960s, would file for bankruptcy in 2009?

Not just General Motors, but the entire North American automobile market failed to comprehend the changing tastes of motorists. Their answer to sagging sales in the 1950s was more chrome, higher fins, and a wide variety of paint combinations. During the 1960s, the answer was simply more horsepower, with engines that would have been more suited to propelling aircraft.

It took a 1970s politically motivated fuel crisis in the Middle East to get Detroit's attention and force the design of sensible cars...but by then it was too late. European (particularly German) automakers, as well as their Asian counterparts, had been waiting for just this moment...and the rest is both automotive and economic history.

In the context of the automobile's 125 year history, that fifteen year period from 1955-1970 seems a short ride...but what a ride it was!

Ladies and Gentlemen...

I READ SOMEWHERE THAT ACCORDING TO AN EXTENSIVE POLL, public speaking is at the top of the list of most people's greatest fears. I would imagine public singing to be just as nerve-wracking.

When I was in elementary school, the annual music festival was held each June in the local township arena. I was in grade three the first time I participated in this musical marathon that endured for an entire day and evening as well. The song our age group was to perform was "Little Nut Tree."

Never heard of it? Well, three or four weeks preceding the festival, we began practising. Any student who could hold two notes in succession seemed to qualify. It didn't take a lot of practice, since the song was just a few lines.

Finally, the big day! Imagine four classes with between three and four dozen kids. Now try to visualize each one singing the same damned song. Then there was the class for boys with changing voices, the duet class, and don't forget the quartet category. Mom went regularly to these festival marathons.... and stayed all day. How she survived, I have no idea!

This particular festival began with 30 kids singing "Good Morning Mr. Sunshine." Then my group followed with "Little Nut Tree." Our order of performance had been pre-selected. I was number four.

"David Turner, from U.S.S. # 11 Wallace."

At the announcer's cue, I took my place centre stage. Our musical director, Mr. Gedcke, played the introduction and nodded for me to begin.

> *I had a little nut tree, nothing would it bear but a silver nutmeg and a golden pear.*
> *The King and Queen's daughter came to visit me, and all for the sake of my little nut tree.*

I don't recall the second verse, but you get the idea. How I sounded, or if I was heard at all, I haven't a clue—but I finished without fainting, vomiting, forgetting the words, bawling, or falling off the stage. I also wasn't picked as one of the four finalists to perform in the evening concert.

After that trial there was nothing more to do but return to our mommies and wait for the day to grind to a conclusion. Another batch of pupils warbled "A White Tent Pitched by a Glassy Lake," followed by a similar performance of "Jim the Carter Lad." Then, mercifully, it was over...until evening.

There were no finalists whatsoever from U.S.S. # 11. The sole reason for showing up at all for the evening's performance, other than pride, was the chorale reading...and according to the adjudicator, our reading of "The Christmas Story" was a woeful performance.

"Spotty, lack of cohesion, incoherent, and unrehearsed," were some of his comments, as I recall. If we stood any chance at all, it was dashed when a neighbouring school (one we didn't particularly care for) performed an absolutely electrifying rendition of "The Highwayman."

Perhaps it didn't fall into the category of "public speaking," but "memory work" was a major focus of elementary education fifty years ago. It began in the early grades, with just a few lines of poetry, and gradually increased to perhaps 250 lines by grade eight. One didn't have to face the classroom, just the teacher—since your selection was recited usually during recess hours or after school. I had no trouble memorizing poetry, although, unlike my father, my recollections lasted weeks, rather than years. A favourite of mine was "The House with Nobody in It," by Joyce Kilmer. I recited that passage three years in a row, until my teacher Mrs. Ashmore suggested I widen my scope.

Real public speaking meant just that...and it started when we reached first semester in grade five. Except for a few lines of recitation, during a Christmas concert perhaps, this was our initial major public speaking exercise. Regulations stipulated a three or four minute address, with a historical figure as its subject. I had always been a fan of David Livingstone, the nineteenth century British doctor who spent thirty years in Africa, teaching Christianity. In my mind, trying to halt the slave trade while exploring further and further into the interior of the "Dark Continent" made him an interesting character.

What really connected the famous explorer to my community was the fact our Perth County Health Officer was his nephew. When the inspector made his twice-yearly visit to test our school's water supply, Mrs. Ashmore would invariably press him for a comment about his legendary uncle. He always seemed a little embarrassed, I thought, but would generally come up with some personal anecdote. In fact, Mrs. Ashmore's worship of the explorer was a strong reason for my choice of topics. I figured I might score a few bonus points.

When the fateful day arrived, my stomach was a bundle of nerves. There were four of us in the class, and by random choice I would be last. Mary Patterson did well, only referring to her notes three or four times. "A little short," commented Mrs. Ashmore, "but all in all a valiant effort."

Allan Bender, the next speaker, was a basket case. He was so nervous he was barely able to hold on to his notes. He remembered the opening paragraph, but then it was all downhill. After staring blankly at the audience for a couple of minutes, he was asked to read the remainder.

Larry Hamilton began with gusto, racing through the opening two paragraphs. In fact, he had to be told to slow down in order to make himself understood. Choosing a historical figure with whom no one was familiar—John Jay— didn't help either. Mrs. Ashmore's interruption completely destroyed his concentration, and like Allan he ended up reading the balance of his text.

The classroom appeared enormous as I took my position in front of the blackboards. The 30 kids looked like 300.

"Madame Teacher, fellow students…the subject on which I've chosen to speak…" When I passed my first paragraph or two without difficulty, I knew I was set. The words tumbled from my memory bank clearly, as if I had been reading the pages. There was no way to know how literary content was contributing to my grade, but if presentation was worth 50 percent, I was halfway home. The minutes rushed passed and then it was over.

Before I could take my seat, a standing ovation erupted! Well, maybe not standing, and maybe not an ovation...but at least an enthusiastic response. Although my face was probably the colour of the morning sunrise, I was somewhere in the stratosphere. This euphoric state lingered long after I received my 93 percent mark. Looking back with the perspective of nearly sixty years, however, I realize the competition was lean in many respects. I now suspect it was Mrs. Ashmore who instigated the "spontaneous" ovation.

When you start at the pinnacle, there's only one direction to go. My first attempt at public speaking proved to be a watershed. I was never able to recapture that magical moment. Oh, I made a couple of decent speeches while still in elementary school...one about the Portuguese explorer Ferdinand Magellan, and another on Canada's first Prime Minister, Sir John A. MacDonald (another hero of Mrs. Ashmore). But an element was missing.

For a variety of reasons, secondary school proved to be a major challenge for me...both socially and academically. With my confidence tanking, I struggled for even mediocre grades. Nowhere was this educational regression more apparent than in my literary abilities.

"Your writing lacks any hint of imagination," wrote my English Literature teacher during one critique.

It was a fair assumption, given the material I was producing during that period. I recall one speaking endeavour concerned a ten minute monologue on the prairie provinces...not exactly an audience grabber I suppose. I plodded along, spouting an endless array of dry details; upon completion, Miss Scott focused her attention on a boy in the front row.

"Ron, what was the population of Saskatchewan in 1958?"

Ron searched his memory and came up empty.

"Neil?" She got the same response.

"I'm not surprised," Miss Scott continued. "One would need an adding machine to keep track of all the figures that were thrown at us. David had the provincial population figures calculated to every last chicken. His account was as dry as the prairie dust he was discussing. I don't recall a more boring speech!"

She obviously didn't hear the one I presented to French class. It of course had to be recited *en Français*. The presentation continued longer than anticipated, and when I finally droned to a conclusion, the only comment Mr. Perrault offered was that he'd counted 32 examples of the phrase "nous avons."

Other lowlights of that era included a discourse on the flight paths of migratory birds as well as an examination on the origin of rubber.

Definitely no standing ovations....During that period of literary staleness, any influence or inspiration garnered from the aforementioned nineteenth-century African explorer would certainly have been appreciated.

Battle of the Ballot

GLANCING THROUGH LIFE'S REAR-VIEW MIRROR AT CANADA'S electoral scene since 1867, it's not difficult to conclude that affiliation for a particular political party is a strongly contested issue. I was reminded of this fact while tracing my own ancestral roots.

Just eleven years old but already an avid student of Canadian history and politics, my grandfather William Carruthers was filled with anticipation upon learning that prime-ministerial candidate Sir Wilfred Laurier would be speaking at Toronto's City Hall on the eve of the 1896 federal election.

In the twenty-nine years following Confederation, Canada's Conservative party ruled for all but four, but that final five year span beginning in 1891 had yielded as many Prime Ministers. Sir John A. MacDonald was in poor health when he won his final election and died a year later. John Abbott served but one year and then resigned. John

Thompson occupied the chair for two years before expiring from a heart attack. Next in line was Mackenzie Bowell, who, at age 75, never really wanted the post, and within months conceded to Charles Tupper.

With the Conservative Party in disarray, the Liberals seized the moment. Laurier had been involved in the political arena for 25 years...half of that as opposition leader. Three issues spearheading the 1896 election resound with striking familiarity today: free trade, language rights, and religious instruction.

Like many political advocates of his day, Laurier was a superb orator; from the moment of his arrival at City Hall, he had his audience's full attention, regaling them for over an hour with tales of his party's merits and the disastrous record of his opponents. But Laurier's "sixty-minute special" paled in comparison with marathon speeches of a decade or so earlier, when debaters such as himself and the aforementioned Charles Tupper would command the floor for four or five hours at a time. Mr. Tupper's personal opinion was that a speech of less than five hours was simply not worth the effort.

Today's parliamentary squabbles are mere sandbox scuffles in comparison. Members of that era fought with every oratorical tool available: screaming, desk pounding, foot stomping, projectile tossing, half-truths, lies, personal accusations, and insinuations were all accepted practice. The verbal assaults hurled across the parliamentary floor were unrestrained, uncompromising, unrelenting, and unflinching in their zeal. Every MP from rookies to seasoned veterans recognized and understood the most important component of political deliberation: never apologize to anyone for anything on behalf of your party or yourself, and maintain absolute and unconditional denial of any political wrongdoing, misconduct, immorality, or impropriety...no matter how damaging the evidence.

Canada was obviously seeking a new direction as the nineteenth century drew to a close and Wilfred Laurier led his Liberal party to a landslide win...although a week passed before the outcome was proclaimed official. Our present system isn't without its rough edges—as witnessed in a recent federal election—but computerized automatic dialing, or "robocalls," pale in comparison with ballot burning, voter impersonation, voter intimidation, and bribery. In this era, voters with known party affiliation were often detained on their way to the polls by opposing party zealots, and threatened to "rethink" their voting preferences.

Alcohol was another staple of Election Day festivities. Public drunkenness reached epidemic proportions, more often than not inflamed by electioneers themselves. For anyone wavering on which way to cast their vote, a couple of free drinks courtesy of a local candidate were usually sufficient to get the recipient to mark their "X" in the appropriate box. It wasn't uncommon for personnel manning the ballot box to succumb to the over-consumption of spirits themselves and leave their station unattended.

However results were achieved, the Laurier win would certainly have been accepted with favour by my ancestral heritage...diehard Liberal supporters from the moment they disembarked the boat from Scotland. Any other vote was considered treasonous.

It's therefore interesting to imagine the fallout when my grandfather jumped ship for an undefined period and joined the Conservative ranks. In hushed whispers, family members would confer among themselves, asking, "Is Will still Conservative?" as though he'd contracted some contagious disease. Whatever caused his disenchantment was never made clear, but the issue was inevitably resolved, and my grandfather got back in line. Family embarrassment, if not forgotten, was at least forgiven.

Today's political parties struggle to secure a 50 percent voter turnout, more often languishing in the 30-40 percent range; but for most of the twentieth century, voting was the most important contribution a person could make. Who became Prime Minister or provincial premier might be the ultimate goal, but it was only the final piece of the puzzle. It was at the local municipalities where political waves were the most pronounced and achieved the most impact.

Local candidates seized every opportunity to make their pitch. In rural settings, schoolhouse gatherings proved popular for political rhetoric. Farm auctions could earn a candidate several points if handled well...unlike the one my father attended, where an aspiring Liberal candidate jumped onto a manure spreader to address the crowd, joking that this was his first time he had a chance to speak from a "Conservative platform." While his followers enjoyed a hearty laugh, somebody obviously from the opposing camp yelled, "Throw it in gear!"

Heated discussions erupted wherever political candidates gathered. Hence friends, neighbours, even family members would fail to speak to one another for days or even weeks following an election...and no one was better acquainted with this phenomenon than my parents.

In Grey County in the 1920s and 30s, no one's political star shone brighter than school-teacher-turned-politician, Agnes MacPhail. Following World War One, Miss MacPhail joined a co-operative movement known as the

United Farmers of Ontario, whose philosophies of collective marketing coincided exactly with her own.

"You can't expect others to solve your problems," she told area farmers, "when it is they who have gained their wealth and power by legally robbing you of your just portion."

It was this oratorical style that endeared her to the rural population, who set aside their regular political affiliations and encouraged her to campaign in the 1921 federal election...an election that held the distinction of being the first where a woman was even allowed to vote. Despite overwhelming odds, MacPhail won against ten men and became the first female Member of Parliament, subsequently winning every election until 1940.

It was by no means a smooth road when she finally did reach Ottawa. Instead of sending their news correspondents to relay parliament happenings, newspapers alternately referred their fashion column editors to critique MacPhail's wardrobe. Male counterparts gave her little parliamentary respect as well. "Don't you wish you were a man?" one asked. "Don't you wish you were?" MacPhail retorted.

Another hurled a barb concerning her marital status. "Why aren't you home looking for a husband?" Her response? "Because I might find one like you!"

When asked if she would ever consider joining the Senate, Agnes quickly answered, "No, when I die I want to be buried."

However, after nearly two decades of success, both Agnes and her UFO party found themselves fighting for their political existence in the 1940 election against Walter Harris, a Markdale lawyer running on the Liberal ticket. Although he'd lived in the village of Markdale for a decade, Harris was considered a "city boy," as he'd practised law in Toronto for many years until economics forced him to move.

Well...the towns and villages could do as they pleased; Agnes MacPhail was still the chosen candidate up and down the concession roads of rural Grey County. As they had from the beginning, the Turner clan would certainly be supporting her...well, most of them. My parents, just married, were living with Dad's parents in their Artemesia Township homestead. To the elder generation's disbelief, it was determined Dad and Mom were planning on voting for Walter Harris!

Between a decade of the most severe economic downturn in history, and a world now perched on the precipice of another world war, my parents were of the opinion the UFO party was mired in issues no longer relevant, and that a new political direction was crucial.

A more intriguing reason for their allegiance was that Walter Harris was related to my mother...second cousin or something. There's nothing like nepotism when it comes to choosing political sides! Frequently while attending Osgoode Hall Law School, Walter would visit with Mom's family in Toronto, and as a teenager my mother considered the young graduate charming beyond description.

To the family's way of thinking, there was no more selfish reason to turn your back on Agnes McPhail. Dad's parents may have expected as much from my mother—after all, "city types" stick together—but my father...he was the real disappointment. Had he forgotten everything Agnes had done for the local farming community, and for the well-being of agriculture in general? Voting against Agnes MacPhail! The family Chevrolet had once been owned by the UFO candidate, and for that reason alone the car was always considered special.

But their pleas fell on deaf ears. My parents cast their vote and Walter won his seat. As it turned out, Mom and Dad exhibited significant foresight in their political choice; Harris not only won that 1940 election, but every election for the next seventeen years. He even secured the high-powered Minister of Finance seat in Louis St. Laurent's Liberal party along the way.

Liberals and Conservatives had basically taken turns running the country the first quarter of the twentieth century, but starting in 1921 and continuing through 1948, Canada was run by basically one political institution (Liberal) and one man (William Lyon Mackenzie King).

There was a period in the early 1930s when the Conservatives regained power, but lost the following election in a landslide. To be fair, this was in the midst of the Great Depression, and it probably wouldn't have mattered who was in power. The Liberals of course blamed the continued stagnation fully on the shoulders of the governing party.

Following King's reign, Louis St. Laurent extended the Liberal dynasty until 1957. It was during this election campaign that I became aware of political emotions within my own family. Political events boiled over that year concerning a pipeline the Liberal government planned to construct to carry natural gas from Alberta to central Canada (another debate with familiar overtones).

The Conservative Party under leader John Diefenbaker thought the eighty-million dollar project far too expensive, and placed every obstruction and roadblock within their power to stop it. In an act of defiance, the Liberals dusted off a little-known and hardly used legality known as "closure," effectively halting all future debate. Diefenbaker was furious but helpless, and the pipeline project went ahead.

During the election drive of 1957, Diefenbaker campaigned with a vengeance, often mentioning the Liberal's "Nazi tactics" concerning the pipeline dispute. Our parents—especially Mom, who was the "true Liberal" in our family (Dad once said if Adolf Hitler had been a Liberal, Mom would have voted for him)—made sure we were in attendance when the PM made his campaign whistle stop in Palmerston. We even got to miss an hour of school! I was just eight years old, and all I recall is an old man giving a boring speech. I guess it wasn't just me...according to political analysts at the time, St. Laurent operated a feeble campaign, having little doubt his personal reputation and party accomplishments would easily defeat the unknown upstart lawyer from Saskatchewan.

Louis St. Laurent was 75 years old by this time, although he hadn't become a Liberal until 1941. Until then he had been a leading and well-respected Quebec lawyer. He was coaxed by then-Prime Minister Mackenzie King to accept the role of Minister of Justice. Four years later he was promoted to Minister of External Affairs, a post he kept until becoming PM in 1948, when King retired. Thus St. Laurent became the second French-Canadian PM in Canadian history (the first was Wilfred Laurier, back in 1896). By 1957, St. Laurent was ready to retire, but was persuaded by his Liberal supporters to undertake just one more campaign. It was apparent throughout the campaign that his heart wasn't in it.

When returning to school that afternoon, I recall our peers gathering to ask about our political foray into town. I also recall how our teacher Mrs. Ashmore paid little interest to the conversation. As a stalwart Conservative, this was no surprise. If John Diefenbaker had hit town we would have got the entire day off!

I guess people were ready for change, for the Conservatives posted a minority win. That "unknown upstart" and "prairie hayseed lawyer" was making inroads into what had been impenetrable territory for decades. And Diefenbaker, despite Liberal denunciations, was anything but an "upstart." He'd been hardened to the rough art of politics since the 1920s, running unsuccessfully in elections until 1940. He'd become party leader just the previous year, and according to him, running for PM in 1957 was "just another in a series of political battles."

Liberal name-calling and questioning his political integrity only deepened Diefenbaker's commitment. "Mud-slinging is the final whimper of a lost party and their election promises are as cheap as the paper they're written upon!" Diefenbaker thundered. "Liberals refer to their election promises as platforms; because when the election is over they can simply hop the next train and leave them all behind!"

Up until that day, a tiny photo of the current Prime Minister had been tacked unobtrusively into a corner of the school bulletin board. Following the Conservative's modest win, an 8x10 photo of new Prime Minister was placed front and centre above the blackboard.

A series of missteps plagued the Liberals the following year...scandals, economic recession, indecision, and just plain stupidity. Within a year, there was another election.

In our family, everyone except Mom ("There's no way I'm going to waste my time seeing him!") joined the crowd in Listowel when the Prime Minister of just one year made his stop to garner support. But despite Dad initiating the trip to see Diefenbaker, it was Mom's influence that counted on voting day. "I'll just cancel your vote!" Mom threatened when Dad casually mentioned he might vote for the Conservative leader.

It wouldn't have mattered. The Conservatives destroyed the Liberals, 208 to 49. With his tall, erect stature, piercing blue eyes, seemingly unlimited energy, and evangelical speaking style, John Diefenbaker captured the hearts of Canadians from coast to coast. Canadians—particularly western, northern, and maritime voters—were drawn to his "one Canada" vision of "a government for *all* the people!"

I guess Mrs. Ashmore felt that the Conservative sweep called for particular attention. By the time we returned to school the following day, the bulletin board portrait of John Diefenbaker had miraculously doubled in size, replaced by a sixteen-by-twenty-inch poster!

Although Brian Mulroney's majority election win in an expanded House of Commons twenty-five years later would garner more seats, John Diefenbaker's 1958 victory remains the largest in Canadian political history, percentage-wise.

Time of course would pen its own legacy of the Tory chief; historians now refer to Diefenbaker as one of the greatest Canadians of our century...but one of the worst Prime Ministers. However, that "upstart lawyer" and "prairie hayseed" so ridiculed by his opponents at the time certainly had the last laugh...for a while at least.

Water From the Wells of Home

I SOMETIMES RECEIVE MY INSPIRATION FOR STORIES IN UNUSUAL places. I was in the shower this morning when it occurred to me how we seemingly take for granted a never-ending water supply. I read recently that Canada's renewable water resources have shrunk 10 percent in the last thirty years, causing some analysts to predict that water will be a more valuable commodity than oil as the decades progress. Here in the rural areas, far away from metering systems and flow restrictions, we utilize water almost without thinking. Just turn the faucet.

Back at the beginning of the last century, when my great-grandfather Solomon Turner staked his claim on 200 acres in northern Grey County, the first issue he addressed once the trees were cleared and the largest rocks were removed was...water. He hired a professional drilling team to bore through more than a hundred feet of topsoil, gravel, sand, stones, and bedrock before reaching the clear liquid.

Of course there were no water pressure systems supplying water through a maze of pipes back then. Every gallon consumed had to be manually extracted by the hand pump on top of the well. Water was carried to the horses, chickens, sheep, pigs, etc. A large cement trough in the barnyard generally served the cattle. Strategically positioned beneath the downspout of the barn's network of gutters, it counted on Mother Nature to keep it replenished. However, that was fine only in periods of frequent showers. Most of the time it was fed by buckets filled from the pump at the well. During winter, the swamp situated at the northern fringe of the farm was utilized, necessitating the cattle herd to be sent each morning to tank up. In sub-freezing weather, it was someone's task to chop a hole in the pond's surface beforehand.

A cistern—usually a cement tank in the house basement—collected rainwater from the eaves, or surface water when it was available. This provided soft water for washing clothes, dishes, and personal hygiene (for what it was worth). A small hand pump situated somewhere in the kitchen drew the water from its storage supply. But water for drinking and cooking had to be retrieved from the well outside.

I recall my mother, who was city-born and raised, telling me how when she was first married and living with her in-laws, she felt forever out of step as far as adapting to rural culture. While her mother-in-law was away in town one day, Mom thought it would be a nice gesture to wash the dishes. Bad move. She put detergent in the water, if you can imagine—ruining it, according to her mother-in-law, who walked in at the conclusion. After all, every country girl knew that once the dishes were completed, the dishwater was sent to the barn to be poured over the grain that fed the pigs. With the addition of soap, this was out of the question, and the pigs simply out of luck!

The most important inconvenience of no running water was of course no bathroom. In order to answer nature's call, one had to make a pilgrimage outside and across the lawn, to the faithful old outhouse beyond the lilac bush. On winter nights, a person was sure they would perish on that frosty seat before the job was completed. Granted, the stay was more hospitable during the other seasons, but especially in the darkness, one had to be on guard for snakes and spiders. It wasn't uncommon to see a snake slither off the seat when the door was opened.

In 1941, my parents moved to Brampton, Ontario, just west of Toronto, where Dad had found work on a large dairy farm. Part of the hiring package included a new house with hot- and cold-running water and a bathroom. This was a blessing to Mom no doubt, especially as she already had two young kids. Two years later, Dad secured a job as herdsman for a dairy operation near the little village of Bond Head in Simcoe County, and while waiting for their new residence to be built, moved into a tiny house with no water features once again. By this time, however, a world war was causing major shortages, building materials being just one. Nearly three years would pass before my parents received their promised new house, with conveniences that once again placed them back in the twentieth century.

But after seven years in that house, enjoying piped water, our family, which included five kids by this time, moved to our own farm—which had always been Dad's dream, but maybe not Mom's. You guessed it: there was no bathroom and no running water...unless you count running for water back and forth from the pump outside the back door.

So let's summarize. Mom grew up in Toronto, with indoor plumbing and hot- and cold-running water. She had neither when first married and living in Eugenia, but had both at Brampton. The first house at Bond Head had neither, but the second house again had both. Now, here she was again with neither. The way these features were repeatedly offered, then yanked away, seems almost cruel, doesn't it?

As a peace offering, perhaps, Dad constructed sort of an indoor-outdoor combination toilet in one corner of the woodshed. Although still pretty frosty, it was at least under cover, and certainly beat dashing through the snow to the regular "one-holer." On the coldest nights, we shared a chamber pot—or "po," as we called it. Different families had different names for the pot; "Johnny," some called it, or "Jimmy," or "potty," or "the vessel." Perhaps the "thunderjug" for the less proper. Once as common as screen doors, fly stickers, and homemade butter, the big porcelain jug has long since disappeared into the pages of history.

One item that our new farm did have going for it was a windmill. When winds were favourable, the cement trough that supplied the cattle was kept brimming automatically. During periods of calm, the "Armstrong method" had to be employed. A twenty-five dollar electric pump would have solved the problem in these instances, but that was twenty-five dollars our struggling farm couldn't spare at the time.

No running water certainly made washday an endurance test, especially during winter. Every drop had to be carried from the well outside and poured into the reservoir on the cook stove to be heated. Pumping, carrying, heating, washing, and hanging consumed a full Monday. Adding to the marathon, the wringer washer had to be bailed out by hand. It had an electric pump, but that never worked. It would be dark when the clothes, frozen stiff, were retrieved from the clothesline. I always thought it very amusing the way the "long johns" stood at attention like cotton statues against the kitchen wall.

Summer brought its own challenges. After a long hot sweaty day harvesting, haying, or whatever, there was no refreshing shower to look forward to, but it was surprising how many body parts one could reach with just a washcloth. One's choices were basically the tepid contents of the water trough situated beside the barn, or a cold bucket of water poured over you, courtesy the well pump at the house.

A warm soaking bath to ease away the aches and pains of those laborious days would have been welcome relief, but that was only a dream. As noted, any heated water had to come from the cook stove reservoir. A large quantity of wood generating a lot of heat was needed to warm water... heat no one wanted or needed in those pre-air conditioning days. Saturday nights were the only exception. A little body odour wasn't objectionable through the week, as everyone smelled the same. But a bath for next morning's church service was a must. When every gallon was carried by hand, water conservation was paramount. No frivolous car washing, that's for sure—that's what rain was for.

To save on the labour of heating water during the summer months, we kids often bathed outside when the weather was favourable. Mom would drag out a couple of her galvanized Beatty wash tubs and fill them with water. The afternoon sun would heat the water sufficiently, providing a pleasant bathing experience. Once the actual bath and shampoo were dispensed with, it was time for fun. Splashes and laughter with naked little bodies racing all over the lawn. I recall some of our city cousins joining us for one of these Saturday night frolics. They had a real bathtub at home, but according to them, our system was much better.

It wasn't until 1957, when we moved to Perth County, that we finally had running water. Our new house featured hot- and cold-running water, plus a true-to-life bathroom. The barn was fitted with automatic water bowls, as well as a hot water heater in the milk house. No more lugging heavy pails from the trough to water the cattle each day during the winter months. Yet time would forecast that piped water didn't solve all our problems. Indeed, it often created new ones.

Our first winter in Perth County proved to be unusually severe, with drifts high enough to block the driveway by mid-November. The first week of December's record-cold temperatures froze the water line between house and barn. The plumber worked half the night to thaw the pipes, only to have them freeze again a couple of nights later. After another thaw, followed by yet another freezing, Dad said he had had enough of this great invention known as running water. For the duration of the winter we elected to carry water from the barn to accommodate our household needs.

We eventually discovered frozen pipes to be a chronic condition. Not until a new water line was installed at nearly twice the depth did that particular headache disappear. However, we were still saddled with our quota of frozen pipes and water bowls in the barn itself. A cloth soaked with hot water from the milk house was usually sufficient to free the pipes of ice. As for the water bowls, hot water poured directly into the bowl was the quickest method—although not always the best, as there was always a chance of one splitting open with this process. When Dad dreamed of a farm with all the modern water conveniences, I'm sure problems like this never entered the picture.

Even under favourable weather conditions, we never seemed to be able to escape from some sort of water interruption. A lot of it was simply time running out on our aged Beatty pump. Not helping the cause was the cattle barn's constant humidity, which played havoc with the electrical components. But when everything was in tune, there was no colder or better-tasting water in the township. Up in a steel-roofed haymow, where the temperature could often top one hundred degrees Fahrenheit on a summer afternoon, the thought of that ice-cold refreshment after each load of hay was sometimes all that sustained us.

As time wore on, introducing more modern and dependable pumps and supply tanks, as well as more efficient ways to stave off winter's fury (insulation, heat lamps, etc.), our water problems slowly but gradually decreased. About the only time we have a difficulty now is during a hydro outage. Just this spring, a severe evening thunderstorm caused a several-hour interruption that carried well into the next day. No shower, no porridge, no coffee, no teeth brushing, no toilet or dishwasher…what an absolute calamity!

I can almost imagine my ancestors shaking their heads, contemplating what our generation refer to as a "water problem." If only they had been so lucky!

What's in a Name

In 1966 I purchased my first car, a '58 Volkswagen, for ninety-nine dollars. It was fine for a starter vehicle to drive for the summer, but as it had serious cold weather issues—like no heater or defroster—a more appropriate all-season car was needed.

I loved Volkswagens, so a new model was my first choice. By this time the German wonder car had a gasoline-powered heater to warm the interior as well as any "normal" car. I commissioned a salesman from Mount Forest to quote a price on a '67 Deluxe, offering my '58 as a trade. My father suggested a pickup might be a more practical choice, serving dual duty as a car for me and a much-needed truck for the farm. In turn, he said he'd help with the financing. That part sounded fine, so a pickup it was.

Long story short, I drove a pickup for a while. But after a year or so I still wanted a "real" vehicle. In other words…a car. Unlike today, when pickups rival luxury cars for style, comfort, and convenience, four or five decades ago most pickups were entry-level, bare-boned, get-the-job-done haulers.

When my desire for a car returned, I methodically began checking the local lots around our neighbourhood. My initial aim was high: I wanted a two-door hardtop loaded with options and a large V-8 engine. Money being the ultimate equalizer, reality dictated a somewhat more pedestrian model.

At McRae's Chrysler-Plymouth, a four-year-old Mercury Comet caught my attention. With four doors, six cylinders, and a three-speed manual transmission, perhaps it didn't quite hit the stylish mark I'd envisioned. And with its anemic 100 horsepower engine, it was certainly no racer. What did strike a chord was the flawless black finish and beautiful red-and-black plaid interior—a color combination for which I'd always entertained a weakness.

The car had been locally owned by an elderly couple, who'd traded on a new Plymouth Valiant. The Comet had been kept in impeccable condition. The salesman allowed me to try it out for the weekend, and while sitting at a stoplight in Listowel Sunday morning, some idiot rammed into the back of me. The collision wasn't as bad as feared...just a busted taillight housing and lens, which the idiot—I mean other driver—agreed to replace without hassle.

Perhaps this is a good time for an historical update for those unfamiliar with the Comet brand.

The car was introduced in 1961 in Canada as a deluxe version of the extremely popular Ford Falcon. Originally, the Comet was planned as a compact Edsel, but plans changed when the full-sized Edsel drowned in a sea of controversy and red ink early in the 1960 model year. Ford did some minor re-styling, most notably scuttling the proposed divided grille, a key characteristic of the Edsel from the beginning. The car was then shuffled over to its new home at Mercury division. Some parts, like parking-light lenses and various dashboard knobs, were lifted directly from the 1960 Edsel. Even the ignition key was borrowed from the Edsel; the manufacturer merely removed the centre of the "E," converting it to a "C."

The reassessed and re-evaluated Comet was met with an enthusiastic response, selling more cars in its initial year than the Edsel did in its entirety, and providing a much-needed stimulant to the entire Mercury line, which was struggling at that point.

My particular Comet was built in Oakville, Ontario, at the only Canadian factory building the car. In 1964, the Comet enjoyed a major restyle, acquiring the crispness of its senior sister lines, Mercury and Lincoln. In fact, at the time I recall pretending I was driving sort of a "junior Lincoln."

My Comet proved to be one of those cars that looked like a million dollars, especially when I added a set of Atlas whitewall tires. Unfortunately the car didn't perform that well, mechanically.

The car had a hard time starting when the weather was cold, and often overheated when temperatures soared. On certain road surfaces, the suspension emitted a mysterious groaning and rumbling sound that no mechanic could understand, much less fix. The gas tank leaked; the engine used oil to such a degree that I had a "ring job" performed. I don't know why I didn't simply let it burn oil; at the time pollution wasn't an issue we thought much about, and there were no emissions tests.

I also installed a new clutch. Probably because of the elderly former owners, the Comet's powertrain was completely unaccustomed to my quick starts. With that puny engine, I figured the car needed all the help it could get!

Then there was the afternoon the car caught fire (possibly due to that leaking gas tank) and burned the entire trunk area inside and out, as well as a portion of the back seat. Let's just say that the beautiful red-and-black plaid interior didn't fare well.

Anyone who ever drove a Comet of that era, with its anemic six-cylinder engine, probably wondered why Ford Motor Company named the car after the astronomical body with the huge tail that blazes across the heavens. When in the vicinity of earth, celestial comets generally travel about twenty-four miles a second—when nearing the sun they can increase to four times that speed. Earthly comets, on the other hand, seemingly took two hours to accelerate from zero to sixty miles an hour.

Perhaps understandably, the origin of the name had nothing whatsoever to do with blazing heavenly bodies. Following the Edsel debacle, Ford lost interest in procuring an imaginative moniker for their new car and merely purchased the name from the Comet Manufacturing Company, a Memphis, Tennessee establishment who converted production automobiles to ambulances and limousines. As CMC was in the process of changing their title, Ford simply bought the old name...pretty exciting, eh?

Considering the unadventurous, unassuming, conservative personality Comets of that era projected, it's interesting to note that besides ambulances and limousines...another speciality of the Comet Company was the manufacture of funeral coaches!

How appropriate...

Old Cars and Diesels

It's interesting how routine moments can generate long-range impact.

Percy and Gertie Magee were a great uncle and aunt of mine; I think I've mentioned their names before. It was at their farm near the Grey County crossroads community of Rock Mills where I developed my addiction to old metal. They always had a dozen or so 1930s-40s vintage vehicles strewn across the pasture field behind their barn.

On a seemingly routine visit my brother Richard had noticed the abandoned cars and trucks. Upon disembarking from our car he quietly asked Dad if we could check them out. I was probably about five years old at the time. Nowadays one would probably have to file an application of intent before even temporary permission and approval were granted. Only after a team of lawyers investigated all possible insurance legalities, including public safety, environmental disruption, health concerns, and child welfare, would the appeal be considered...and certainly denied.

In the mid-1950s things were a lot simpler.

"Of course they can!" was Percy Magee's answer to Dad's request. Sure there were jagged fenders and shards of broken glass to gash an arm or leg as well as rusted sheet metal and sharp bolts to puncture unsuspecting skin—that's the reason our tetanus shots were kept up to date. Snakes, spiders, rats, wasps, ill-tempered geese, thistles, burdocks, plus a variety of noxious weeds only added ambiance. "Just be careful," Dad said as we departed on our adventure. So what else needed saying?

Percy and Gertie's youngest son Ken drove the first car that truly impressed me...a 1948 yellow Pontiac convertible with brown leather interior. I think it was the summer of 1953 when Ken visited our Simcoe County farm while on his honeymoon, and I remember being mesmerized by his shiny "rag top." Our family chariot at the time was a 1947 Pontiac sedan, which, except for a slightly different grille, was identical with the 1948 model. Stylistically, however, the convertible made our sedan seem frumpy.

Now, Ken's brother, Bill, could have been driving anything. In the mid-1940s, while barely eighteen, he'd gone to Toronto to advance what would become a lifelong career selling cars. Bill had been buying and selling in his home neighbourhood before he had a driver's license. His first sale had been a 1928 Oldsmobile coupe, and he had originally owned the Pontiac convertible his brother drove on his honeymoon. Bill Magee never kept any car for long. If there was a prospective buyer...it was gone.

Eldon Turner was Dad's youngest brother. His first vehicle was a 1948 GMC pickup for which he forfeited five dollars cash and a ninety-five dollar cheque for the privilege of driving it home. At this point the truck was in fairly rough shape and painted dark blue. But Eldon improved it considerably, adding a new maroon finish, yellow wheels, and painted-on whitewall tires. The result was a real "girl catcher" (according to Eldon).

In 1953, when we moved from Bond Head to Bradford, Eldon loaned the truck to Dad for a week, in exchange for our Pontiac. During one of the many trips between the two sites, the spare-tire assembly, complete with yellow wheel and painted whitewall tire, dislodged from its location on the side of the truck, and disappeared, never to be found. I recall the brakes giving up the ghost that week as well.

Eldon followed the GMC with a 1949 Monarch. The Monarch was a medium-priced car exclusively sold through Canadian Ford dealers. Like many Ford Motor Company engines of that era, Eldon's V8 entertained a healthy appetite for oil, necessitating a supply of quart oil cans to be carried in the trunk.

Eldon's navy blue-and-white 1956 Dodge Regent was a sharp car; it was top of the Dodge model line that year, and much more accommodating when it came to oil consumption...probably because in most weather it simply wouldn't run. "If the weather was cold, hot, wet, foggy or even just damp," Eldon reflected, "that Dodge would refuse to start. Sometimes just a cloud in the sky was all it took!"

An experience concerning Doug Turner, Eldon's older brother, occurred one afternoon while on my way home from public school. I was walking down the centre of the asphalt approach leading to the 400 highway overpass that bordered our farm, lost in the fantasy world of a six year old. From somewhere I became aware of a sound just barely audible...sort of a whisper. I also detected a slight ticking sound. These sounds persisted, and finally, almost subconsciously, I glanced back...and stared straight into the chrome grille of a 1948 Chevrolet, just a few feet behind me!

I took a mighty leap toward the ditch and managed to land in the weeds unscathed. Peering from my vantage point, I observed the Chevy that had so nearly run me over, stopped on the road directly in front of me. I then recognized the occupants: my Uncle Doug and Aunt Muriel, who'd apparently followed me for some distance as the old Chevy's six-cylinder engine idled almost noiselessly behind me.

I got in and rode the rest of the way home. Doug, still enjoying the moment, immediately related the story to Mom and Dad.

"David should audition for the Olympics this year; I believe he could win the running broad jump easily. He never even touched ground between the car and ditch!"

Aunt Muriel must have sensed I was going to start bawling, and tried some consolation.

"Well, I didn't think it was very funny. Poor little fellow could have had a heart attack."

In all honesty, the attack I nearly suffered in my dash towards the ditch that afternoon was a little lower down!

That old Chevrolet is the only car I can recall my uncle driving during that period of my life. It was a Fleetline "Aero-Sedan", the moniker General Motors gave their "fastback" styled automobiles of that era, and was finished in a pleasing two-tone green. Purchased when barely two years old, it ran for more than a decade before the Department of Transportation hauled it off the road due to "hazardous and disintegrating" metal issues.

Winter always provided additional strain to vehicular operation and performance. How many times did we walk the quarter-mile length of our rural laneway to the road where our old Pontiac was stationed during the winter, only to discover it wouldn't start? Dad would then have to trudge back to the barn and get the tractor. One morning while Dad was towing our Pontiac down our side road with the tractor, the chain broke.

Anyone who has witnessed the fracture of a link on a chain under tension is well aware of the force unleashed. In a split second the clevis securing the chain to the tractor's drawbar let go at about 200 mph, skimming over the roof of the car and landing some fifty feet behind. An inch or two lower and the heavy metal clevis would have blasted completely through the driver's windshield directly where Mom was sitting!

I recall the day Mom was driving us to school...a very uncommon occurrence, as Mom didn't have a driver's license, and was never comfortable driving under even ideal circumstances. It was a bitterly cold morning...probably the reason we were being chauffeured. Where Dad was, I don't know. What I do recall, and vividly, was the Pontiac's accelerator pedal stuck to the floor, the car roaring out our laneway, crossing the side road, bouncing through the ditch, and finally coming to a rest up against a woven-wire fence.

Just for the record, Mom hardly ever swore...and I mean ever. On extreme occasions she might offer a "be damned" about something about which she felt strongly, but that was it.

This particular morning hadn't gone well from the start. The alarm clock had failed to do its job, which meant a hurried breakfast. The washing machine had ceased operation in the midst of the Monday morning ritual, and one of us kids, looking for something in the china cabinet, had busted the handle off a favourite cup. Thus a whole host of human and inanimate objects became innocent victims of the "d" word that morning: the washing machine, us kids, Dad, the Pontiac, the ditch, winter...and generally just life itself.

Although no help in starting an uncooperative engine, tire chains offered regular aid to winter driving once the car was underway. Before snow tires became routine, these awkward appendages, which one strapped to the rear wheels, were common in the rural region where I grew up. For safety concerns, road speed was limited to about 35 mph, so the steel traction boosters were mainly for rural back roads and laneways. I can remember driving with my father the two miles to the Bradford highway, where he'd remove the chains and stash them in the trunk. Upon returning, as soon as we turned onto our side road, Dad would retrieve the rattling, clumsy gadgets from the trunk and re-install them before proceeding home.

At times, winter provided challenges seemingly beyond human durability. Trying to breathe life into obstinate and disobliging engines in frigid temperatures was endlessly exhausting. When I was a kid, our Allis-Chalmers tractor was gasoline-powered, like most tractors of that period. For whatever reason...whether it was general practice or that we simply couldn't afford it...Dad never used antifreeze.

Hauling milk cans to the road for pickup by the local dairy was a daily winter challenge for our Allis-Chalmers. In cold weather, not using antifreeze meant draining the tractor's radiator and block at the end of each day. Retrieving two or three gallons of hot water from the reservoir of the kitchen stove was therefore standard daily procedure; this tried-and-true formula would sufficiently warm the engine block and provide ignition.

When our farm switched to diesel power in the early 1960s, we had to adapt to a new convention for starting cold engines. Although much more efficient to operate than gasoline-powered engines, diesels were also much more difficult to fire up in cold weather, due to factors like engine block density and compression ratios. Our Massey-Ferguson, like most diesel tractors of that era, relied on a winter starting system that used glow plugs, which pre-heated the combustion chamber, similar to the way a toaster operates. In cold weather, the operator would turn on the glow plugs for usually thirty seconds or so, and then start the tractor as usual.

This system worked relatively well for the first two or three years, when the tractor was new and electrical system in good working order. Then things gradually deteriorated. A battery that seemed perfectly capable in October completely abandoned all starting intentions with the arrival of January and February. Different approaches to combat this challenge were tried…usually with limited success.

A warm battery was the obvious solution, but retrieving the 75-pound unit from its deep battery well and loosening its myriad of brackets and rusty bolts was a challenge in itself. During one extremely cold period, I realized the tractor would not start the following day without help. So I removed the battery from its stubborn compartment and transferred it to the warmer climate of our house basement. The next morning I had to reinstall the warm battery in order to clear the laneway of snow to allow access for the feed truck. I was in the process of hoisting the battery to its location under the hood when it slipped out of my hand and the goddamned thing fell to the cement floor, busting a corner out of the battery casing, immediately spilling sulphuric acid and whatever else onto the garage floor. Long story short…I had to hire my neighbour to blow the snow from the laneway that morning while I went to the Massey-Ferguson dealer to purchase a new battery.

On another occasion, rather than deal with the wretched removal exercise, I got the idea to simply place a heat lamp over the battery. Brilliant! Except I guess the lamp was too hot and too close to the battery. It melted the entire casing. It's a wonder the battery didn't explode and torch the tractor, the garage, and everything else in the vicinity!

If you think that's a hard-luck story, let me tell you about my brother's tractor, an International B-275. This was a British-built, three plow model that International Harvester manufactured for a decade beginning in 1958. This particular tractor sat hub-deep in water and mud the latter part of the autumn of 1964, before freezing completely into the ground when winter came. The main problem had been the mud, which caused the tractor to become stuck in the first place. Then it wouldn't start. The cold weather simply compounded the misery...but let's begin at the beginning.

The tractor was purchased through our friend/neighbour/trucker/dealer Doug Hamilton, who promised he could find something in my brother's specified $1500-1800 price range. Shortly after, Bill met Doug at a farm sale, and Doug explained that he'd just bought a tractor, which was in the back of his livestock truck that very moment.

"I'll start it," Doug volunteered. He settled himself onto the seat, staring blankly at the controls and finally locating the starter lever. The starter growled away for a while with nothing more than black smoke to show for his effort. Doug tried several more times before disappearing completely in the black cloud of diesel smoke.

During a coughing fit Doug stated that he must be

doing something wrong, and promised to check the owner's manual when he got home.

Later that day, Doug backed his truck into the front yard of his neighbour and co-driver Wes Bender, where the combination of a steep hill and a deep ditch afforded an ideal unloading dock.

"Not one of those!" Wes drawled as he spied the tractor.

Doug shot him a not-too-friendly glance. "Why...what's wrong with them?"

Realizing he may have spoken out of turn, Wes merely shrugged. "I just heard they were a little hard to start sometimes."

In hindsight, perhaps that's the moment Bill should have walked away. I recall years later someone commenting that "those tractors weren't worth the powder to blow them up!"

While perusing the manual, Doug discovered that the glow plugs had to be activated. This was not news, of course, since the engine was a diesel...except this was September! This was another clue that Bill should have noticed. Nevertheless, once heat was applied, the tractor roared to life in a cloud of black smoke that would have made a locomotive envious.

As autumn progressed and the days turned colder, Bill's tractor became steadily more cantankerous. Longer and longer periods of pre-heating were required, which played havoc with the two six-volt batteries that were the heart of the tractor's electrical system. Finally, it became more comfortable and less time-consuming to simply "pull start" the tractor each morning.

Bill summoned Doug Hamilton one morning to witness the starting (or, more accurately, non-starting) ritual. Doug provided no useful input except to suggest a new battery...

an avenue Bill had already explored. I guess any warranty had ended the moment Bill's cheque cleared the bank!

Finally, as mentioned, the tractor became mired in mud in the middle of a ten-acre field, surrounded by water and then ice as the winter of 1964-65 closed in.

With the arrival of spring, Bill and I made a concentrated effort to revive the stricken machine, slogging across the field with newly-charged batteries on numerous occasions. We drained fuel, added fuel, bled the fuel system, pre-heated the injectors far beyond the recommended time interval, changed fuel filters, and continually boosted batteries. We spent many frustrating hours working on that tractor—as many as the array of adjectives we heaped upon it!

Bill even brought two brand-new "severe service" International Harvester batteries to the site, only to drop one in the "lake" that surrounded the tractor. The water was probably two feet deep, and we had a bear of a time finding the fallen battery! We still had no luck getting the tractor started, and guessed that perhaps the new batteries were duds. We retrieved another pair, and finally...success.

As the cool days of autumn...never mind winter... returned, it was the same tired story. Bill invested in the best battery International Harvester offered—the same grade that powered bulldozers and other construction equipment that worked in extreme conditions—but with only modest improvement.

The crux of the problem was simply the design of the engine. It was designed to be started by pre-heating which in turn required plenty of electrical power. Built in Europe, it seemingly wasn't formulated for extreme Canadian temperatures. Nowadays we wouldn't think of operating a diesel in cold weather without the aid of a block heater, but in that era diesels were still relatively novel, requiring a good deal of trial and error.

When Bill was in the midst of this chronic dilemma, I recall the owner of the International Harvester dealership in Palmerston wondering if perhaps the entire shipment of batteries he'd been receiving were defective, as he'd had other complaints as well.

"Next time the IH salesman comes," he told Bill, "I'm going to tell him he can shove every last one of those batteries right up his ass!"

I'm certain my brother would have been more than happy to assist in the procedure.

What Could Go Wrong?

In April of 1967, my cousin Doug Watt had just finished his third year of a four-year course at the University of Toronto, and was looking for a summer job. How much energy Doug applied to find employment in Toronto I don't know, but he ended up boarding at our place while working for a local drainage contractor. Although born and raised in Ontario's capital, Doug seemed to have a lot of rural blood flowing through his veins, no doubt from the many summers spent at our place.

The contractor with whom he was employed that particular season was working in the counties of Lambton and Middlesex, so following his recess from university in May, and until resumption of studies in September, a daily ritual began. I'd fire up my Fargo pickup about a quarter-to-six and we'd make a fifteen-minute run to the neighbouring town of Fordwich, where Doug hitched a ride to the jobsite with a fellow worker.

His co-worker Jerry drove a '58 Plymouth that suffered a variety of issues, foremost being chronic stalling at the most inopportune times, followed by reluctance to restart. Other shortcomings included flat tires and empty gas tanks. Few days passed without at least one flat, or without the tank going dry (it was kept only quarter full, as anything above that level simply leaked out). Jerry delivered Doug home each evening at a time dependent upon the mood of the Plymouth and the length of time spent enjoying the hospitality of the local taverns along the way.

The drainage game, according to Doug, was enjoyable when the weather cooperated, and miserable when it didn't. His employer utilized a clay tile machine as opposed to plastic in use today. This meant walking and standing in eighteen-inch-wide trenches for hours on end laying tile, often with mud and water to your knees. Mom had the lucky job of laundering Doug's clothes, which all had to be pre-washed to remove the accumulation of sticky clay, which had a consistency resembling wet cement.

The following year, Doug and I saw even more of each other, as he spent practically the entire summer at our place. Officially, he was looking for a job, but mostly we just enjoyed each other's company. I believe he returned with the intention of working with the tile contractor again, but something went sour, the details of which escape me.

With four years of university education, Doug was clearly overqualified for any local jobs. Openings for graduates of meteorology and anthropology were few and far between. Employment opportunities in our area centred around the newly-opened Campbell Soup plant, Spinrite Yarns, or Rothsay Concentrates (an innocent name for a rendering plant).

My strongest recollection of that year is from March, when Doug phoned to ask if I'd be interested in accompanying him to Montreal the upcoming weekend. The idea of driving in a strange city notorious for its less-than-attentive drivers, coupled with March's unpredictable weather, left me somewhat hesitant. However, when he mentioned travelling by bus, my interest piqued.

"I think it would be more interesting to take the local bus don't you?" he asked.

"What's the difference?"

Doug explained how the local bus took highway No. 2 along Lake Ontario and the St. Lawrence River, while the express simply barrelled straight down the 401. I agreed that the local sounded more scenic, and promised to meet him Saturday.

"Two tickets to Montreal...the local bus," Doug requested of the agent in charge.

"You mean the express bus?"

"No...the local bus," Doug repeated.

"Are you sure?"

"Yes I'm sure!"

The ticket agent shrugged his shoulders and processed the fare. Dozens of buses to destinations all over North America stood in an angled row inside the huge Toronto terminal. We finally located the Montreal-bound bus (which oddly displayed "Kingston" above the windshield) and climbed the two steps, handing our tickets to the driver.

"You should be on the express bus," he declared.

"No, we want the local bus!"

"I'm getting a little tired of all this free advice," Doug grumbled as he took his seat. "We're the ones buying the tickets. If we want to take the local bus, it's our bloody business!"

Clouds hung heavily over the city and mist obscured most of Lake Ontario as the partially-filled coach eased out onto Lakeshore Boulevard. With each passing town the sky turned a darker shade of grey. Soon light rain began along with thickening fog.

Our visibility was hampered in another way as well... by people. Every few miles the bus would stop to allow someone else to embark. Grey Coach weren't kidding when they designated this route "local." By the time we reached Belleville, not even halfway to our destination, every seat was taken, and the aisle was crowded to capacity. Perhaps we should've been more receptive to the free advice concerning the express route.

We at last landed in Kingston, the halfway point, and disembarked—eager for a good lunch and a chance to stretch our legs. At that point our driver informed us that any passengers bound for Montreal would transfer to the express bus for the remainder of the trip. Maybe it was just my imagination, but I'd swear he was staring straight at Doug and me.

Well, we didn't much care at this point. The express coach would be a welcome respite from the stop-and-go, three-and-a-half-hour trial we'd just endured. It was then we discovered the Montreal bus would depart at one o'clock...just a little over twenty minutes away. We wondered aloud why they'd allow only a half-hour break for the entire busload. Someone pointed out how the passengers on the express bus were treated to an hour-long respite as they arrived a half hour earlier from Toronto.

Retrieving our two overnight bags from the bus floor, we joined the throng at the lunch counter. Since we were pressed for time, we simply ordered a sandwich. At ten-minutes-to-one we were still waiting when our waitress sauntered over. "Now...what can I get for you boys?"

"We've already ordered!" we answered in unison.

She mumbled to herself as she leafed through her slips. "Hmm...I don't see it here. Would you like to re-order?"

"We haven't got time," I said, "Our bus leaves at one." She nodded then wiggled off towards more promising prospects.

"Boy, this is turning into a great trip!" Doug spoke in disgust. "Let's just get a chocolate bar to eat on the bus."

Suddenly Doug's face turned pale. "My wallet's gone!" he cried, frantically checking and re-checking his pockets. "It's got to be on the bus!" Making a dash towards the door, we were crushed to discover that the bus had departed for Toronto. Just then we were informed by an elderly man and woman whom we recalled seeing on the bus that the driver had found a wallet and taken it to the ticket counter. Leaving me to guard the luggage, Doug chased down the lead, returning in just a couple of minutes with the errant wallet. "Well, maybe our luck is changing," he sighed, as the billfold seemed untouched and intact. By now it was three-minutes-to-one.

"Alright, give it back!" I looked at my cousin, unclear as to what he meant. "My bag—give it back! I'm in no mood for games."

I guess the vacant look on my face conveyed my innocence.

"You mean you don't have it?" Doug pounded his fist against his forehead. "I don't believe it! What in hell kind of place is this?" I couldn't believe it either...I'd been sitting right next to it.

"Last call for Montreal!" crackled the voice from the loudspeaker. It went unheeded. We spent the next hour searching and asking questions, but to no avail. The bag was gone and we'd missed our bus. At this point we seriously debated returning to Toronto before events got any worse—although it was doubtful that they could. However, we still had our tickets, and figured we might as well play out our hand.

The next bus left Kingston for Montreal at 6:30. So what does one do in Kingston for four hours? First we ate; at least now there was no hurry.

"So what was in the bag?" I asked between mouthfuls of mashed potatoes and roast beef.

"Nothing important," answered Doug sarcastically. "Just my electric razor and alarm clock and camera and transistor radio and some magazines and a pair of pants and a couple of shirts..."

Upon leaving the restaurant we happened to see the same couple who'd helped Doug retrieve his wallet. Doug asked if they knew anything about his overnight bag. I could only imagine what they were thinking. Talk about a pair of losers...lost both a wallet and luggage and only halfway to Montreal! The couple were no help this time, but Doug was unconvinced.

"You notice the way they grin all the time. There's something strange about those two. I'm sure they know something about my bag. I'll bet they had something to do with my wallet's disappearance too!"

I failed to comprehend why anyone would return a wallet full of money while keeping a stupid overnight bag, but kept the thought to myself.

To pass the time we decided to take a walking tour of Kingston. The bus depot was in the heart of town, and since many of the city's historical buildings were located in that area, it seemed like the ideal chance for some sightseeing.

Yesterday's Moments...Today's Memories

At least it would have been if it hadn't started raining. It had been raining lightly for several hours, and now a steady downpour began. So now we were in the middle of downtown Kingston and soaking wet. A theatre marquee advertising *Guess Who's Coming to Dinner?* beckoned, so we allowed Spencer Tracy and Katharine Hepburn to help us forget our troubles for the next two hours.

The rain seemed to have no intention of easing, and we received another soaking on the way back to the depot. Obviously expecting a daylight journey, I had looked forward to this portion of the trip, especially as we neared Montreal. Instead, I peered through a rain streaked window into darkness.

Doug had booked a room beforehand, and at the hotel lobby the bellhop asked if he could carry our luggage. "Thanks, but we're travelling light," Doug quipped. The rain continued to beat down, so after a light supper in the hotel restaurant we spent the remainder of the evening eating popcorn and potato chips and watching television... what else was there to do?

Part of our plan had been to take a tour of the city, but it was still raining when we awoke. We opted instead for the deluxe three-hour bus excursion. I had little idea where we were most of the time, but I do recall going down Dorchester Blvd...wherever that was. The tour guide explained how many ancient and historical buildings had been demolished to transform this avenue into one lined with skyscrapers. "The most famous is Place Ville Marie," he boasted. "It's forty-five stories tall!" Because of the settling fog, the top third of the building was invisible, but we took his word for it.

Up on Mount Royal, we meandered through tree-lined

arteries of the cities of Westmount and Outremont, noted for their beautiful homes and gardens. This may have been true on a nice day, but somehow the combination of grey skies, brown leftover snow banks, a cold winter rain, and barren trees dispelled any notion of this being so.

On the summit of Mount Royal the bus stopped, while we all stared into the greyness that completely enveloped everything.

"It's a shame the visibility is so poor," apologized our guide, "for this is one of the most beautiful parts of our city. The St. Lawrence River on the south side, and Riviere des Prairies on the north, provide a picture taker's paradise. We usually stop here for half an hour...but today..." his voice trailed off as he motioned for the driver to continue. We all peered at our opaque surroundings once more before leaving. The balance of the tour was the same...fog and rain.

Later in the afternoon the rain finally subsided and Doug decided he'd like to visit McGill University. But no sooner had we began our tour of the university campus when the rain returned. We'd been soaked so many times in the past twenty-four hours we barely noticed.

As we took our seats for the return journey, the bus felt like a furnace. Fifty passengers in various degrees of dampness had steamed up the interior until it resembled the atmosphere of a sauna. Between the heat and humidity, both Doug and I were close to nausea by the time we reached Kingston.

Certain we'd endured every kind of bad luck during the previous thirty-six hours, no sooner were we underway when the rain that had plagued us from the beginning transformed to sleet and freezing rain, slowing the bus to a crawl. And that's the way it was all the way to Toronto.

The slow pace coupled with scores of accidents added an additional two hours to the schedule...all we needed for this nightmare disguised as a weekend trip!

In the following years, Doug and I talked about returning to Montreal some weekend when it wasn't raining, when the sun shone warmly and brightly, and everything would go exactly as planned. That trip never happened; but if it had it would have been nothing to write about.

Midnight at Molly's

I WAS NINE WHEN I FIRST MET DOUG HAMILTON. ALTHOUGH fifteen years my senior, he eventually became one of my closest friends, a relationship that lasted five decades.

Doug had a lucrative livestock trucking business, and was a buyer for several meat-packing plants in the Toronto-Hamilton region. Apart from Christmas and New Year's, it was an unrelenting schedule...two loads of livestock a day, five days a week, fifty-two weeks a year. I'd be home from work in time for the second load. Thus every month or so you'd find me in the passenger seat of the Mack, and after our load was delivered (which could happen anytime between 9:00 p.m. and midnight) we'd stop for supper.

Molly's Truck and Trailer Café was situated at the bottom of a long grade, and on a clear evening the flashing neon sign beckoned for miles. To this day, the recollection of that restaurant brings to mind the unmistakable odour of frying onions, which was noticeable the second you stepped from the cab, courtesy of a large kitchen exhaust fan that emptied into the parking lot.

Inside, two dozen booths fashioned in a recurring theme of vinyl, chrome, and plastic were spaced throughout the L-shaped room, while calendars of vintage vehicles and Nashville and Hollywood legends graced the turquoise and cream-painted walls.

Dispersed among this assortment of wall material were various messages and slogans:

"In God We Trust...All Others Must Pay."

"My Best Is None Too Good...Don't Bring Out The Worst In Me."

"Don't Go Away Mad...Just Go Away."

The daily special was written in red script that hadn't changed in years. "Piece of Pie: $1.50. Peace of Mind: Free."

These messages weren't confined to the dining area. Neatly written above the washroom urinal was a sign that advocated the benefits of cleanliness and proper hygiene, requesting that its patrons "Please Stand Close to the Urinal...It's Shorter Than You Think."

Molly Hanlon had operated at this location for thirty years. She'd been threatening to sell the restaurant ever since her husband died a decade before, but never acted. "I'm just not ready," was her stock answer when pressed. "This is my home and family."

Molly's "family" were an eclectic mix, and that certainly included Doug. He'd been a consistent customer through the years, and she felt obligated to endure his endless questions.

"Molly, did you make this soup? Did you bake these biscuits? Is this town water or do you have your own well? Is this 18 percent or 10 percent cream? How often do you have garbage pickup? Do you think last night's rain will hurt the rhubarb? Do you heat with gas or oil? Do you use white or brown eggs? What do you think of the East European situation? What's your view on Britain's new lady Prime Minister?"

One evening Molly turned to me. "Does Doug yap constantly like this in the truck, or have you simply learned to tune him out?"

Another "family" member was Delmar, a machinist who worked the 3-11:00 p.m. shift at a metal fabricating company, and stopped in on his way home. Delmar always studied the menu in great detail. Why, I don't know, as his order was as consistent as Doug's questions: a glass of water, a coffee and a hot turkey sandwich.

Delmar enjoyed taxing his brain on crossword puzzles and related word games from the *Toronto Star* newspaper he bought without fail. Borrowing a page from Doug's playbook, he'd seldom miss an opportunity to question certain words or phrases.

"I wonder why 'abbreviation' is such a long word. What do they call a male ladybug? Isn't it strange that most sandwich meat is round when bread is square? And why does a round pizza always arrive in a square box? How do you suppose MacDonald's gets the sesame seeds to stick to their buns?" Delmar referred to these as "mind puzzlers."

Then there was Harris, a truck driver who'd reminisce about his forty years driving the roads of southwestern Ontario. Name any letter of the alphabet and Harris would name a product that he'd hauled—from asphalt to zinc oxide.

Harris was a big man in every direction; probably close to three hundred pounds and several inches over six feet. Partly because of his size, but mostly because he didn't believe in them, Harris wouldn't wear a seatbelt. His philosophy was that it was safer to be thrown out of the truck cab than trapped in it. With his mass, most observers figured he wouldn't be thrown far.

His friends relished telling the story of the time Harris was stopped by police conducting their roadside seatbelt compliance program. There were a couple of vehicles ahead, giving Harris just enough time to fasten his belt.

"Do you always wear your seatbelt?" the officer asked when Harris pulled up.

"Always."

"You don't find it uncomfortable?"

Harris thought it a strange question but answered with a shake of his head.

"It must be difficult to drive," continued the cop, pointing at the steering wheel. At this point Harris noticed that in his haste he'd fastened the belt around the steering wheel instead of himself!

Like most truckers, Harris had hundreds of stories. There was the time his brakes failed in Barrie, and he just " missed going into the drink." Sometimes when he repeated that particular story he actually did go "into the drink." Then there was the night he crossed the double train tracks near Schomberg in thick fog, and the freight "couldn't have missed me by more than a foot!" Often when that tale was recounted the distance was reduced to "just an inch or two."

Another story was about a produce truck that upset its load of oranges directly in front of him. When Harris retold that one, the fruits and vegetables often grew in size. Oranges were supplanted by tomatoes, grapefruit, pumpkins...even watermelons.

We'd heard all of Harris' stories...only the details

changed as the years passed, his imagination wandered, and his memory weakened.

Another Molly's regular was Wesley. When the waitress asked, "What can I get for you?" he always began by answering, "Well I don't see your name on the menu E.J., so I'll guess I'll have..." This was forever followed by a hearty laugh. The exchange had grown tiresome but Wesley was a good tipper so E.J. was always able to force a laugh.

Whatever he ordered, Wesley always requested gravy on the side, which he'd dribble a spoonful at a time on whatever he was eating. Dessert was apple pie...but not Dutch apple...just regular apple.

"I've nothing against the Dutch, I just don't like the way they make pie!"

When I first met E.J. she was probably in her late thirties...it was hard to tell. Close to six feet tall, she had eyes as brown as Belgium chocolate, raven black hair that flowed over her shoulders, and a body that would cause any man to dream. Nobody knew what E.J. stood for. Ellie Jane? Edna Jean? Emma Jean? It didn't matter...to everyone she was simply E.J.

E.J. didn't talk much about her personal life, but the story around Molly's was that she'd been married at least twice. Her first husband, according to those who knew him, spent his time "searching for direction...instead of a job." The second seemingly had alcohol consumption issues. There was rumour of a third, but no one seemed to know much about him.

Secretly, every man in the place loved E.J., and none could figure why she'd struck out so often. Most would have given anything for even one swing of the bat.

"She's got it all," sighed Wesley. "Beautiful eyes, beautiful hair, beautiful skin, beautiful smile, a nice rack, and a great ass!" Wesley's description may have been crudely stated, but not a guy in the room would have disagreed.

E.J. certainly had her suitors...or, more aptly, predators. She'd been the recipient of every pick-up line invented, but took it all good-naturedly, in return providing just enough fun and flirtation to keep the tips flowing.

Most understood the boundaries, and for those who didn't, the lesson was soon learned. Clint, a trucker for National Grocers, put his hand up E.J.'s skirt one night while she was bent over cleaning a table. It was probably three weeks before he regained full use of his hand.

There was Cornell, who came in every night at precisely 10:00 p.m. on his way to work at Kodak. Cornell worked the overnight shift in the dark room and claimed that from when the time changed in November until it reversed in March, he never saw the sun. He'd pick up the newspaper on his way through the door, consuming the editorials and articles while he ate.

All somebody had to say was, "So, Cornell, how's the world look today?"

"These goddam politicians," Cornell would begin. "No matter what level of government, they don't care about anyone but themselves. Just lapping at the public trough of taxpayer money as long as they can until their fat pensions click in! Now I agree there's a bit of larceny in us all, but this is just pure greed...listen to this..."

Conservatives, Liberals, or NDP, federal or provincial, city councillors, rural councillors, county planners, educational trustees, striking teachers, the airlines, the postal system, the OPP takeover of small-town police forces, consumer groups, Sunday shopping, farmland expropriation, municipal amalgamation...these were all subjects about which Cornell was passionate.

Another member of Molly's diversified family was Herman, a man of slight stature with thick black hair and equally thick glasses. Herman and his guests patronized Molly's establishment on a regular basis, always reserving booth No. 16, which was in the farthest corner of the restaurant. Sometimes the meeting lasted just long enough for a cup of coffee—other times a full-course meal—but Herman always paid the tab.

Herman's associates seemed to be laden with baggage from life's wars. Over time I discovered that Herman was a lawyer and those he dined with were clients. Apparently Herman had an office in the city, but if clients preferred the restaurant's relaxed forum, and perhaps a meal, so be it.

From the outset something about Herman seemed familiar, and one evening, just to emphasize what a small world we live in, chance conversation confirmed that he and I had attended high school together. Although he had been engaged in the technical/commercial program, and I in the academic, we shared a couple of subjects throughout a semester in the early 1960s.

Herman was a person of few words, so our high school relationship was remote. But back then, something about him appeared to be out of focus. Behind those thick glasses his eyes telegraphed a turbulent personality. He got into frequent scuffles with school authority—allegedly tossing a fellow student head-first down the stairs on one occasion. (Herman claimed he tripped.) After an incident arising from an assault in the school parking lot, Herman was briefly consigned to Guelph Reformatory.

Later, another encounter—a variety store robbery as

I recall—netted Herman some time at a real prison. His lawyer pleaded for leniency because it was only a replica gun. Once released, Herman appeared to have regained his footing, securing a job as an electrician's apprentice with a company in the Niagara area. Then one evening he came home to discover his live-in girlfriend in the midst of a mattress encounter with a co-worker. The circumstances concerning the girlfriend remained unclear, but the confrontation left the co-worker unconscious and near death in an alley outside Herman's apartment.

After serving a little over two years of a seven-year sentence, Herman won an appeal with the parole board. His case was helped considerably by his former boss, who believed Herman had been a victim of circumstance, and that he was truly a good man. This former boss offered to vouch for Herman by re-hiring him at his old job.

Another thing in Herman's favour was the fact that he used his incarceration to his advantage, utilizing the prison library system to study the intricacies of the legal system. Once paroled, working by day and diligently continuing his studies at night, Herman soon joined a small legal firm. His speciality was aiding individuals who'd fallen through the cracks of the regular court system. Several years later, Herman opened his own practice so he could devote himself to "helping those who need the most help" (as he put it).

Who'd have thought that Herman, that supposedly unreachable, inaccessible, unpredictable personality behind the thick glasses, would have become a lawyer? Who indeed!

No way could I close the book on this litany of Molly's customers without including Carl, the restaurant's resident storyteller. Carl had a soft voice, but when he began a yarn, everyone listened. Whereas Harris' truck driver stories were generally straightforward, Carl's tales were elusive narratives that often centred on the vague and indefinite.

I'd heard dozens of Carl's stories, but one I recall was of his Uncle Morgan and Aunt Susan, who farmed a section and a half in southern Saskatchewan during the 1930s. For three straight years they watched their farm literally blow away in the dust storms that ravaged the prairies of that era. With crops amounting to next to nothing, about the only thing sustaining the couple was the garden, in which Susan took special pride.

"As long as we can eat, we'll survive!" she had stated. Another delight was her flowers, especially roses. "A red rose is one of the most beautiful, most delicate living things in this world!"

Susan nursed her garden and roses through the sun-baked summers, while Morgan hauled water in oak barrels from three miles away, since their well had long ago succumbed to drought.

"Then some fever was making the rounds," continued Carl, "and Susan died. Uncle Morgan buried her in the lilac-lined cemetery plot a hundred yards from the house, the final resting place for three generations of their family.

"Morgan struggled on for another year, but with the bank foreclosing on the mortgage, the county suing for unpaid taxes, and his wife gone, he eventually went to live with relatives in Ontario, leaving the farm to disappear in prairie dust. Three years later, he relocated to British Columbia, stopping at the old farm on his way through.

"Morgan had no idea why he stopped, as there was nothing there, since the place had been left to the elements. The barn was just a pile of scattered timber, and the house had not fared much better. Everywhere sand was piled like snowdrifts."

"Except for a couple of lilac bushes, the sole survivors of a grove that had once provided shelter for the tiny cemetery, there wasn't a hint of greenery as far as the eye could see, until something caught his eye out beyond those lilacs."

Carl paused, enjoying the silence in the room.

"Once establishing the location of the old cemetery, and more importantly Susan's grave, Morgan discovered what had drawn his attention. Growing out of the drought-ravaged, waist-deep sand that covered Susan's grave was a red rose...a red rose as vibrant and glorious as one could imagine!"

The story ended the way all Carl's stories ended...as an unrestricted parable free from definition, allowing the audience to draw their own conclusion.

One evening after he had delivered one of his signature ramblings, and allowing for a reverent pause, I said, "I've got one for you, Carl." Carl turned to me in anticipation.

"For a long time now," I began, "my brothers and I have been taking a yearly day trip. Mostly to visit steam shows, car shows, or agricultural museums of some kind. Well, last weekend we visited an antique agriculture/automobile show in southwest Huron County, and on the way home we stopped in the town of Lucan. Are you familiar with Lucan, Carl?"

"Of course," he replied. "It was the home of the Donnelly family, who were murdered by a vigilante group one winter night back in the late 1800s."

"Exactly," I went on. "In fact, our plan was to visit the Donnelly museum, but it had closed for the day. Well, on the south side of the town lies the cemetery where the Donnelly family is buried, and as you probably know, on the original headstone, beneath the names of the family members who met their fate that day, the word 'murdered' had been carved deep into the granite finish."

Carl nodded, and I continued.

For anyone listening, I explained how, following years of "souvenir hunters" chipping away pieces of the granite legend, the headstone was removed by surviving family members, and replaced by a less volatile monument, replacing the word "murdered" with "died."

"Anyway," I concluded, "as we pulled up in front of the cemetery, our attention was drawn to a large black cat sitting in the entranceway, staring as only a cat can. We made some comment about the significance of this graveyard greeter, and then our minds wandered to other subjects, as we slowly threaded our way through the hundreds of memorials towards the rear of the cemetery. However, when we got to the Donnelly gravesite…guess who was there staring at us directly in front of the monument?"

Following Carl's lead, I said no more, simply allowing audience imagination and creativity to furnish an appropriate epilogue.

Carl shook his head. "Don't you just love unexplainable incidents like that?" he asked. "Of all the tombstones to pick, isn't it eerie the cat would choose the Donnelly stone! Did you get a picture?"

I shook my head.

Wesley, who'd been silent up to this point, spoke up. "That's too bad…a photo would've been valuable. Then you'd know if it was really a cat."

"What are you rambling about, Wesley?" scoffed E.J., who'd been pouring coffee and listening to the exchange. "I guess Dave would know if it was a cat or not!"

"No. I mean maybe it wasn't a cat…perhaps it was

merely an apparition. If nothing showed up on film, you'd know it was a ghost, because ghosts don't photograph!"

Silence filled the room as that last remark was digested.

"You know," Wesley continued, "people were always claiming they saw Donnelly ghosts around Lucan. Legend has it that for years you couldn't drive a horse down that road after dark!"

I shrugged my shoulders. "Ghosts...legends...simple coincidence...your guess is good as mine."

Carl nodded, agreeing there was no logical conclusion for this particular story. Then all conversation returned to where it had been a few minutes earlier, and the world moved on...

The aroma of frying onions followed Doug and I to the parking lot and lingered in the cab of the Mack seemingly for miles. After a lengthy discussion of the evening's events, and a search for some kind of explanation concerning the rose and cat stories, we fell silent.

After a while, Doug broke the solitude. "You know, David...there's times when a person just has to let life figure itself out."

Highways and Holidays

R‍ECENTLY I WAS IN CONVERSATION WITH A BUSINESS EXECUTIVE acquaintance who was about to retire. The subject of vacations arose, and he mentioned that he was entitled to eight weeks of paid vacation, plus the accumulation of two weeks' worth of sick days. I reflected that this generous reward approached that of politicians.

For the most part over the years, "vacation" was an unknown word in our family's vocabulary. For 40 years I contracted a courier service for the Ontario Ministry of Health. During the first 20 years I took one week of vacation per year, while during the final two decades I never took a holiday at all. Being self-employed, I decided it wasn't worth the aggravation every twelve months of having to search out and train someone willing to do just a week's work...especially since I enjoyed the job.

My grandfather worked at Massey-Harris for 40 years, and with the exception of the last two or three, never received more than a week's vacation. Holidays were limited for my father as well. Beginning in 1943, he was employed as herdsman for a dairy operation in Bond Head, Ontario, and received one week per year paid holiday for the decade he was there.

Due to commodity restrictions—mainly fuel and rubber—widespread travel was impossible during the war years, but in 1947 Mom and Dad utilized their allotted vacation time to drive to Quebec City, their first extended trip since their honeymoon eight years earlier. In 1953, after purchasing their own farm, so-called vacations became even rarer.

When I was young, day trips were the extent of our recreational activity. With our family of seven squeezed into the passenger compartment of our Pontiac, and a picnic lunch stashed in the trunk, we'd head out after church on Sunday to nowhere in particular, eventually stopping at one of the numerous roadside parks that dotted Ontario's highways. "Fast-food" chains such as MacDonald's and Tim Horton's have replaced the picnic-by-the-side-of-the-road experience of a half-century ago. With a plastic table cloth spread over a wooden table beneath the inviting shade of a maple, we'd enjoy our hard-boiled eggs, salmon sandwiches, and Kool-Aid.

I recall one Sunday when we went to Wasaga Beach on Georgian Bay. Beach outings had been few for most families of this era, and with valid reason: parents were afraid. For as long as they could remember, wherever large crowds gathered during the hot days of summer, there was the potential for new outbreaks of polio. In 1952, there were nearly 70,000 cases...the highest in recorded history. Usually the disease affected children in the four-to-fourteen age range.

In 1949, three Harvard University bacteriologists developed a practical method to grow the polio virus outside the body, making it possible to produce the large quantities needed to make a vaccine. In 1953, Jonas Salk, a scientist at the University of Pittsburgh, developed the first vaccine, and although there were some serious problems at the outset, by autumn 1954 it was declared safe and effective for public use. Many, my father included, disagreed with the theory of using live viruses to treat healthy kids. But majority ruled, and that autumn, I and my sister and brothers, along with two million other schoolchildren, received the Salk vaccine. Although it had not been cured, a disease traced back to the Ancient Egyptians had at least been brought under control.

Although our parents may have been deprived of holidays, there was never any shortage of friends and relatives anxious to spend their free time with us. These visits could last several hours or several days. There were regulars, such as our city and country cousins, but there were always a few of whom we had no idea who they were and never felt it important enough to ask. This minority contingent would show up with yearly regularity Maybe they were second or third cousins. Maybe their parents were simply friends or neighbours of our parents in some other era. Who would know?

Whoever they were, the barn was always a suitable starting point for childhood activity. Hide-and-seek in the hayloft was a perennial favourite. But inevitably the attraction that proved irresistible was the superhighway on the western boundary of our farm. If one development symbolized the great post-war recreational invasion of Simcoe County, it was the construction of Highway

400 from Toronto to Barrie—often referred as "Ontario's Vacationland Freeway."

With an increasing need to lessen the traffic flow off Highways 11 and 27, which were the only routes from Toronto to Barrie and points northward, construction on the proposed highway began immediately after the war in 1946. My brother Bill recalls riding with Dad on the new highway when it still featured several gravelled sections. By December a single paved lane on either side of the thirty-foot grassy median was in place, and during July of 1952, paving was completed and the 400 officially became a four-lane highway.

Beginning late Friday afternoon in the summer season, the cottage-goers would begin their migration northward and my brothers and I would be out in the hilly pasture field that paralleled the highway, debating the pros and cons of the stream of metal passing before us.

We had animated arguments as we discussed the models of our dreams. Both dual-tone and triple-tone colour configurations were becoming fashionable in the mid-fifties. My particular favourite, a Desoto hardtop, had a pink/black/ivory combination. Another aspiration was a turquoise-and-white Chevrolet Belair.

Not just Friday afternoons, but long into the night, a steady stream of headlights provided a constant beam through the south window glass of the bedroom I shared with my brothers. Sunday evening, the tide would reverse as bumper-to-bumper traffic wound its way back to Ontario's capital. The 401 was just beginning construction in the Toronto area at this point and no other major routes throughout the city existed. With limited opportunity to siphon off incoming traffic, the flow from the 400 naturally slowed to a crawl when it hit the city.

Add an accident or two into the mix and the backup would be tremendous. Seldom did a Sunday evening pass without some sort of issue bringing traffic to a standstill. Since we lived less than 1000 feet from the superhighway, on hot summer nights the heavy air would easily carry the voices of stranded motorists to our front yard. It almost felt as though we were eavesdropping.

During the mid-1950s, I recall only one gas station on the entire Toronto to Barrie stretch: a British-American Centre at Cookstown, just a few miles north of our place. Due to the shortage of service centres and because we lived in such close proximity to the highway, strangers walking across our pasture field in search of a gallon of gas for a dry tank, some water for a boiling radiator, or, if more serious, the use of our telephone was a regular occurrence.

One June day two or three years ago while on a Sunday drive through Simcoe County, I found myself in the vicinity of our old farm. As I passed beneath the ninth concession bridge below the 400, I couldn't help but be reminded of that walk home in the torrential rain so many years before—the night Hurricane Hazel came to call.

I stopped at the end of the laneway, which at first glance appeared pretty much as remembered. One of the cement pillars that marked the entranceway lay neglected in the long grass beside the driveway, but its mate remained firmly anchored. The current owners were very receptive, kindly letting me roam the property while reliving past memories. However, the orchard I knew was completely gone—no cherries, plums, apples, pears, or gooseberries now, but as before, a row of spruce trees crowded the fenced yard west of the house, and in the yard itself, lilacs still bloomed in abundance.

Time hadn't been kind to the old windmill, as only the frame remained, and the wooden silo that had guarded the northwest corner of the barn had been replaced by a cement structure. I found little familiar about the stable itself, as it had been completely gutted and a couple of chickens were walking around what used to be the milking area.

Upstairs, the barn was empty and silent, except for pigeons and sparrows. The hay fork remained suspended from the ceiling, as it had for decades, and it wasn't difficult to envision our old Pontiac, rope attached to its sturdy bumper shuttling up and down the steep slope of the gangway as it operated the giant fork lifting loose hay from the wagon into the hayloft.

And what about that ribbon of asphalt? Well, over the years the highway had expanded to six lanes, with more, noisier, and faster traffic, and was now seemingly dominated by Asian- and European-built automobiles. Interestingly, the hill we as kids climbed to the highway's boundary didn't seem as steep as remembered, despite the advancing years.

Watching the traffic race by, my mind returned to that Saturday in March 1957, sitting in the passenger seat of the truck beside my father. I recalled the sadness that swept over me as we drove beneath the 400 overpass and both the highway and our farm gradually disappeared from view. We were on our way to a new farm in a new county and I figured I'd never see that highway again—a highway that been instrumental in both entertainment and education, and an integral part of childhood.

Leaning against the woven-wire barrier, lost in thought, I needed little imagination to envision myself in this exact station nearly sixty years earlier. It had been a simple and uncomplicated time, when youthful dreams involved nothing more than a triple-toned Desoto or a turquoise-and-white Chevrolet Belair.

Yesterday's Moments...Today's Memories

Thomas and Mary Carruthers with (left to right) sons William, Dave, George (1900)

The Carruthers sisters: Jean, Lillian, Alma, Evelyn, Lois (1938)

David Turner

My parents (1938)

Billy and Vivien (1948)

Yesterday's Moments...Today's Memories

Richard and Vivien (1952)

Vivien with Tim McIsaac (1954)

Oliver and Mamie Turner (1955)

Don at the controls of a Massey-Harris tractor (1960)

Verdun (Mac) McIssac (1960)

Yesterday's Moments...Today's Memories

Evelyn MacDonald and brothers Harold, Doug, Eldon (1962)

My grandmother Reba Carruthers and daughters (1960)

Aubrey and Evelyn MacDonald (early 1960s)

David and brother-in-law Glen Cober (1972)

Yesterday's Moments...Today's Memories

Harvest time (1972)

Cousins Doug Watt, Richard, David, Dan McIssac, and uncle Don Valentine (1984)

The launch of Beyond the Moon (1993)

Three brothers: Doug, Harold, Eldon (1995)

Lifelong friend Doug Hamilton

Mom and Dad at Palmerston farm (Thanksgiving, 1996)

Author off for another day on the road (1997)

David poses with his summer car (2004)

Author poses beside driveway pillar of childhood Simcoe County home (2007)

Barn built in 1900 still stands on Turner's Hill

South Wind

In a previous chapter I wrote an account of my 1977 journey deep beneath the Mason-Dixon Line in search of southern culture and philosophy.

At the time, with great anticipation and high expectation, I foresaw two weeks of sugar and cotton plantations, southern mansions, southern drawls, magnolia blossoms, Stephen Foster songs and paddle-wheelers lazily navigating the Mississippi River.

In a little town in Alabama however, I was reminded of another side of southern hospitality; one that just a decade or two before was quite comfortable with segregation and its inherent blemishes and imperfections. I'm sure I was aware of this darker flank but conveniently chose to ignore it. So in honesty this discovery was not so much a disappointment, but an awakening.

My intention, however, had been to gain a wide-angled lens of this historical region. That I did; Alabama's famous "black belt," where cotton once ruled; cities like Montgomery, where the seeds of the Civil War were sown and flourished, as well as the colourful coastal towns and cities of southern Mississippi.

Unfortunately, I saw New Orleans in the pouring rain and the Mississippi River shrouded by thick fog—both were sights to which I'd especially looked forward. And then there was that motel just north of New Orleans that to put it kindly had a few "issues."

Upon leaving the abovementioned motel that April morning in 1977, my initial plan was to return to New Orleans and resume where I had left off during the previous day's wash-out. But with the forecast sounding anything but promising for the Gulf region, I decided to continue northward up Highway 61 towards Baton Rouge. My luck began to change and by the time I reached Louisiana's capital, the sun was breaking through the clouds.

There was no question as to my first point of interest. "Old Man River" would not deny me twice. The sky by now was clear and blue and I sat down on a bench alongside River Road, where from practically any vantage point the great waterway that spawned so many songs, stories, and legends is visible. Like Tom Sawyer and Huckleberry Finn, as a kid I envisioned myself rafting down the Mississippi and listening to the deep-throated whistles of the paddle-wheelers echoing across the muddy water.

Regardless of size, every river begins somewhere; a small stream starting up in northern Minnesota is the source of the Mississippi. With major tributaries like the Missouri, Illinois, and Ohio, as well as their branches and offshoots, it becomes a waterway a mile wide and a hundred feet deep in places. A huge amount of topsoil, sand, and gravel is carried by this river, and when deposited on the bottom it raises the bed, causing flooding during periods of sustained rain.

One solution to this chronic problem has been the construction of levees—earthen dams strengthened with steel cables built along the river's sides to hold back the water. Many of these levees were constructed decades ago, built not by machine but hand labour (prison gangs, mostly).

Another solution is dredging. Down at the river's mouth, a worker told me that enough silt accumulated each day to make dredging a twenty-four-hour-a day-job just to keep even. I never thought to ask him what they do with it!

Baton Rouge is somewhat unique, featuring two state capitol buildings. One was built in 1847 and used until 1932, when a new building was constructed during Governor Huey Long's reign.

The name of Huey Long appears frequently in the study of Louisiana history. He built a powerful political organization during the 1920s and was elected governor of the state in 1928. Although ruling more as a dictator, Long helped develop the state with vigorous programs of roadbuilding (including the new "Airline Highway" linking New Orleans and Baton Rouge), hospital construction, free textbooks for school children, and night school for illiterate citizens.

In 1930 Long was elected to the senate, backing President Roosevelt's Democratic Party. Over time, a major disagreement in political policies caused Long to run for the top job himself in the upcoming 1936 election, threatening to split the Democratic vote. His erratic and unpredictable philosophies garnered many political enemies on both sides of the political arena; death threats, arsons, and drive-by shootings were all part of Huey Long's world during this period, and in September 1935 he was assassinated while inside the capitol building.

Baton Rouge's new capitol building looks like a smaller version of New York's Empire State Building, rising 34 floors above some of the most beautiful parks and gardens anywhere. An elevator hoists visitors to an observation deck, affording an excellent view of the city, and particularly the Mississippi River. Each step leading to the Capitol building is engraved with the name of a state, in order of their admission to the Union. A statue of Governor Long marks his gravesite outside the building, and on the ground floor tour, guides enthusiastically point out the actual spot where Huey Long was gunned down.

I crossed the bridge over to the west bank of the Mississippi, turning south on the state highway. At that time (the mid-1970s), several old estates could be found in this area. Some were still situated on active plantations, dispelling the notion this way of life had vanished.

I passed the better part of an afternoon at Avery Island, on the Gulf of Mexico, some 150 miles west of New Orleans, deep in Louisiana's bayou country. Avery, a roughly three-mile-long, three-mile-wide island, is actually a huge salt dome; during the American Civil War the island produced over 10,000 tons of rock salt for the Confederacy. Salt is no longer mined, and today the island is a tropical refuge for many bird species. At one point I saw at least a half dozen pelicans fishing for their dinner, and heron sightings are common. The island's most popular tenants are snowy egrets, which gather by the tens of thousands. According to studies, roughly half the wild ducks and geese in North America winter in Louisiana's bayous.

If a person wishes to discover natural Louisiana, Avery

Island is the place. Cypress trees sporting beards of Spanish moss dominate the island. Anyone unfamiliar with the phenomenon might guess the trees had been inflicted with a fungus infestation; but the moss is actually a flowering plant of the pineapple family, which has no roots and absorbs moisture directly from the air. When I stared at it long enough it made me itchy.

One travels in Louisiana's swampy bayous on the "pirogue," a small, flat-bottomed boat propelled by a pole. Primarily designed to navigate the shallow marshland waterways of Lower Louisiana, it was used by fur trappers to approach their traps with minimal noise.

The state's farm commodities seem to fall into four main categories. Cotton grew in the north; sugarcane in the lower, more tropical regions; rice along the Gulf shore; and though technically not a farm crop, fishing and trapping were carried out in the lower bayou swampland.

It was interesting to listen to the farm broadcasts by Louisiana's rural radio stations. The grain and oilseed markets seemed to be given only a brief summary, while a major portion of the program would be dedicated to fishing and related topics. Locals would phone in to relate where they were making a good catch of perch, bass, or catfish.

Over in Bayou Boeuf, a listener bragged how he'd snagged "a dandy bunch of juicy channel cats," and how another had latched onto a catch of bigmouth bass using a lure of bacon rinds and I forget what else.

The king of the Louisiana swamp is the alligator. One afternoon I spied one dozing on a riverbank about fifty feet away. "Gators" were scarce when I visited, having fallen prey to hide hunters and sport hunting. Subsequently, alligators became a protected species until their numbers increased to an acceptable level. Today, there are an estimated two million wild alligators in Louisiana's swamplands. Roughly 5 percent are harvested each year by licensed hunters. There are also some 300,000 raised on alligator farms, and marketed similarly as any other agricultural commodity.

I saw only one building on Avery Island—an ivy-covered brick structure used to manufacture tabasco sauce. Louisianans seemingly inject this spicy red pepper sauce, often referred to as Louisiana Hot Sauce, into most everything they eat. I once had turtle soup spiked with a liberal amount. One slurp of soup...one gulp of water...another slurp of soup...another gulp of water.

The McIlhenny Company was established in 1868 and manufactured their famous sauce exclusively on the island for a century. To handle the increased volume and meet demand, a modern factory was built in New Iberia, just a few miles away, and although many of the ingredients are now outsourced, pepper groves still thrive on the island, and limited manufacturing continues in the old building, as it has for nearly 150 years.

So if you care to sample the ultimate in tabasco sauce, insist it says McIlhenny's from New Iberia on the label. Just make sure you have a pitcher of water handy!

At Lake Charles, I headed northeast through the heavily wooded areas of west central Louisiana, crossing the Red River at Alexandria. The river is aptly named—the dark reddish brown sediment it carries is striking. Late in the day I sighted the "Big River" once again and crossed the bridge into the state of Mississippi and the city of Natchez.

Natchez is the oldest city on the Mississippi River and due to the growth of the cotton industry it became the centre of wealth and culture until the Civil War. Because the cotton industry was little threat to Ulysses Grant's invading Union troops, Natchez escaped what befell many of its sister cities, which had been torched to blackness. Thankfully some eighty registered pre-Civil War homes exist in and around Natchez, many open to the public.

Some are over 200 years old. A few offer bed and breakfast for guests. Some were relatively small and cozy, others breathtaking in their magnitude. *Longbranch*, a huge domed affair, sat unfinished, exactly as when the Civil War interrupted its construction 120 years earlier.

A leisurely drive up highway 61 brought me to Vicksburg, Mississippi's most important city during the war. The city and the river itself were controlled by Confederate forces until the battle of Vicksburg, which began in May 1863. Being pounded by cannons from land, and gunboats from the river, residents dug into the city's sandy hillside caves for protection. Out of food, and completely estranged from the rest of the country, they ate whatever they could find: horses, mules, dogs, cats, even rats. After forty-eight unbelievable days, Vicksburg finally surrendered. I toured the city but saw few reminders of the old south. That forty-eight day battle more than a century earlier had seen to that.

Over the next couple of days I continued my homeward trek up through northeastern Mississippi, following the highway known as the Natchez Trace. The "Trace" runs all the way from Natchez to Nashville, Tennessee, close to 500 miles. During the Civil War the Trace was an important supply route for Confederate troops and new settlers to the Gulf States used this route with regularity.

Perhaps it has changed, but in 1977 what I discovered was a two-lane highway of smooth pavement and clipped debris-free roadsides. It was a road not merely to get from point to point, but a road upon which to linger and enjoy; the posted speed limit was a leisurely 45 mph and commercial trucks were restricted. Frequent roadside picnic areas and historical plaques beckoned travellers along its entirety.

One didn't have to travel far in this region to be reminded of the racial instability prevalent just a decade earlier. The pretty town of Oxford is just one example. On the western outskirts stands the University of Mississippi, where fourteen years earlier, in 1963, James Meredith attempted to become the first black student to enroll at that institute. "Attempted" is the key word; Mississippi Governor Ross Barnett, along with other political dignitaries, blocked the doorway. The National Guard was deployed, and students both black and white clashed, resulting in millions of dollars in property damage to the university and campus, scores injured, and two dead.

The final stop on my two-week excursion into the heart of Dixie was Shiloh National Military Park, just over the Mississippi border, in Tennessee. A spectacular setting of rolling forested hills, it's difficult to imagine how this place once witnessed such terrible human sacrifice. During a two-day period in 1862, over 25,000 soldiers were killed. Altogether nearly half-a-million soldiers died from battle wounds during the Civil War, and it's been estimated that many again died from disease, exposure, malnutrition, and even snakebite.

Reflecting on what transpired on battlefields all across the US during that conflict, I couldn't help but wonder why the south held on so long to an elusive dream of victory. What began with such exuberance on April 12, 1861, ended in bitter defeat almost to the day four years later, when General Robert E. Lee surrendered what was left of his shattered army to General Ulysses S. Grant.

When one watches Alex Haley's *Roots* saga, despite the distaste, repugnance, and embarrassment of slavery, one can't help but have some compassion for the plantation owners. As the war concludes they are left with nothing more than a mansion falling into ruins, their cotton and sugarcane crops burned to blackness by Grant's Union troops. Their slaves are free to go wherever they want; they are bankrupt, have no credit, their confederate money is worthless, everything they worked for is gone. So they merely pack up their few belongings and ride off into the unknown; victims of a way of life that shattered before their eyes. So although this war may have begun as a battle of north-versus-south, union-versus-secession, it quickly became much larger. An entire way of life was being threatened.

Then there were the Confederate soldiers. It wasn't long into the war before most forgot what they were fighting for. Few ever knew, let alone owned a slave. Most of the recruits were poor cotton farmers and factory workers, and seven dollars a week, a uniform, three meals a day, and a rifle to retain when the war was over, was the best offer they would ever see.

I had seen and learned plenty in that two-week period, and even if I perceived an imagined rather than actual way of life, my memories of the south will always be alive with antebellum mansions, black delta cotton land, and sugarcane plantations; the unforgettable aroma of magnolia blossoms; white picket fences surrounding gardens of azaleas; a warm Gulf breeze drifting off the blue waters of Mobile Bay; and mammoth oak trees standing after three centuries. I will always remember the romance of the grandest river of them all, and the old-world charm of New Orleans despite the rain.

On second thought...maybe it isn't that difficult to understand why the south fought so hard for so long against such overwhelming odds.

Jennifer, God, and Me

THE SCENE WAS A SATURDAY AFTERNOON IN JACKSON MISSISsippi, when a storefront sign advertising "Bibles, Books and Records" caught my attention. It was during my two-week road trip to the southern United States in the mid-1970s that I happened to stop at the little shop, and while browsing through the gospel music section, a pretty girl who introduced herself as Jen inquired if I needed assistance.

With her walnut-brown eyes, suntanned skin, and shoulder-length auburn hair, the only assistance I needed was to not fall in love that very moment. As we chatted about our musical tastes, conversation turned to my "accent."

"You're not from around here!" Jen drawled. She was astonished I'd driven over 2,000 miles in ten days, and was interested in my experiences on the road. Half in jest, and half in seriousness, I asked her to join me later for supper, and she agreed. I'd made it to first base!

During the meal, Jen continued with questions about

life on the road. I embellished some of the story, and some aspects I simply made up as I went along. Supposedly she was beginning a thesis on the Civil War, with emphasis on her native state. Over breaded shrimp and scallops, we talked for an hour and a half. While settling up the bill, Jen leaned across the table. "Maybe I could come back to your motel...and we could talk some more?" Second base! A variety of fantasies leapt to mind as I contemplated the possibility of this southern belle in my motel bed.

Back in my room, I casually asked if she would care for something to drink. "Pepsi? Beer?" Jen answered that she never drank alcohol; I responded I didn't either, that I was merely taking this case of Schlitz home as a souvenir. Despite my temperature gauge being in the hot zone, I wasn't naïve to the dangers of getting too quickly involved with strange women, so I treaded carefully.

I asked Jen about herself, and learned that she was finishing her high school tenure and had been accepted at Jackson University, where she planned to study political science and history. She and a fellow student shared an apartment near the university. I also learned that she taught Sunday school at the local Baptist church, where her father was the minister, no less!

For a girl who supposedly subscribed to family values, her signals seemed to be waving me on to third base as the evening progressed. "I've never done anything like this before," she confessed.

"Anything like what?"

"Well...inviting myself to a perfect stranger's motel room, for one thing!"

"I'm not perfect," I answered, "but then who is?"

Jen laughed at my attempt at humour, than continued.

"I realize we just met, but there's something about you I find appealing. I can't explain it—maybe it's your smile. Has anyone ever mentioned you have a wonderful smile?"

"I seem to recall a public school teacher from long ago writing that on a report card."

"I'll bet you've captured a lot of hearts with that smile."

"Hundreds!"

"You're lying."

Honesty seemed the correct route with this girl.

"You're right," I said. "I'm actually very shy."

"Doesn't it feel good to be honest? Because God knows when we lie."

A lengthy pause followed.

"I'm essentially shy, too," she said. "In fact…I've never been…I can't believe I'm telling you this! I've never…you know…been with a man."

She reddened, her eyes turning to some imaginary object on the opposite wall before continuing.

"I'm sure you think it hilarious: an eighteen-year-old in this day and age who hasn't had sex."

I paused for breath myself, wondering how I would respond to this declaration.

"Do you see me laughing?" I said at length.

She returned her gaze to me.

"Well, you're too much of a gentleman."

"Far from it. Actually, right now I'm imagining you naked."

"You're embarrassing me, David!"

"I'm sorry. You can put your clothes back on!"

"Now you're making fun of me—not that I blame you!"

"I'm not making fun of you, Jen," I answered, somewhat frustrated. "I'm just getting a lot of conflicting signs."

"I understand that, believe me I do." There was another long pause. "I can't even imagine why I'm saying this—but I do want to make love to you."

Around third and heading for home!

"Well, I think I do," she added then. "But I couldn't bear to think your only memory of me would be telling your friends back home about this Mississippi broad with which you had a one-night stand."

"I'd enjoy telling that story," I answered. "And you could do the same."

Right away I realized that comment was ill-conceived, if not just plain stupid.

"Yes, that's right," she continued, sarcastically. "I'll just tell them about meeting this guy in the record store, inviting myself to his motel room, and spending the night in his bed! Who am I going to tell? My Sunday school class? My father? He probably thinks his sweet little girl is at the library right now!"

"Jen, you're thinking too much. Relax! You're a grown woman, able to make your own choices and decisions."

I retrieved another Pepsi from my portable cooler and handed it to her. I couldn't believe I had this magnificent young woman so close to saying "yes," yet all indications appeared I was stuck at third base.

However, Jen must have been reading my mind. We looked into each other's eyes, like they do in those afternoon soap operas, and our lips met. We kissed, and then kissed again. She pressed against me and there was no resistance as I began to caress the softness of her skin beneath her blouse. A few more minutes and I'd be sliding into home plate!

Then she pulled away. "I'm sorry, David. I know where

this is headed and I can't do it! I'm sure it would be great—I *know* it would be great. But something so warm and intimate—well, it shouldn't be just one night. And besides, it goes against everything I have ever been taught or I try to teach others. How could I face my Sunday school class tomorrow morning, knowing I had sex with an almost total stranger?" Jen was in tears by this point.

"Well you said yourself you're probably the only girl your age who hasn't."

"That doesn't make it right!" Jen fired back.

I tried another tactic. "How about you tell your class that God was testing you—and you simply failed. Tell them there's nothing wrong with failure. Compare it to school examinations. Sometimes we pass, and sometimes we don't. It doesn't make us any less of a person!"

Even in desperation I thought this was a reasonable argument!

So intent was I upon separating Jen from her blouse and Levis, I think I might have promised to apply for US citizenship and move permanently to Mississippi. And it's with no sense of pride that I recall how I considered, however briefly, the thought of having sex with her whether she wanted to or not. But I had to face the fact I'd been thrown out at the plate. Morality and virtue had triumphed over lust and sin. Chalk up another for God's side!

"I've got to go," Jen said, looking around for her purse. "I've completely embarrassed myself. You must think I'm a nutcase!"

By now that scenario had certainly occurred to me. Tears were streaming down her cheeks as she headed for the door. My mind searched for something to ease this uncomfortable situation. "Just sit down Jen. I don't want you go. Not like this."

"I have to. I've ruined your evening. You could have had some normal girl with whom to spend the night."

I placed my hand on the couch and slowly she sat down. Neither of us spoke while she continued to dab her eyes with a Kleenex. The silence was deafening—each of us was waiting for the other to re-establish conversation. Unable to generate some thoughtful, insightful, or even humorous phrase to relieve the tension, again I decided to go with simple honesty

"Do you know what I'd probably be doing tonight if I hadn't met you? Reading *Motor Trend* or studying road maps while listening to Johnny Cash or Tom T. Hall tapes."

"You're just saying that to make me feel better," Jen answered, forcing a smile. "God knows when you're lying."

"Yes, you mentioned that, but it's the truth. Let's put on some music and we won't broach the subject again, unless you say so."

I inserted an 8-track tape into the portable player that I took everywhere, and we talked and talked. I talked about growing up on a farm, going to a one-room school, my failure at farming, and the changes I would make given a second chance.

"Who wouldn't want a second chance at life's poor decisions?" Jen interjected. "The truth is we'd probably just find different ways to make the same mistakes."

Then Jen talked—about her school years, and how they differed so widely from mine; about being raised in one of the most racist states in the union during one of the most volatile decades in recent history; about anti-war demonstrations, student protests, flag burnings, draft card burnings, segregation, inequality, freedom marches, and Martin Luther King Jr.

Jen talked about her mother (who died when Jen was twelve) and her father's carpentry shop, which over the years evolved into a successful lumber business before he laid it aside to "follow Jesus." She shared stories about her three older brothers—two of whom had gone to Vietnam, and one of whom who never returned.

"I'll never forget that day, standing beside my father while he read the telegram saying my brother had been killed in some unknown village 10,000 miles from Jackson. Through that terrible time I believe it was only my father's faith and his church that sustained him."

"There's a sign that hangs on the wall of my father's office that's been there as long as I can remember: 'Behind the dark clouds the sun is still shining.'"

Since religion was never far from her mind, Jen asked about my family's spiritual upbringing. After a brief outline, she brightened. "You know what would be a great idea? You should come to our church tomorrow!"

I groaned inwardly at the thought, and began a mild protest, indicating that I wanted to get an early start in the morning.

"Our first service is over at ten, which gives you plenty of time. It would be good for both of us. It would cleanse our souls"

"We didn't do anything to get them dirty," I replied.

"Well, our thoughts weren't pure." I confessed mine still weren't.

"All the more reason to attend church!" Jen concluded.

I argued that I would feel out of place and uncomfortable.

"Nonsense," she said. "I'll be right beside you."

I tried again. "I don't have a suit."

"Do you think God cares what you are wearing?"

I couldn't think of any more excuses, weak or otherwise, so I reluctantly agreed. I may have had a naïve notion that romantic involvement was still on the table, and that perhaps a "yes vote" might tip the scales. But it wasn't to be. Sex had been permanently removed from the ballot.

I drove the half dozen blocks to Jen's apartment, and walked her to the door. After unlocking it, she turned to me.

"I realize this evening didn't turn out as you planned. But I can't remember an evening I enjoyed more." I recall thinking she must have had some extraordinary dates if she considered this one notable!

"It's comforting," she continued, "to realize there are still gentlemen in this world."

"Don't give me any false credit," I replied, offering my best smile. "I still have this vision of you and me naked on my motel bed! It's still not too late, you know."

She just laughed, and, before closing the door, whispered, "Sweet dreams!"

All I could do was shake my head as I walked away. Frustration? Exasperation? Neither of those came close to describing how I felt!

Next morning I joined a couple hundred worshippers in the white-framed Baptist church, two blocks from my motel. I eased into a seat near the back, where Jen joined me upon the conclusion of her Sunday school class. I noticed while waiting for the service to commence that the pews filled from the front—just the opposite of our Presbyterian church at home. (I recall Dad wanting to get to church early simply so he could brag he was the first one out the door following the service.)

Jen's father was a big powerful man with a voice to match. Following referral to various Scripture chapters, he talked at length about the sad state of the world today, how we were lost sheep without benefit of shepherds, wandering aimlessly, finding false gratification in alcohol, sex, drugs, lust, and other scenes of corruption.

"But don't think you're all high and mighty," he boomed from his pulpit, "shaking your heads as if everyone is on the road to Hell except you. God knows better! And more importantly—you know better!"

He then began asking members of the congregation if they could honestly admit being without sin. Recalling the fantasies I had imagined with his daughter, I slunk low in my pew, daring not to meet his eyes, convinced beyond all doubt he could read my mind!

With the sermon concluded, a couple more songs sung and the contribution plate passed for a second time, my introduction to the Baptist church was complete. "So what did you think?" Jen asked, as we made our way towards the exit.

I hesitated before answering. "I liked the music."

At the front door, we met her father, and Jen introduced me simply as her "Canadian friend." He looked slightly surprised and asked a couple of general questions as to how we had met.

After furnishing a couple of vague answers, I wanted to blurt out, "I didn't have sex with your daughter! Well, maybe in my mind. But I never touched her! Well, we did kiss—but that's all. Well, maybe I felt her up just a little. But she said it was okay! Well, at first she did, but then she changed her mind. But it was her idea to come to my motel!"

I don't remember what I actually said. While my mind was babbling an incoherent jumble of guilt, confession, and other misguided thoughts, Jen's father simply offered a solid handshake, and expressed his appreciation for choosing his family's church to visit.

I had checked out of my motel before leaving for church, and was anxious to hit the road. After giving me a hug, then looking around to make sure no one was watching, Jen gave me a sensuous kiss. "Thanks for everything. I'm proud of the way we resisted temptation last night."

"Yeah, me too!"

"There's no need for sarcasm—that's almost the same as lying."

"Do you want to hear about the dream I had about you last night?"

"You shouldn't be talking or even thinking about things like that, especially on the Sabbath!"

"How do you know what I was dreaming?

"I have a pretty good idea."

"Tell me," I whispered. "I'll bet you had some fantasies about me as well?"

"No, I did not!"

"Then why are you blushing? Remember, Jen—God knows when you're lying."

"Did you glean nothing from my father's message this morning?"

"Well, when he mentioned sex and lust I thought about you." Jen tried to look disgusted, but smiled in spite of herself. "You're incorrigible!"

"Incorrigible?"

"Yes. It means—"

"I know what it means. So you think there's no hope for me?"

"If you believe in God there's always hope. Yesterday

may be lost, but tomorrow's still to be won. Resisting temptation is not easy; believe me. If it were, anyone could do it. Just put your faith in God and He will take care of the rest. Remember—God never promised smooth sailing, only a safe journey."

"Well Jen," I said, inserting the key in the ignition. "Your philosophy is interesting, but I've always believed a person has to find their own direction. I suppose an occasional fragment of divine intervention couldn't hurt. Anyway, it's definitely been a thought-provoking twenty-four hours, if nothing else! You're right it didn't turn out the way I hoped. But on the other hand I won't forget it anytime soon! So I guess that's worth something. Anyway, take care and good luck with that Civil War thesis."

"What?"

"The Civil War thesis—the reason you came to my motel, right?"

Jen's face turned thoughtful. "I'm thinking maybe I might head in a completely different direction."

"Like what?"

"Oh, I don't know. Maybe something more topical and familiar. Perhaps life's lost opportunities?"

I couldn't help but laugh. "We could write that one together! I've had this thought in my mind for years about writing a book. Perhaps the experiences of the last twenty-four hours might make an entertaining chapter. Do you think anyone would believe it?" This time it was Jen who laughed.

"I pray God will see you safely home!" she called as I pulled from the church parking lot. "Remember. He loves you!"

If it was Jen's intention to at least get me thinking about religion and its numerous side channels, she succeeded. As the miles clicked by on my homeward journey, I recalled the contradictory forces which Jen confessed facing each day in her quest to follow the Bible's teachings. Her struggles reminded me of my own personal opinions, doubts, and beliefs on this controversial and complicated subject. I think Jen would have been impressed with my thought process on how I might reconnect with some of the convictions and principles she valued, and from which I had perhaps drifted.

She would have been less impressed had she realized that the majority of my reflections weren't remotely connected to religion, but rather to Jen's Mississippi accent, dark chocolate eyes, warm lips, soft skin, and fragrant perfume. Fantasizing of how events might have otherwise concluded in that motel room in Jackson would haunt me for months.

Fair-Weathered Friend

THE SUN WAS JUST BEGINNING ITS ASCENT INTO THE EASTERN sky as I walked across the yard to survey the site. A few chunks of what had been structural beams continued to smoulder. All else was quiet. A variety of implements stored in the upstairs area now lay on the stable floor, welded and distorted by extreme heat and dozens of steel support posts that stood like headstones. The concrete silo was cracked and blackened, appearing tall and foreboding as it towered above the charred ruins, while scores of sheets of roofing steel blanketed the burnt-out site. I felt a wave of sadness as I imagined the countless man-hours that had gone into the construction of this building.

"Frame a barn with elm and it will be standing in a hundred years," the foreman had said when he set out the framing plans for our barn in the autumn of 1907. Throughout that winter my family had worked cutting trees and skidding the de-limbed trunks to the local saw mill. Once the snow melted, the logs were squared to the desired dimensions and hauled back to the building site. At this point all the proper mortises and tenors were cut and formed, and countless holes were drilled into the newly cut timbers. This was exacting work with no margin for error—like a jigsaw puzzle, every piece marked and numbered for proper assembly.

One of the great events of that era was the day of the actual barn-raising, when forty or fifty men would arrive for the construction, and almost as many women to provide the banquet. With an undertaking of this magnitude, food and beverage were paramount. The wooden sills that lay atop the stone walls and the floor had been roughly laid by the time the main framing began. Each section of frame was assembled on the ground, and with the aid of poles, bars, cables, winches, ropes, and sheer muscle, it was hoisted into position. While these sections were held in place, others hurried about on the newly installed beams, hammering wooden pegs into the pre-drilled holes. Once the main frame was secured, the rafters and other support braces were fitted, and by day's end, a fully framed structure of hardwood timber stood watch over Lot 23, Concession 9, of Wallace Township.

Our barn was already a half-century old by the time I became aware of its magic. I remember the windmill that was positioned just outside the building's west wall. A small wooden enclosure surrounded the base, and for a little boy, it was a wonderful place to be on a humid summer afternoon, watching the sucker rods cycling up and down, and listening to the water gurgle away to the huge cement trough in the stable.

I recall the hayloft on a minus-thirty-degree February

evening, when the steel roof would pop and crack as it expanded and contracted in the frigid air, or its extreme heat on a July afternoon. I remember someone brought a thermometer and placed it against the underside of the steel sheeting. The mercury registered 110 degrees Fahrenheit.

The stable of the barn enjoyed an atmosphere of its own—an eclectic aroma of hay, grain, manure, and molasses, providing an inviting ambiance only a person raised in a rural environment could appreciate. The air was always humid, regardless of the season. During winter, heat from the animals, in conjunction with the frigid outside air, made the windows permanently opaque with frost.

The dairy barn was much more than just a shelter for food and animals. It was a forum where current and world events, politics, weather, family problems, crop analysis, milk production, financial obligations, and a dozen other subjects could be discussed and debated. It was a centre for the congregation of friends, neighbours, cattle buyers, rural and urban relatives, and sales personnel pitching everything from alfalfa seed to zinc supplement.

When recalling milking time, I remember sounds as much as images. For instance, two rows of Holsteins, shuffling about in their stalls, neck chains rattling, impatiently waiting for their share of the season's harvest. Calves bawling their heads off, while a clatter of pails signaled someone was readying their meal to shut them up. A dozen cats swarming around, eagerly waiting that first pail of warm milk. And Dad making it clear that most of them should be out "mousing" rather than lazily hanging around the cat dish. Other sounds included the suction of the milking-machine pulsators, CKNX crackling from the tubes of our Stromberg-Carlson radio, the Surge vacuum pump droning away in the background, and often several people talking at once.

As a farm kid knows only too well, cleaning stables is the most time-consuming job in a dairy barn—an operation handled at our place by a litter carrier. Some guy from the city must have figured "litter" was a more proper word than manure—but regardless of the name, and however undignified the task, removing tons of waste from the gutters was simple necessity. When a stable cleaner salesman would visit, Dad would end his sales pitch right away, nodding toward us boys "I don't need a stable cleaner. I have all I need."

Fashioned from galvanized steel, the carrier bucket in many regards resembled an old fashioned bathtub. It was lowered to the floor on a chain by a winding mechanism, and when loaded, was raised to a height some four feet off the ground. A simple shove would send the outfit clattering along a steel track suspended from the ceiling. Once outside, a long, swinging pole allowed the track to arc to any degree. A tug on the release lever dumped the bucket—although ours was overly sensitive, and often unloaded prematurely, causing some under-the-breath four-letter remarks.

It is easy to look back forty or fifty years and paint a wonderfully warm portrait of our old barn, conveniently discounting what made it less-than-perfect. Nevertheless, by the 1960s it was showing its age, especially where younger cattle were concerned. Our homemade wooden and wire gate partitions were forever being challenged by spirited animals, who could entertain themselves all winter with escape attempts. Baler twine was our main fastener, but with time and patience, an enterprising heifer soon learned that twine could be severed by chewing.

The old stable was eventually updated with steel partitions, and support beams, ventilating fans, and, despite our father's resistance, an automatic stable cleaner. Yet although the interior had undergone a makeover, the unmistakable presence that only a barn can convey remained intact—at least until that fateful September afternoon.

Just after 1 o'clock, a spark from an unknown source burst onto the thresh floor. It took only a few seconds for the loose chaff to ignite, and in no time a carpet of flame had spread across the straw-laden floor. Almost immediately the entire upstairs section was turned into an opaque, white cloud of smoke, its thickening plume billowing from every crack and crevice. By now the seventy-year-old timbers were supplying all the fuel needed to feed the fire. When the fire department arrived minutes later, the entire barn had been consumed by a huge orange ball of flame. Only the superstructure remained. The silo appeared as a giant smokestack. A few more minutes passed, and the main structural beams yielded to the inferno, sending a shower of fire-laden debris into the air as they fell. At this point, I could do nothing but stand alongside the gathered crowd and watch.

This morning I'm standing within the weathered walls of my neighbour's barn, or, more accurately, what remains of it. The farm was sold many years ago, and the barn ignored and forgotten, except for pigeons and sparrows. With each passing year it decays further. Huge doors that protected decades of produce swing on rusted hinges, while loosened sheets of corroded steel scrape quietly overhead. The structure groans and creaks at every joint, as the wind sifts through the numerous missing sideboards. Much of the thresh floor, once able to support a year's harvest, is now rotted and collapsed, as endless seasons of rain, snow, temperature, and humidity have taken their toll.

Why this empty building should affect me as it does, I don't know. Barns such as this exist all across Ontario. I observe them every day in my travels. Barns once full of feed and livestock stand desolate and dilapidated, reminders of the rural families that have left to pursue some other avenue. Maybe the reason is simply that I have to look at this particular building every day. As I witness its agonizing decay, my mind returns to the fate of our own barn. As traumatic and tragic as it was at the time, its demise came quickly. Perhaps that wasn't such a bad way to go. Anything would be better than what this particular fragment of Canadian history is experiencing at the moment.

Come to the Parade

It's March 21 as I write this, the first day of spring. But this story is not about spring, but parades. It just so happens there's one in progress in a neighbouring town this very day: Listowel's "Paddyfest" parade. March is not a month conducive to parades in Canada, so I guess the particulars bear some comment.

The idea for "Paddyfest" was hatched in 1977, when someone suggested Listowel needed an event to overcome the winter doldrums, and at the same time provide promotion for the town. Neighbouring municipalities celebrated winter with snowmobile rallies, ice sculpting, syrup collecting, Christmas light tours, even weather prognostication.

Listowel Ontario received its name from its sister city, in County Kerry, Ireland. Since Patrick, the Emerald Isle's patron saint, is commemorated each March 17 (the day of his death), and since a significant proportion of the town's residents claimed Irish ancestry, why not celebrate the town's Irish heritage with a winter festival?

My wife Mary's Paddyfest origins date back to that first parade nearly forty years ago. Although she wasn't a parade participant, her car was. Officials were looking for a convertible to chauffeur a couple of town dignitaries, the first Paddyfest queen, and the festival's mascot (an Irish setter). In the spirit of the occasion, Mary offered her 1972 Oldsmobile Cutlass. This caused much consternation for her mechanic, who'd serviced and babied the car almost to the point of fanaticism.

Split-roof fabric, cracked rear-window glass, bent struts—all were probable consequences from opening the canvas roof in sub-freezing temperatures. This is not to mention riders with their asses perched on the convertible's vinyl boot, and the potential of leather seats being chewed or clawed by an exuberant canine. In a last-minute compromise, the Texaco service station owner insisted the Oldsmobile remain in the relative warmth of one of his garage bays the night preceding the parade. Although frosty temperatures prevailed the following day, the sun shone brightly on the parade route, and anxieties concerning a roof catastrophe or shredded upholstery proved unwarranted.

On the subject of parades with an Irish flavour, during the 1950s and 60s our family never missed the annual Orange Parade. As they had for generations, every decent-sized town of that era staged a July 12 celebration. Ours was hosted by Beeton, Ontario. My father especially enjoyed the Orange Parade. As a kid I had no idea of its significance. It was just another parade, filled with participants with red faces huffing, puffing, panting, and wheezing their way along the street under a blazing mid-summer sun.

As time passed, my parents seemed to have a greater degree of discussion of what this parade represented. "It's a good parade," Dad would say.

"Yes, but I don't think we should be glorifying it," Mom would counter.

"I'm not glorifying it. I just think it's a good parade!"

"There are enough bad feelings in Ireland without stirring up more trouble here!"

"I've nothing against the Catholics. I just think it's a good parade!"

And so the conversation would go each year. In time, I learned that July 12 was the observed anniversary of the Battle of the Boyne—a decisive struggle for control of Ireland, between Catholic ex-King James II of England, and his Protestant successor, William III. In the Revolution of 1688, a majority of English, led by William III (or William of Orange, as he was known), had deposed King James and installed William as king. This naturally didn't sit well with Irish Catholics. But on July 12, 1690, they were soundly beaten on the banks of the River Boyne.

I don't know where a person would go to see a July 12 parade today, although I'm sure they still exist. The last time I attended one was in the 1960s, although I think Dad might have continued on into the 1970s. Two decades later, when he was in his eighties, the subject of the orange and green resurfaced; at the end of the discussion, Dad merely commented "I still say it was a good parade!"

Parades were important during my youth. One that comes to mind was the Eaton Santa Claus parade. My initial experiences with that Toronto tradition were via radio. That probably sounds strange: listening to a parade. On the contrary; it was actually kind of fun. The announcer described the various floats and everyone in the radio audience could form their own interpretation.

When I was six or seven, a neighbour invited our family to watch the spectacle on their television—in glorious black and white, of course. No longer did we have to employ our imaginations. All that was required was the announcer describing the colours.

At the opposite end of the scale were the local fall fair parades. The Beeton Fall Fair was a significant event in our area, considering its small population. Parades of that era meant marching—lots of marching. To a short-legged kid it seemed like miles. We'd be dressed in our finest clothes—preferably white shirts and blouses and dark pants and skirts, accented by cardboard caps and sashes advertising our individual school colours and number. It was always important to me that I spied Mom and Dad somewhere along the parade route, so I could wave and have them return the greeting.

As well as platoons of marching students, the fair featured numerous bands; horses decked in their finest harnesses, with tails braided and decorated with crepe paper; new cars and old cars; steam tractors that never failed to sound their ear-splitting whistle until they were directly in front of you; Majorettes and clowns; and of course that one parade participant who appeared regularly, with the sole purpose of terrifying youngsters.

I'm speaking of the "Peanut Man." You're familiar with his countenance on packages of Planters peanuts. He wore black pants, a black top hat, and white gloves, and had a peanut for a body. He walked on stilts that made him eight or nine feet tall. I didn't realize he was on stilts, I just figured that was his true height. Little wonder I was scared silly!

But it was more than just being tall; everything about this creature I found frightening. He had a face that could peer directly into a crowd and pick out little boys, even those trying to hide. One afternoon he spotted me and extended a white glove, full of salted peanuts. Much to the embarrassment of my family, I began screaming at the top of my lungs!

I suffered nightmares for a long time following that episode. It was always the same scene: I'd be standing at the top of our stairs, while the Peanut Man stood at the bottom. With one of his white-gloved fingers, he'd beckon me. With my heart racing, I'd back up against the wall, but some invisible force would inevitably draw me towards the top step...closer...closer...and all the time he'd be grinning and continuing to motion for me to come forward. Finally I would come hurtling down the stairs headfirst, directly into his gloved hands. Then I would wake up.

The Peanut Man is still occasionally seen on prime-time television, and although the Planters mascot doesn't seem nearly as tall and foreboding as I recall, I'm still not certain if I could bring myself to shake his hand. Maybe if he'd remove those white gloves.

When we moved from Simcoe to Perth County, rather than marching, local farmers donated a wagon for individual school floats. Our teacher, Mrs. Ashmore, always entertained ambitious ideas of what our float should represent. Most importantly, it must showcase *all* the students. Her insistence on including everyone was often its downfall—as during the year "an old-fashioned schoolhouse" was the theme chosen.

Slate blackboards, world maps, shelves stacked with books, oil lanterns, a clock displaying Roman numerals, wooden desks, and a cast-iron stove competed for space. With nearly thirty students on board, our props disappeared, and the float simply became a bunch of kids on a wagon. The school that claimed first prize (one we didn't particularly care for incidentally) employed a "maypole" for its theme. A gleaming white pole set on a green carpet to simulate grass, and three or four kids skipping around the pole.

The maypole apparently had its origins in Europe—Germany in particular. The actual significance of the maypole has intrigued scholars for centuries. Most think it was a fertility festival held on the first day of May to celebrate the arrival of spring, new growth, and romance. Some have even gone as far as depicting the maypole as a phallic symbol. Apparently children and young adults dance around the pole holding coloured streamers attached to the pole's apex. As the dancers circle and revolve, moving in opposite directions, the streamers intertwine, further substantiating the fertility festival theory.

I doubt that commemorating a centuries-old "sex festival" was the intention of the school in question, but whatever they were attempting to celebrate, these few kids bouncing around the aforementioned pole was the extent of their float. Mrs. Ashmore's review was short and sarcastic. "A few kids, fake grass, and a white pole—what imagination!"

And she was absolutely livid the year we got disqualified. Apparently we were unaware, or didn't care, that when the floats pulled into the fairgrounds, the final destination point of the parade was where the judging commenced. Anxious to get to the fair, everyone abandoned the float, and when the parade judges arrived with their clipboards at the U.S.S. # 11 exhibit, all that remained was an empty wagon with a few scattered props!

Then there was the year of our "autumn" float. Two or three afternoons preceding the event were spent cutting out bristle board "leaves" of various colours. The night before the parade, a half-dozen jute feed bags, lifted from someone's granary, were filled with "real" leaves gathered from the school playground. The cardboard leaves were methodically stapled around the perimeter of the wagon, while the real ones were deposited over the surface of the wagon floor just prior to departure.

Straw bales and cornstalks were placed strategically around the platform for an added touch. We even half-buried a few of the youngest kids in piles of leaves to create the impression of children at play. Several others stood around with rakes, and I believe we even featured a wheelbarrow full of leaves. An inordinate amount of time was expended on the project, but a float depicting nature at its finest was the result. We might have won, too—if gale-force winds hadn't sprung up en route, blowing most of it away.

Beans, Tales, and Rusty Nails

After my barn burnt to the ground that September day in 1973, I had many decisions to face concerning a replacement. My first thought was a modern one-storey stable, incorporating all the latest features and technology, and improving in areas where the former barn had failed. Erecting a building of that status, however, demanded twice the reparation my insurance would allow on the destroyed barn. My financial scaffolding was already on the verge of collapse, and added debt was simply out of the question.

My insurance company was flexible on replacement buildings, however, and so upon ascertaining that my agricultural future lay in cash crops, I erected a thirty-two-by-sixty-four-foot implement shed and a 5,000 bushel steel granary to replace the lost barn storage.

Since deciding against livestock, I next had to figure out which crops to grow. I'd downsized my machinery inventory and dropped all rented land, and a second mortgage went a long way in freeing me from the narrow economic margins under which I was operating at the time.

I was talking to my friend Horace Wells one day, and he suggested including white beans in my 1974 crop plans. Though I'd spent countless hours helping him the previous year, I'd never considered them as an option for myself.

"I made a lot of money on those beans," Horace said. He wasn't gloating, but merely stating fact. Horace had entered the white-bean market at its strongest. Various estimates of how much Horace actually netted were tossed around by the morning coffee crowd for weeks. Whatever the actual number, I know he had paid off his mortgage.

"Beans don't require near the amount of fertilizer as corn," Horace continued. "They're harvested a month earlier, and the herbicides leave no residue. Also, the elevator will incur all seed and herbicide costs, and simply take it out of your harvest receipts."

I mentioned Horace's suggestion to Dad, and he thought it was worth trying. He'd never been an advocate of corn anyway, although he suggested a small acreage until I "learned the ropes." However, I reasoned that if I had to buy bean equipment, my entire acreage may as well be utilized. Besides, there was no sense making just a little money when there was a fortune waiting!

The following afternoon I drove the thirty-mile distance to Thompson's Elevators in Mitchell, our closest elevator site for bean contracts, and signed on for the upcoming season. The only stipulation on my part was compulsory crop insurance. At this point I don't believe I was even aware this kind of insurance existed. (What a difference that would have made for that 1972 horror story disguised as a corn crop.)

As white beans manufacture their own nitrogen, fertilizer consisted of phosphorous and potash only, hauled by wagon in four ton lots from Mitchell behind my Fargo pickup.

While I broadcast the fertilizer, Dad incorporated with the cultivator. Then I followed with the planter. Because of the high market value of beans at that time, seed and herbicide costs increased dramatically. And it wasn't only crop input; the previous year Horace Wells purchased a bean hiller, puller, and windrower for $2,000, but with demand for equipment at a premium, the price nearly doubled. When questioned as to the severe price spike, the dealer merely laughed. "Don't worry, you'll still be making tons of money with this market!" I wish I could have gotten that in writing!

I finished planting by June 20, and with no additional farm chores to occupy my time for three months, I took a job with a small construction firm. I'd stopped in at the local restaurant one afternoon, and ran into Wanda Becker, who I hadn't seen for some time. I'd rented her farm the previous two years, but it had become a casualty of my forced downsizing. Over coffee, Wanda talked about life in general who was currently renting the farm, and that her daughter Nicki was working as a veterinarian's assistant on a ranch somewhere in the foothills of Alberta. (Recalling Nicki certainly rekindled memories...but that story has been told.)

During our conversation, Wanda mentioned how this guy she knew was looking for help for his construction business. I'd never done anything but farm and so wasn't too responsive when Wanda suggested I go see him about employment. I began listing my excuses when she interrupted.

"It sounds to me that until your beans are harvested you're doing nothing but sitting on your ass! His name is Blake Kincaid—here's his number."

I learned long ago that it was easier to agree with Wanda then argue, so a couple of nights later, somewhat reluctantly, I met with Blake Kincaid. He was about my age, and his company, Kincaid Construction, poured cement floors and walls, installed steel roofing and siding, and performed general barn reconstruction.

"What would I need to start?" I asked.

"Just a hammer," Blake answered, "and I suppose a hard hat."

Wages were neither mentioned nor asked but recall it was about $150 a week.

At the job site two mornings later I met the "gang"—or, more accurately, "the family." Besides Blake, there was his brother Jerome, his father Royce, his nephew Linwood, his brother-in-law Rayburn, and Rayburn's brother Wilfred. How I conquered the family rampart I don't know.

The program was simple enough that first day. A couple of wooden beams had cracked under the weight of an upstairs granary, and two or three posts had been jammed underneath to keep the second floor from caving in. While several thick hardwood planks were nailed together to create two new beams, hydraulic jacks raised the floor slightly while the old beam was removed with a chainsaw. With plenty of muscle working in unison, the new timbers were put into place. I'd had experience in this line with our own barn.

Being in the employment of Kincaid Construction that summer rekindled my passion for working with wood. Not that I was or ever would be a great carpenter. But I simply loved the odour of new lumber. Whether cutting spruce for roof strapping, pine boards for barn siding, or hemlock planks for floors and beams, I think the unmistakable essence of fresh-cut lumber is one of the most intoxicating aromas available to one's olfactory senses.

I quickly learned Wilfred was the designated comedian and storyteller of our little band. Humorous stories about his own experiences, or those of his cousin Owen, would provide refreshment on many a long hot day.

"Owen was so ugly his Mom had morning sickness *after* he was born. Where Owen works, his boss quit allowing him coffee breaks—he says it takes too long to retrain him."

Despite my initial trepidation, I fared well in my new vocation. Steel roof installation was one of our more regular endeavours. Once the first row of wooden strapping was nailed to the lower edge of the roof, it was easy to proceed from there. Each row made a step as you worked your way up the roof incline, thirty inches at a time. Once the framework was nailed, it didn't take long to install the metal sheeting. Roofing was hardest on windy days, or on hot sunny days, when the reflection off the shiny steel was not only blinding, but seemingly doubled the temperature.

"Several years ago," Wilfred began, "I was roofing at my place. The weather had been threatening all afternoon, but suddenly, out of nowhere, this huge gust of wind appeared. I was nailing a sheet of steel when the gust lifted me into the air, sheet and all. I held onto the sheet for dear life. It acted like a magic carpet, and I glided all the way to my neighbour's farm next door, landing in the manure pile behind his barn. Man, what an emotional rush that was!"

One afternoon Jerome was complaining about the heat and humidity.

"It's hot alright," said Wilfred. "This morning I noticed a dog chasing a cat, and they were both walking! But heat beats cold. I remember one bitter winter years ago, when, in order to cope with the extreme cold, the fire department advised people to set their houses on fire."

Probably because we were the youngest, and because Jerome suffered from chronic back problems, Linwood and I seemed to get most of the high-climbing jobs. Up until this point, I only considered myself an average climber, but it soon became second nature. It mattered little whether I was walking the peak of a barn, forty or fifty feet off the ground, or hanging onto the side wall, nailing steel. I learned how to jam my knees between the wooden framing, thereby leaving both arms free to work. It was kind of a neat feeling leaning out over nothing but space.

"According to the weather bureau, that winter was one of the coldest on record. It was so cold at our place," Wilfred continued, "that Mom kept the fridge door open to heat the kitchen."

The three months I worked for Kincaid Construction, I don't recall seeing a safety rope on anybody, no matter the height or steepness of the roof. "Be careful" was the extent of our safety program. One day we were installing steel siding on a barn. The hydro wires were anchored to the wall on which we were working. So to attach the steel sheets, the bracket securing the wires had to be released in order for the new sheet to slide underneath. I was loosening the bracket bolts when suddenly I felt a strong tingle in the back of my neck. It seemed to vibrate through my entire body. I dropped my wrench and at the same time my hard hat dislodged and fell to the ground.

"Are you okay?" Blake asked, quickly. I didn't really know at that moment, and still felt kind of funny. It was a strange sensation—not a pulsating shock, as from an electric fence, but rather a strong rippling effect that seemed to flow from head to toe. I guess it was fortunate I was standing on a wooden ladder as opposed to aluminum.

"You look a little pale," said Blake. "Maybe you'd better come down."

"Well, at least now you won't have to pay to get your hair curled," commented Wilfred, trying to restore some levity. As Linwood and I were relocating the ladder for the next sheet, I overheard Blake say to Wilfred, "I guess by rights we should've turned the power off."

Most of the time the crew brought their own lunches, and we simply ate wherever we were. Under the shade of a convenient tree, or the sheltered side of a building, or maybe sitting on the rack of a wagon—wherever we were, mealtime seemed to be Wilfred's favourite setting for tall tales.

Unwrapping his bologna sandwich, Wilfred began. "Well Owen's in deep shit now! I guess he and the old lady next door really got into it last night."

"I thought they got along pretty well?" someone responded.

"Well they did—until last night. Evidently Owen's old hound Rufus ate her pet bird. I can't remember if it was a budgie or a parrot. But whatever the hell it was I guess it was sort of valuable—it even talked. That's what upset the old lady to such a degree; apparently the damn bird kept hollering, 'Stop! Stop! Stop!' all the way down!"

Whether we were replacing barn floors, removing old boards or steel from the sides of buildings, or removing old shingles or steel from roofs, we encountered an endless supply of rusty, bent nails. While working we'd simply let them fall where they may, then after each job we'd retrieve the nails with this neat gadget known as a magnet sweeper. About three feet wide, it sort of resembled one of those old-time push lawnmowers. The spent nails were placed in 5-gallon capacity cans, and Blake took them home with him. What he did with them I have no idea and never bothered to ask.

One afternoon, Wilfred was watching me pick up nails. "That reminds me of an incident when we were nailing down a new floor. The nail gun went off accidently and nailed my hand to one of the floor planks. Prying that nail from the floor up through my hand—I'll tell you, that stung!"

We got onto a familiar subject one afternoon: women and their idiosyncrasies. After listening to a lengthy discussion, Wilfred shook his head. "Well, women are a mystery, alright. Take my cousin Owen, for instance. He went out a couple of times for coffee with this girl, and then a night or so later she calls and says to come over cause there's nobody home. Well, needless to say, Owen's pretty excited. So he goes over to her place but there was nobody home".

"Now Sadie and I," Wilfred continued, "we've been married twenty-five years. Right from the start we forged an agreement that she was responsible for the minor decisions and I the major decisions."

"So how did that work out?" someone ventured.

Wilfred paused before continuing. "Well, so far there haven't been any major decisions."

"Oh, we've had our problems," he went on. "What marriage doesn't? I recall the time—this was a few years ago—Sadie kept bugging me about getting the garage roof re-shingled. I mean, I said I would do it—there was no need to remind me every six months! I was working on a more interesting project of my own at the time, so told her to quit hounding me and that I needed some space."

"How'd that go over?" Blake asked.

"She locked me outside in the yard all night!"

Since many of our discussions concerned women, it was only natural that sex would be a related topic. At that time Linwood had just started dating a girl and was anxious to move things along.

"Don't be in too much of a hurry, Linwood," Wilfred cautioned. "It's much more satisfying when you take your time. Just remember—sexual foreplay is more than 'do you want to screw' or 'are you awake?'"

"My brother Harley's gotten himself into a bit of a situation," Wilfred continued. "I guess he got the hots for his next-door-neighbour's wife. Her husband works the night shift, and Harley thinks he should too. I told him to smarten up and remember that tenth commandment."

"Which one is that?" Blake questioned.

"Thou shalt not covet thy neighbour's wife or her ass—or something like that."

Despite Wilfred's comedic monologues, we worked hard. Our biggest and most ambitious project that summer was the construction of a concrete horizontal silo. More than 100 cubic yards of concrete went into the structure just to form the walls and floor, plus more for the support abutments that lined either sidewall. As the new silo was adjacent to the barn, the cement for one entire wall had to be handled manually, with good old-fashioned wheelbarrows!

Nearly two full days were consumed building the scaffolding for the one-wheeled carriers. It was a tricky exercise wielding a fully loaded wheelbarrow up a steep plank incline and then across a narrow plywood platform stretching along the entire length of the wall. Wilfred suggested a correction in the way Linwood and I had laid the plywood.

"How about we overlap the sheets this way—I'd rather trip with an empty wheelbarrow than a full one." Up on the wall with an ungainly wheelbarrow, toting a heavy semi-liquid load, I couldn't have agreed more.

At the end of one particularly busy day of cementing, we were washing the wheelbarrows, shovels, trowels, etc., when Linwood noticed his radio was missing. No matter what job we were doing or where we were, Linwood always brought along his transistor radio, permanently tuned to CKGL, Kitchener-Waterloo's FM country music station at the time.

"I recall when Owen got his first AM radio years ago," commented Wilfred. "He had it for months before he learned he could listen to it in the afternoon as well."

Linwood's radio had been up on the wall that particular day, and at first he thought someone had merely hidden it. However, when a grilling of each person yielded nothing, the obvious answer was that the radio had toppled off its perch and fallen into the crevice, which by now was a newly formed wall of wet concrete.

That was over forty years ago, and somewhere down the line, someone will bulldoze that silo and wonder about the turquoise transistor radio entombed in the wall.

"Speaking of radios," Wilfred interjected, "I heard on the news this morning that thieves cleaned out the safe at the Laundromat in Listowel last night. According to the police they got away clean."

As promised at the outset, upon completion of that job I bade farewell to the crew, so I could return to farming. Over the course of the summer, the guys had become quite familiar with my track record in farming, and upon my departure wished me the best of success with my bean crop.

"It's a tough struggle, this farming," Wilfred confessed one afternoon. "A fellow hardly knows what to grow these days. Now take Owen, for instance. He has tried everything, but nothing seems to go right. He gets these big ideas, and some of them are pretty good, but for whatever reason, they fail to get off the ground. I thought for sure his concept of growing olives with the palmetto already in them would be a hit!"

Despite the drier-than-normal summer, my first attempt at growing beans was encouraging. I figured I could net in the vicinity of $25,000. However, these past four years had taught me the realities of agricultural life. I felt as though I were riding a pendulum, forever cycling between hopelessness and optimism. I wasn't asking for a miracle—just a little luck.

The custom combine operator came exactly when needed. The weather was perfect—a plus, as bean-pulling consumed much more time than anticipated. I'd begin after dark, when the dew was falling, thereby lessening the chances of the pods shattering. Generally I worked until about midnight. I'd then return to the field about 5am and continue pulling until the dew lifted by mid-morning. During the day, when the beans were being combined, either Dad or I would haul the harvested beans by wagon to the Mitchell elevator.

I'd been under the impression that I could expect a $10,000 initial payment upon final delivery of my crop, plus two roughly equal payments in the $6000-7000 range the following spring and fall, if all went well. It didn't.

"An unstable market with lower than anticipated prices has lowered your initial payment," began the form letter from the Bean Producers Association. Once the rhetoric, apologies, alibis, and excuses were filed, the result was an installment cheque only half the expected amount.

The market continued its shaky existence throughout the winter and I conservatively re-calculated my March payment in the $4000-5000 range. Wrong again!

"These are very difficult times for Ontario bean producers," said the next letter. Then followed another gloomy account defining the elements of supply and demand and examinations of how production had tripled compared to the previous year. Similar circumstances in Michigan, Ontario's largest competitor, were also blamed for the decline. I was almost afraid to look inside the envelope. The payment barely totalled $3,000. The final November installment was every bit as depressing.

I couldn't help but contemplate if there was a curse upon me when it came to farming. First it was the pork market falling through the floor. Next was the aforementioned corn crop calamity. The following year saw my financial credit for crop input axed partway through the planting season; a final kick in the ass that year was the loss of the barn to fire. Now, I'd grown a promising bean crop, only to witness that market collapse.

Following the bean downfall, I discussed my agricultural future with my brother Bill. "Maybe you should try ginseng," he suggested, "or garlic, or peanuts, or sunflowers, or cucumbers, or ginger, or pumpkins, or olives..."

My agricultural experiences reminded me of one of Wilfred's monologues, in which a group of men from many different vocations were discussing what they'd do if they won the 15 million dollar lottery jackpot that weekend. A yacht, a chalet in the mountains, a house by the ocean, a horse farm in Kentucky, a Mercedes Benz, an ocean cruise, the purchase of an island in the South Pacific, all formed part of the dream for those assembled.

"We haven't heard from you, Harlan!" someone said to the farmer in the group. Harlan thought long and hard.

"Well, I'm not much for ocean cruises, fancy boats, or cars. I think I'd just keep on farming until the money was gone."

It may come as a surprise, but despite the agricultural strife and financial pitfalls, that particular summer proved to be an enjoyable experience. Sometimes a person has to be forcibly removed from their everyday environment in order to gain a fresh focus on life. Although farming had been a series of disasters, at least it was predictable—hence my reluctance to venture into unfamiliar territory when the opportunity to hire on with Kincaid Construction was offered.

However, working with the Kincaid gang provided a chance to leave these challenges behind for a few hours each day. And no one did more to expand this new perspective than Wilfred. His daily chronicles on life proved to be the exact prescription I needed, and his legacy of anecdotes, tall-tales, jokes, and stories were remembered long after. Years later, if I was having a particularly challenging day, or things simply weren't going as planned, I'd recall one of Wilfred's witticisms from that long-ago summer, and find myself smiling.

"This horse walks into a bar, and the bartender says, 'So why the long face?'"

News Travels Fast

As the seventh decade of the twentieth century got underway, my attention was reallocated from agriculture to other endeavours. This shift in focus wasn't some long-planned, well-thought-out venture lurking in the recesses of my mind, eager to emerge at the perfect moment. It was much less grandiose; induced simply by financial factors, triggered by commodity market collapses and weather extremes. This alternative presented itself in the form of a medical courier route serving health institutions in southwestern Ontario, thanks to Palmerston entrepreneurs Don Ganner and Helen Woods.

I began my allotted two-day training program, courtesy of another G & W driver, Jake Allison. The company provided me with a brand new Chevrolet Vega station wagon and a two-dollar-an-hour wage contract. I recall my first week's pay was fifty-one dollars.

I didn't realize it at the time, but I was in effect

taking Allison's job. Jake, I learned, had "a little drinking problem," and G & W had already experienced a few issues with him—one was an altercation with another car, while driving a similar route. On the route in which I was being trained, he'd apparently kept an erratic schedule, necessitating frequent calls to area hospitals to track him down. On one occasion he'd apparently been delayed while stopping to help some kids build a snowman.

When I returned from the route just a few days after being on my own, Jake flagged me down on Palmerston's main street, requesting a ride to the liquor store at the edge of town. He emerged with a bottle of Gold Stripe rye and asked to be dropped at the Texaco station. On the way downtown we met the town police cruiser, and Jake waved his bottle through the windshield. The cop either didn't see him or didn't care.

"Join me for a drink, Dave?"

I answered that I should be getting home, but Jake insisted.

"Ah, come on—just one."

I followed him to a back room of the service station, where he proceeded to half-fill two Styrofoam coffee cups. Jake raised his glass to mine and downed its contents in one gulp. I took one swallow, feeling the whisky burn all the way down my throat and into my gut.

"Another one, Dave?"

"No, that's plenty, Jake," I whispered. Unaccustomed to liquor of any variety or amount, the rye left me practically without voice or breath. At that moment, the proprietor appeared and glanced at the two of us.

"How can you guys drink that stuff straight?"

"We're drinking it like men!" Jake said. I closed my

eyes, took one more swallow and waved goodbye. I still couldn't talk.

Jake hung around town for a few weeks, performing part-time taxi service for G & W. Then he mysteriously disappeared. Whether by his own volition or otherwise, I never asked.

Along with driving taxi, Jake had also been helping somewhat sporadically with a mobile newspaper delivery service G & W operated—so when he left, I was offered the position. The job consisted of delivering newspapers for the Kitchener-Waterloo Record, the area's most popular daily news source. The newspapers, rolled and secured in brown paper that resembled butcher wrap, were delivered to G & W's depot in bundles of roughly fifty papers each at 4:00 p.m. every afternoon—a schedule coinciding perfectly with the completion of my courier route.

The job proved to be an exciting venture, as the papers were designed to be delivered on the go. Throwing the wrapped papers wasn't especially difficult—the challenge was getting them to land in the customer's driveway rather than the ditch.

The concept was simple enough: load as many newspapers as possible in the Vega's passenger seat, and put the balance in back. And then, away you went, as fast as you could. It was more like a road rally than a newspaper delivery. All forerunners of this occupation subscribed to this aggressive driving formula, so I felt inclined to follow tradition.

As a majority of the roads were gravel, eighty kilometres an hour proved to be a good average speed. At this rate the route could usually be completed in two hours. Only one hand was available for steering; the other was continually gathering papers from the seat beside you. When it was time to throw, the right hand took over driving duties while the left fired the paper either straight out the driver's window or over the roof of the car, depending on which side of the road the customer lived.

Those over-the-roof throws took a little extra practice to properly calculate the correct trajectory of the paper in relation to the car's momentum. But once established I was good for 95 percent accuracy, providing wind direction and velocity were taken into account. A strong crosswind in conjunction with a light paper could play havoc with marksmanship. My motto: "the more news the better the throw."

Accuracy was also affected by the laneways themselves. A narrow entranceway or deep side-ditch constituted compulsory velocity adjustment. On rainy days, one had to be sure the papers did not land in puddles. Occasionally I'd receive a call from an irate customer wondering what they were supposed to do with their waterlogged newspaper! I had an idea but kept it to myself.

The route was strictly a windows-down, six-days-a-week, fifty-two-weeks-a-year operation. Summer dust, autumn rains, spring mud, and winter's frigid blast all contributed to the challenge. Winter especially; if a day was missed due to closed roads (or, more accurately, blocked roads, as roads were never officially closed in that era), then it was double the number of newspapers to deliver and keep track of the following day.

I recall a ferocious April storm in 1975, when the weather necessitated three days of product to be delivered in one session. My brother Don accompanied me—not without resistance—to help sort out the mountain of newspapers that had accumulated. Along with the extra workload, we managed to get stuck no less than six times! We shovelled ourselves free four times, a farmer pulled us out once with his tractor, and the township snow plow rescued us the other. Don admits he can still recall the chill in his feet when reminded of that ordeal.

In those days, many of the problems encountered on snow-clogged roads were simply due to vehicle size. The Chevrolet Vega and the Ford Pinto were both hand-me-downs from my courier route—after changing to medium or full-sized cars it was a much-improved exercise.

Part of the job description was collecting. Customers had three choices for subscription rate: a four dollar monthly rate, a semi-annual twenty-two dollar rate, and a yearly forty dollar rate. Collecting was a pain-in-the-rump, as several tries were often needed to find customers at home.

The biggest gripe I had with collecting was personal. These collection breaks ruined that important, never-slow-down, rhythm-of-the-road atmosphere—delivering as many papers as possible, as fast as possible, in the least amount of time!

Architects of Harvest

THERE'S A WELL-RECOGNIZED FRENCH OIL PAINTING FROM THE 1850s titled "The Gleaners," depicting a trio of peasant women picking up stray kernels of grain in a recently harvested field. I saw a copy of this painting in an agricultural exhibit recently and couldn't help but be reminded of the evolution in grain gathering techniques through the decades.

Many enterprising personalities who are credited with being the inventor of a certain product will themselves admit that their creation was merely the culmination of following, then improving upon, the ideas of other less-successful personnel with similar goals.

Take Cyrus McCormick, for instance, the Virginia-born entrepreneur known as "the father of the reaper." McCormick's father, while operating the family farm, spent every free hour trying to perfect a horse-drawn machine that would mechanically cut ripened grain from the field, then group the severed crop into bundles on the ground to be tied. It wasn't until 1837 that his son finally managed to get a seemingly successful prototype in operation and receive a patent.

To say that the public was slow to adapt to this new invention would be an understatement. McCormick sold one unit in 1840, none in 1841, and seven in 1842. Things did not really take off until 1843, when twenty-nine units were sold. Fifty were sold the following year. All machines were manufactured on McCormick's Virginia farm.

Cyrus's contraption replaced the sickle and scythe— basically the harvester's tools of choice for the preceding 5,000 years. Even as late as the 1890s, when my then-teen-aged grandfather vacationed at his uncle's Grey County farm, the scythe was still in use. The young lad would follow along, marvelling at the smooth strokes of the razor-sharp blade as it sliced the ripened grain. It may have been impressive to watch, but it was painstaking to use. McCormick's invention could cut enough in one day to replace fifteen scythe-wielding workers.

As ingenious as the reaper was, by the turn of the century it was outdone by an even more fascinating invention: the binder.

Similar in appearance to the reaper, and pulled usually by three or four horses, the binder, like its predecessor, employed a revolving wooden paddle that gently laid the grain back against a six- or seven-foot knife that moved in a rapid reciprocal motion. As it was cut, the grain fell onto a moving horizontal canvas conveyor, then to a vertical conveyor and the bundling mechanism. It was at this point that this newest invention came into force. Without any human intervention, a mechanical knotting device pulled a length of twine from a tightly wound roll, secured a snug knot, and tossed the bound sheaf onto the ground.

Reaping or binding were only part of the process, of course. The final element was the threshing itself. From its inception in the late 1800s, the threshing machine used sieves and shakers to successfully separate the grain from chaff and straw, at last freeing farm families from the slow and laborious task of hand gleaning. Early threshers simply distributed the mixture of straw, grain, and chaff into an indiscriminate pile on the ground. The invention of fans and blowers was a giant step in producing a clean, chaff- and weed-free sample for elevator or granary storage.

Harvesting techniques basically remained static for the next fifty years, despite efforts to combine the reaping and threshing components into a single operation.

In the late 1930s, Allis-Chalmers introduced their all-crop harvester, a pull-type tractor-driven machine with a five-foot sickle knife that could thresh one acre an hour. With updates, this combine/harvester was manufactured into the early 1960s and earned its A-C designers, Harry Merritt and Charles Scranton, the prestigious Agricultural Society of Agricultural Engineers (ASAE) award.

During the 1920s, Massey-Harris Co. had become interested in a self-propelled combine designed in Australia by the H.V. McKay Co., hoping to adapt the Aussie thresher to meet the needs of North American farms. This challenge proved to be beyond M-H's capabilities at the time.

The Great Depression of the 1930s stifled any further development until later in the decade, when a Massey-Harris engineer learned of a small Italian firm in Argentina that had produced a revolutionary reaper/thresher, driven by a self-contained gasoline engine.

Massey borrowed the idea and quietly went to work developing its own version, and by the early 1940s a self-propelled unit was introduced, meeting with instant success. John Deere, International Harvester, Case, Oliver, Minneapolis-Moline, and Cockshutt followed, but Massey's three-year head start would keep them as the combine leader for the next thirty years.

Whether pull-type or self-propelled, a great advantage of a combine over a stationary threshing machine was the issue of straw. Whereas a combine dropped the straw into a neat windrow upon the ground for baling, a threshing machine blew the straw into a pile within the barn, and straw, by its very nature light and fluffy, had to be manually tramped, packed, and levelled as it was discharged from the thresher's blower pipe.

My father recalled the horror of this job. "A straw mow was an incredibly dirty place, as straw, dust, weed seeds, and especially thistles rained from above. There were no products to control plant disease in that era, so grain fungi such as rust and smut completely saturated the air. Your spit would be black for days!"

By the time we began farming on our own in the early 1950s, combines were fast relegating threshing machines to extinction. A couple of neighbours with their Massey-Harris and John Deere self-propelled units harvested our oats and wheat.

When we moved to Perth County in 1957, Dad elected to work with the former proprietors on sort of a cost/share agreement in order to keep our initial costs in line. Instead of hiring a variety of neighbours to perform a variety of jobs, as we'd done at our former farm, the Nelsons agreed to supply all labour or machinery needed without charge.

In return, Dad and my oldest brother offered their labour for all three Nelson farms. It made for a grueling summer.

One trip down memory lane Dad could have nicely done without was the Nelson's preference for threshing as opposed to combining. After just a few minutes in the loft, he was overcome with dust from the straw and weeds, and was quickly reminded of horrors he had endured in past harvests.

Over the next few years we began to exert our independence by establishing slowly and steadily a line of machinery of our own. It had always been our father's belief that to keep his sons interested in the farm, a good line of machinery was a must. And although that sounds selfish, it was true. We'd all known lads our age who'd become discouraged with "horse era" equipment, and opted for other jobs. By 1964, only silo-filling and grain-swathing required outside help. We even had our own combine!

This machine came via our neighbour, Doug Hamilton, a trucker/dealer who over the years made countless trips across the border to machinery auctions in Michigan and Ohio. The combine we purchased was a John Deere pull-type model, perfectly suited to the power and size of the new Massey-Ferguson tractor Dad had purchased the previous year. Dad paid $600 for the combine, and although miniscule in size by today's standards, for the acreage we shared with my brother Bill, it was ideal until the rains came.

Given an extremely wet August, it was early September when we finally began at Bill's farm. Although the weather slowly began to cooperate, we were in for a surprise—mud! We had a few wet spots at home but were completely unaccustomed to entire fields that retained water like a sponge. We succeeded in getting a few acres harvested, but then our

Massey tractor, even with its oversized tires, could no longer pull the combine without becoming mired to the axles.

Dad and Bill searched in vain for a custom operator with a self-propelled machine to finish, but because of the wet season, the few available were hopelessly behind schedule.

Another week passed, and with the sun finally shining two or three days in succession, Dad and Bill (with Brian and I trailing along) wound up at the used machinery lot of the local Ford dealer. Rydell Crawford, the dealership's only salesman, introduced himself as we entered the lot.

"You wouldn't have a used self-propelled you would rent?" Dad asked.

"No, but I'll sure sell you one at a good price!" Crawford replied.

Because of the wet harvest and increased demand, dealers had farmers exactly where they wanted them. Rydell showed us a weary-looking Massey-Harris at the far end of a row of used combines. It obviously hadn't seen active service this season, given the thick layer of sprouted grain covering the intake area. "You can have that one for $1,600."

Dad certainly wasn't keen on spending much money on an unfamiliar machine with questionable potential, especially when there was nothing wrong with our own combine that some dry fields wouldn't cure. The engine coughed to life, however, and as the rest of the mechanism was put in gear, I became excited by the prospect of what this machine might do for us. I had been the designated operator of the pull-type combine, and could already envision myself at the controls of this Massey-Harris.

Without actually seeing our John Deere, and relying solely on Dad's description, Rydell offered to trade for $1,000 difference. After plenty of head-scratching and soul-searching, Dad accepted the offer. One thousand dollars wasn't much for ownership of a self-propelled combine—but as combines go, it didn't look like much either. As I was underage, Bill drove the combine the seven-mile trip home. As he lumbered off down the highway with our newest possession, Dad, Brian, and I followed in the car.

I had hoped that our neighbours wouldn't miss the combine's grand entrance—and there's no way they could have, as it died just as it turned into our laneway. The dealership mechanic arrived shortly, accompanied by Rydell the salesman, who added nothing to the proceedings except to relate what a great machine this was, and what a good job the machine would do despite this "minor" stalling issue. Following new spark plugs and points, a carburetor cleaning and adjustment, a new fuel filter, plus some minor choke adjustments—fixes that took nearly two hours—the old combine set out for Bill's place.

Excitement mounted as Bill wheeled into the driest wet field available. I could see that my brother wasn't going to relinquish his seat, so I climbed the ladder to the operator's platform and stood beside him. Bill placed the separating mechanism in gear and opened the throttle. I could really feel the excitement now—a deep vibration encompassing the entire machine and penetrating my entire body.

We probably travelled no more than 200 feet when a terrible clatter arose from deep within the combine. We put in another call to the dealership, and out came the same mechanic, again joined by Rydell (the two seemingly inseparable). Inspection revealed that a small stone had passed through the cylinder, but given the racket, it sounded more like a cement block! Dad wasn't in a good mood and let Rydell know it.

"You can't blame the combine if the operator puts a stone through it!" Rydell groused.

"Well," Dad shot back, "I thought I'd bought a combine—not a stone picker!"

While Rydell and our father were sparring, the mechanic, armpit-deep inside the combine, was attempting to dislodge the offending stone. Once extracted, he stated that this rock certainly wasn't the first. The cylinder, according to him, already showed extensive damage.

Dad naturally wanted no part of the deal at this point, and Rydell reluctantly agreed to reclaim the crippled machine.

But wait—they just happened to have a Ford combine for $7500 on their lot. Dad simply wasn't interested in anything that large or expensive and said so.

According to Rydell, the dealership felt bad for the way the deal had concluded, and consequently kept lowering the price until they were somewhere in the vicinity of $5900 (plus our pull-type John Deere). Dad repeatedly tried to convince the exuberant salesman that the combine was oversized for our operation—plus he was wary, as it was a model with questionable resale value. Mostly he was irritated and annoyed with the dealership for offering a machine in such a sorry state, plus the time (and sunshine) wasted.

Instead Dad traded in on a brand-new self-propelled John Deere. This unit was the smallest self-propelled the company offered at the time, but twice the capacity of the pull-type we'd been using. What clinched the deal was a special end-of-season bonus. With the trade-in, nothing more had to be paid until the following year. Dad signed on the dotted line. How to pay for the $4800 balance would be next year's challenge.

As well as a gain in harvest capacity, traction, and

maneuverability, the best part of this new machine was that it possessed that wonderful patented John Deere pickup, which more resembled a carpet sweeper. With its fine wire teeth, it was nearly impossible to pick up a stone. And on the outside chance it did, there was a stone trap just ahead of the cylinder.

We harvested with that combine for a dozen years, and not a stone ever touched the cylinder. I somehow wrangled my way onto the seat that first day and never relinquished it. Compared to today's mighty harvesters, that John Deere was bottom-level basic.

During that era, options were few, and creature comforts non-existent. You inherited a hard metal seat and little else. Every adjustment required a wrench but you were given no tool kit in which to keep it. Sitting on the open platform, you were subject to every whim Mother Nature could offer—from scorching summer sun to chilling autumn winds. Whatever the weather, the operator was soon black from grain dust that constantly billowed up from the header and swirled around the combine, and if the machine plugged from an overload, one was lucky if a half hour cleared the obstruction.

Still, when I think back over the years, there's no other piece of equipment that came close to providing the pride I felt at the wheel of that faithful John Deere.

Today, more than fifty years after that combine first graced our fields, I'm sitting on my veranda watching a new John Deere combine gobble up wheat in those same fields—a harvesting machine that with every pass slices a swath of wheat as wide as a two-lane highway. This machine contains hundreds of computer sensors monitoring grain yield and moisture percentage—even the portion of weed seeds, chaff, or other foreign material in the harvested grain. It can warn of an overheated bearing or slipping belt, alert the user that it is time to change oil or perform other general maintenance issues, monitor tire inflation, and warn when the grain tank is nearing capacity.

Cruise control automatically adjusts the combine's forward speed in relation to the density of the crop. Automatic steering takes over the combine's controls, allowing the operator to retrieve an ice-cold drink from the built-in cooler, or check the day's commodities market activity or the fourteen-day weather forecast on the large computer screen—all from the comfort of an ergonomic, chiropractic-approved leather seat. There is even a "combine hotline," where, via text or phone, one can access information concerning any mechanical issue that might arise while in the field.

As I watched the huge green machine empty its eight-ton load of wheat into a waiting tractor-trailer in a minute and a half, I was in absolute awe of how far harvest technology had journeyed in the last half century alone.

I can't even imagine what Cyrus McCormick might have thought!

Mother Nature Has the Final Word

THROUGHOUT MOST OF THE 1970S, BETWEEN FARMING, DRIVing my courier route, and operating my paper route for Ganner & Woods, I didn't have many concerns about free time. As far as the agricultural component of my schedule, it was strictly cash crop: white beans, corn, or barley grown on a rotational basis. Therefore all field work had to be programmed around my off-farm occupations, which meant it was done on weekends, after supper, or before breakfast.

Since I was full of youthful ambition and energy, this worked for a while. But early in 1977 I was incapacitated with back issues, and while recuperating, I entertained various options for decreasing my workload. As farming had always demanded the most input—be it labour, time, or expense—and the least to show, renting the land seemed the logical choice. My friend and neighbour, Doug Hamilton, was looking for land in close proximity, and offered a three-year contract with a two-year option.

Facing a probable long-term commitment, I chose to unload the remainder of my machinery. My agricultural inventory found new homes in a variety of places, from Wasaga Beach to Tillsonburg. The seed drill and feed mixer—victims of the barn fire—unceremoniously ended their days in the back of a local scrap dealer's truck.

The rental agreement signed with Doug Hamilton assumed even more significance when later that summer I suffered more back distress just as harvest season got underway, and was out of commission for a month.

But what is it about agriculture that's ingrained in our soul? While April's sun was soaking up the previous season's remnants, I felt the itch to be out in the fields. Doug needed extra help but was reticent in asking, as he was unsure of the status concerning my back. I assured him I was fit, even if I hadn't entirely convinced myself. The job he had in mind necessitated the application of nitrogen and herbicide for over 1000 acres of corn, beans, barley, and canola.

The growing of corn in particular had undergone a dramatic change. When I was a lad in the 1950s, our corn acreage consisted of eight acres—enough to fill our small silo. Nitrogen was provided by natural product—cow manure. Then crop specialists and analysts began educating farmers on the benefit of commercial fertilizer, and how just one dollar spent could return three dollars in extra yield.

I recall that my father was skeptical of this promise, but upon applying commercial fertilizer in conjunction with the "real thing," admitted that the boast had merit. The recommendation dictated a 2-12-10 nitrogen-phosphorous-potash blend, delivered in 100-pound plastic-lined paper bags. A decade later, fertilizer was as a consistent a component of crop development on our farm as pedigreed seed or a properly prepared seedbed.

By the 1970s, I'd assumed control of our farm, and my brother Brian was attending Guelph Agricultural College. Part of his curriculum dictated a soil-testing program. Although somewhat doubtful of his assessment, I applied his recommended high phosphorous 13-52-0 fertilizer mélange, broadcasting it on a field seeded to alfalfa for several years. No one was more surprised than I when the crop doubled its yield from the previous season—way to go, Brian!

It wasn't just the fertilizer industry undergoing historical change—herbicide development was also altering the agricultural landscape. When I was a teenager, "hand picking" eradicated mustard, the most common problem in grain fields, while "scuffling" controlled row-crop weeds. This method of cultivation kept weeds under control until the corn crop could provide shade, thus cutting off one of nature's prime principles of growth: sunlight. It seemed a simple enough exercise, and a concept that worked well when crop acreages were small.

Then American chemical company Ciba-Geigy introduced a wonder product known as "atrazine." Here was the answer to farmers with visions of fence line to fence line corn acreages. Just a couple of pounds of this powdered herbicide eliminated pigweed, mustard, ragweed, and thistles—the most common plant pests in corn fields at the time. Add another pound or two, and mix in some variation of vegetable oil to act as a surfactant, and you could rid your fields of twitch grass and quack grass as well.

This was fine until weeds we'd never heard of began to appear. Without the competition of the more common grasses and broadleaf weeds, these new weeds had seldom flourished with enough significance to cause problems. Chemical companies then introduced products that were either grass- or broadleaf-specific. That solved that dilemma until certain weeds and grasses developed a resistance to these selective herbicides, thus necessitating the development of other selective and more aggressive strains—and so it went.

With crop acreage expanding, it became impossible for manure to supply the high levels of nitrogen corn required, so manufactured nitrogen became normal practice. Choices included 34 percent granular ammonium nitrate (the product responsible for burning my barn to the ground) 45 percent urea pellets, 28 percent liquid or 80 percent anhydrous ammonia, a highly concentrated form of nitrogen applied in a gaseous state. Such was the seemingly complicated world of growing corn when I entered the picture in 1978.

For 25 years I remained Hamilton Farm's "herbicide specialist" (as Doug referred to me), a job that developed into a six-week marathon and continuous learning experience each spring. Years of trial and error, experimentation and research, carried us to a point where every acre slated for corn was sprayed twice. The first herbicide application handled grass weeds and was mixed with 28 percent liquid nitrogen before the crop was planted. Upon emergence of the crop, a second application destined for broadleaf weeds was applied.

For the record, that "herbicide specialist" moniker was a bit of a misnomer. Early in my crop-spraying career, when I knew everything, I informed Mom and Dad how much time they were wasting ridding their potato patch of pigweed the old-fashioned way; i.e., with a hoe. I'd discovered this great product "Patoran", an herbicide registered for both beans and potatoes. True to my promise, the herbicide did a terrific job: not a weed was left in the garden—or a potato. If I'd read the label closely I would have discovered that the herbicide was designed for application *before* the potatoes emerged. Sorry!

Back in those unenlightened days it was trial by experience when it came to personal safety in relation to herbicides and pesticides. For instance, spraying wild mustard in barley with 2,4-D. (the most common mustard deterrent at the time) Because of the low volume of water required per acre, sprayer nozzles clogged regularly. Standard procedure was to remove the offending nozzle, the herbicide meanwhile dripping over your fingers. Place the nozzle to your lips and blow out whatever foreign object had obstructed the flow and re-install the nozzle. Wipe your hands on your jeans, climb back on the tractor, and finish the sandwich you were eating before the interruption.

Probably due to such practices becoming more widespread, the Ontario government began compulsory licensing of herbicide applicators in the 1980s. An all-day pesticide course (including a written exam) was now a requirement to apply or even purchase herbicides and pesticides. I received a 99 mark on my initial exam, and recall Doug asking, "99? What did you do wrong? Misspell your name?"

It was a valid query, and something that continually bugged me about those government pesticide courses—the fact you didn't receive your mark on the day of the exam. Maybe the procedure has evolved, but back then it was a couple of weeks following the exam before a form letter would arrive from the Ministry of Agriculture's head office at Queen's Park. Your score, whether 99 or 93 or 83, was the only information furnished; nowhere was there an explanation stating what question or questions you had been unable to solve. Theoretically, one could continue making the same mistake for years, with no chance for correction.

The government no doubt spent millions implementing the legislation and hiring representatives to teach the course, with the intent of educating applicators on the risks involved. But then they provided absolutely no dialogue or follow-up to assure the entire focus of the program—supposedly the safe handling of pesticides—was being carried out.

As bagged fertilizer eventually changed to a bulk-handling system, herbicides likewise underwent transformation. From the days of handling chemical products by 5-gallon metal cans or bags of dusty powder, packaging gradually evolved to dustless granular formulae, or "herbicide packets." These wallet-sized packages are simply tossed into the spray tank. They dissolve in minutes, eliminating the mountain of plastic containers that were supposed to be triple-rinsed before proper disposal (an almost impossible task in the field without a sustained or adequate fresh water supply). For several years we utilized a relatively thick liquid corn herbicide "Primextra" in 10 litre containers at 2 litres per acre. With nearly 700 acres to cover—you can do the calculations on the number of plastic jugs required!

For a substantial portion of my career, I utilized a pull-type 3000 litre tank sprayer with a 45-foot boom operating at five miles an hour. Today's self-propelled sprayers equipped with "auto steer" often triple that speed with booms twice as wide; computer sensors continually calculate dozens of sprayer functions, including booms that automatically compensate for varied topography, as well as individual nozzles that are monitored to prevent over-spraying.

But no matter how technically advanced the application or genetically sophisticated the product, Mother Nature still has the last word on how well a chosen product will perform or a certain crop will respond. Modern herbicides must be applied at key stages in crop development to do the job for which they were designed. Waiting for that window was undoubtedly the most frustrating aspect of herbicide application.

Today's farmers, whether planting seed, applying fertilizer, or spraying herbicides or pesticides, adhere to a concept they refer to as the "4-R Solution": the right product at the right rate at the right time to the right place.

Through twenty-five years of crop-spraying experience, I acquired my own version of this, which I call the "T-7 Theory": it's too wet, too cold, too hot, too dry, or too windy—and if you wait too long, it's too late.

The Bard of Thornhill

I WAS SIFTING THROUGH A BOX OF OLD PHOTOS LAST NIGHT AND came across one of a slight-built man in khaki shorts, heavily flowered shirt, and Mexican sombrero standing beside a Chevrolet station wagon with "God is my Superhero" stencilled in large red letters across the tailgate. The man is Joe Cumming, my wife's uncle, and one of the most fascinating characters I'd ever meet.

I first met Uncle Joe in 1978. He was in his mid-sixties at that point, and I was forewarned that he was "a little different." That was Mary's description; others categorized him as "strange," "eccentric," "an odd duck," "peculiar," "offbeat," and "a nut." Mary's father, never one to waste words, simply stated that he was "full of shit."

Joe and his wife Florence lived a greater part of their lives in the town of Thornhill, now part of the Greater Toronto Area (GTA). In recent years they had wintered at a trailer park in Clearwater Florida. No one really knew what Joe had done for a living; driving a taxi seems to be the only occupation he performed with consistency. Most people figured Florence, a registered nurse all her life, to be the main breadwinner. When Florence died suddenly, Joe, perhaps to escape the memories, spent his final years on the road visiting friends, neighbours, and family. Mary was Joe's favourite niece, so three or four times a year, he'd show up at our place and stay for a couple of days.

Joe talked incessantly with no boundary of subject. Listeners often grew impatient with his endless monologues on life, but Joe and I became close when he discovered that I was an ardent listener.

Some of his questions were so broad they could have taken days to discuss. "So what do you think of technology in general? Where do you think the answer lies pertaining to world hunger? Do you think the Versailles Treaty was the root cause of what would become World War Two?"

On others topics he was only slightly more restrained but every bit as passionate: satellites, astrology, geology, meteorology, crop science, nuclear power, elderberry pie, the history of spaghetti, the cultivation of kohlrabi, the origin of salt, the perplexities of the internal combustion engine, or the folly of Daylight Saving.

First-time acquaintances were met with a barrage of questions. "Where were you born? Where are the roots of your ancestry? What's your occupation? What did your father do? What family have you? What are your goals and ambitions? What do you think you can personally achieve to make this a better world?"

It usually wasn't long into a conversation with Joe Cumming before the subject of China arose; Joe was fascinated with this country's culture, and was a firm believer that most of the world's problems to date could have been remedied through a dedicated remedy of tea and acupuncture.

"The Chinese are so advanced," he'd say. "Relaxation methodology, literature, architecture, cuisine, music, ceramics—they invented ceramics, you know. In fact—now this is interesting—before paper, another Chinese invention, they carved characters on ceramic plates and pots."

"At the beginning of this century," he'd go on, "China utilized at least a dozen different dialects, but most Chinese you hear nowadays is Mandarin. It's the easiest to learn I'm presently studying an eighteen-week home course."

"So have you learned a quite a bit?" I asked.

"So far just 'hello,' but I hope to become fluent."

Music was another major contribution of Chinese culture, according to Joe. "Did I tell you I'm learning to play the Guzheng?" I shook my head. "I discovered one at a garage sale. Can you believe it! No one knew what it was."

I admitted I was in the same category.

"Well, it sort of resembles a zither."

My blank expression called for Joe to explain that a zither was an instrument utilizing about three dozen strings stretched tightly across a wooden board, and plucked like a harp. "The Guzheng is very similar, and one of the oldest musical instruments in the world."

Uncle Joe felt that all tea was great, but that Chinese blends were unparalleled. "Tea's all I drink," he said. "Long ago I quit drinking coffee. It's lethal—and once you add sugar you may as well be drinking dynamite!"

"I've never heard that," I responded.

"Oh yes—coffee beans affect your equilibrium by playing havoc with your brain cells. Sugar only accelerates the process. Now this is interesting—it has been discovered that many of the worst criminals in history consumed high amounts of sweetened coffee. There'd be a lot less crime if people consumed only tea. A cup of tea and a slice of elderberry pie—it just doesn't get any better!" Joe fairly glowed at the mention of elderberry pie. "Are you familiar with the origins of elderberries, Dave?"

Whatever your answer, Joe would proceed to tell you anyway.

"They're grown worldwide, but in the more temperate climates they are much darker, almost black, and grow on large trees—whereas our variety is red, and tends to flourish on smaller lilac-sized bushes. Elderberry yogurt is a favourite in Germany. Other cultures make elderberry wine, elderberry syrup, elderberry marmalade, elderberry soft drinks—the uses are endless. In China, they apply the elderberry for medicinal purposes to combat influenza."

Joe thought most people weren't familiar with the correct brewing technique of tea.

"Boiling the water destroys the beneficial enzymes. 190 degrees Fahrenheit is the perfect temperature. In China, when a cup of tea is offered it's not merely a formality, but an expression of respect; a practise we should perhaps embrace more forcefully in this country."

Joe was in his glory when in the country, where he could enjoy one of his favourite passions: searching the darkened skies for alien life. Upon return from a nocturnal adventure, Joe would be filled with accounts of the celestial activity he'd witnessed. He was fully committed to the idea that there were unidentified flying objects hurtling through the heavens, carrying lifeforms from other planets and solar systems.

Joe owned several vinyl recordings exclusively dedicated

to "space sounds," and carried a series of similarly-themed eight-track tapes in his car. "I like driving alone at night and listening to the music of alien cultures."

Joe played me a portion of one his space tapes; I thought the "music" sounded like some cross-pollination of a pan flute and a saw blade. Joe was convinced he recognized the faint strains of a guzheng. He also claimed to hear voices only he could decipher. It was his conviction our world would be attacked at some point by alien forces.

"Maybe not in my time, but it'll happen. This abundance of meteor showers we're presently experiencing—it's simply these far-off cultures practicing. All these meteorites falling in the ocean or desert—do you think that's coincidence? Once these space civilizations get serious, a meteorite will be able to target a city, like an inter-ballistic missile. Just an average-size meteor would take out a city like Hamilton; a couple would decimate most of Toronto!"

Joe always seemed to have some new health affliction he'd acquired since last encounter. During the time I knew him, he suffered from inflammation of the esophagus, digestive disorder of the lower intestine, infection of the upper ventricle, inflammation of the right clavicle, discourse of the left vertebrae...

His favourite illness was diverticulitis. He loved the word, and he'd pronounce it slowly, emphasizing each syllable with deliberation. A majority of Joe's medical disorders appeared to be no more than passing fads, but diverticulitis was constant. In the nearly twenty years I knew him, the subject of diverticulitis never failed to surface during the conversation.

Joe Cumming had two major nemeses: Bell Canada and Beatrice Foods. During his visits they'd always be singled out for discussion. According to Joe, each in their own way was intent on taking over the world—Bell, through its communication and satellite technology, and Beatrice, through a stranglehold on food production.

Joe was convinced that Bell monitored all his incoming and outgoing phone calls. "And not only that," he added, "but every new phone they install nowadays is equipped with a camera."

Joe's paranoia didn't end there. "Bell's not content with merely recording your calls—with all their satellites they can watch you whether you're driving your car or sitting in your backyard! Even their service vans are fully equipped with monitoring devices."

"And Beatrice...did you know they are the largest food processor and distributor in the world? A multinational company without equal! It doesn't take a genius to realize that a company who controls the world's food supply controls the world. They still pretend they're that little rural creamery that got its start back in Nebraska, flaunting those red, white, and blue American colours in their logo. It's all part of a huge charade!"

Given his obsession, the year he showed up with the lenses of his Chevy's taillights painted in Beatrice's tripletone colours was perplexing. His rather obscure explanation centred on his belief that when Beatrice made their inevitable move for world dominance, his allegiance to their logo might ensure he was "spared, or at least shown some leniency."

It's difficult to pinpoint a particular idiosyncrasy of Joe Cumming, but one that is certainly prominent originated the afternoon his familiar station wagon pulled into our driveway. I was cutting grass, so I stopped and walked over to his car. While pleasantries were being exchanged, I noticed what appeared to be three rocks, each roughly the dimensions of a man's fist, perched atop the driver's side of the dashboard.

I wanted to get back to my lawn, as rain was threatening, but couldn't refrain from asking the obvious.

"Well Dave," Uncle Joe began. "These are Brazilian rocks, and the result of a relatively recent experiment of mine. I was reading my latest copy of *National Geographic* when I came across this article pertaining to the geological structure of South America. As you may or may not be aware, South America's geological roots are the result of an extremely complex volcanic revolution producing an amazingly high-grade rock structure, rich in energy flow. And nowhere is this more pronounced than in rocks from Brazil."

Joe paused, supposedly to allow this information to seep into my brain cells.

"Practically the entire geological structure of South America contains some of these highly desirable qualities, but through research—now this is interesting—I discovered that Brazilian rocks have the highest energy-flow-to-toxic-reduction ratio by far! Well that reminded me of a guy who has a shop in downtown Toronto, who bought, sold, and traded geological merchandise. I met him years ago—in fact I was in his shop the day he got his first shipment of moon rocks!"

Joe paused again, perhaps waiting for some commentary on my part. But what could I say?

"Well, long story short"—too late!—"this fella happened to have three Brazilian rocks left. He claimed Brazilian rocks were one of his best sellers. I figured there had to be some way to harness the positive energy contained within these rocks, so I glued them to my dashboard, theorizing the air from the defroster vents would blow this highly explosive energy with its toxin-reducing qualities back into my face."

Following a long pause, I asked, "So how is it working out?"

"Well, this is just the first week, and the guy at the store claimed it sometimes takes several—but I'm convinced I already feel my energy threshold rising significantly."

At the time, I recall imagining the outcome if Joe got stopped in a routine seat-belt check or RIDE program, and the police officer asked the inevitable question about his "rock collection."

What would be his response? Would he tell the cop the same story he'd told me? What would be the reaction? "Please step out of the car, sir!"

Would the officer request a roadside breathalyser test? Perhaps a chauffeured excursion to the nearest health institution, for an in-depth psychiatric assessment? Knowing the persuasiveness of Joe Cumming's oratories, I suspect that more than likely he'd convince the police officer beyond all doubt that Brazilian rocks were a completely acceptable method of dispelling driver fatigue!

Because Joe Cumming was basically a nonstop conversationalist, I was under the general impression I knew everything about him. After all, anyone who revealed as much of their personality as he couldn't have many secrets.

But one aspect of Joe's life—religion—remained a mystery. Despite his Chevrolet boldly advertising the fact God was his "superhero," Joe hardly, if ever, broached the subject of religion. I assumed that religion was simply a deeply personal experience, and that he chose not to share his beliefs.

Over time, I came to the conclusion that I was probably overanalysing the situation. The solution was obvious;

reduce the complexities of Joe Cumming's character to its simplest form.

As far as the "God is my Superhero" proclamation—Joe may have simply spied the sign at some roadside garage sale or flea market and thought, "Now this is interesting."

Lesson Learned

I WAS SIFTING THROUGH OUR ATTIC THIS MORNING IN SEARCH OF some old farm magazines. Among the scattered clothing, board games, jigsaw puzzles, and faded Christmas decorations, something hidden within a burlap sack caught my attention. I removed the covering and stared at the ninety-year-old rifle, vividly recalling the last time I held this gun in my hands.

The story of this particular rifle can be traced back to September 1925. Eaton's Fall/Winter Catalogue had just arrived. By my father's eleventh birthday, in early November, one page was barely recognizable, worn by the frequency with which he'd shown his father that .22 calibre "Cooey." Persistence triumphed, however, and the birthday wish was fulfilled.

My grandmother had an entirely opposing view of gun ownership at such a tender age. Her concerns were well-founded, since Dad had been offered little (if any) knowledge of firearm safety and operation. It was trial and error only, and practice often consisted of firing out the kitchen door at the outhouse—which was hopefully unoccupied. But despite this shaky beginning, Dad became a crack marksman.

A decade and a half later, we find my father newly married and struggling to make a living in the mink business. The cost of prepared mink feed was prohibitive, and groundhogs were an important supplement. Groundhog burrows dotted the pastures from spring through autumn, and for anyone with a good eye and a reasonably accurate rifle, the supply was unlimited.

After Dad removed the carcass, Mom processed the remains through a regular meat grinder. If not immediately needed, the departed rodents were stored in a cool environment—generally on the stone floor of the house cellar. Recalling those pre-hydro days, my father retains a clear memory of his mother stepping on a corpse in the darkness, and the ensuing colourful language.

Dad garnered no appeal for sport hunting, but throughout the passing years, although the mink enterprise was history, the faithful Cooey soldiered on in the never-ending battle of groundhog reduction. To our father, the rodent's depopulation was a justifiable aspect of farming, no less important than fence mending or machine maintenance. A large burrow could break the leg of an unsuspecting cow, or dislodge a carefully constructed load of baled hay in seconds. Groundhog elimination was therefore the only accepted and allowable use of firearms.

When I struck off on my first hunting expedition, I was about fourteen. The lessons Dad acquired over the years he passed to me: never shoot at anything unless you are certain what it is, and never load your gun until you are ready to use it. Simple and uncomplicated!

Rule number one garnered special meaning the day Dad spied the furry coat of a groundhog sunning itself on a large rock by the creek. "That would be a perfect shot," he thought. Just then the groundhog moved away from its perch. It was me; I'd been sitting with my head propped against the rock, lost in some boyhood dream, and all that was visible from Dad's vantage point was my medium-brown hair. Now the point isn't whether my father would have taken a shot at the "groundhog"—he wouldn't—but rather that he even considered it!

I ventured out with the old rifle three or four times that summer. I never hit a thing, but I always lied when asked, saying, "Yea, I nailed a couple." I had difficulty aligning the sights for some reason (perhaps it was that left eye that "turned-in" on occasion). I remember hiding behind a tree one evening when a groundhog appeared from its burrow just a few yards away. I fired and missed. I probably could have tossed a rock at it with better results.

After that embarrassing episode, I wandered over to our neighbour's clover field, thinking perhaps a change of location might likewise change my luck. I inserted a .22 "mushroom" into the chamber and took a position behind a bale stook of second-cut clover. A few minutes passed when I was startled by Mickey McGivern's booming voice; often it didn't take much to ignite Mickey's temper, so my first thought was he might be angry I was on his property.

"How are you making out?" he asked.

"Uh, pretty good."

"Well, you're welcome to all the little bastards you can shoot. They've made a goddam mess of this field!"

At ease now, I figured a small lie wouldn't go amiss.

"Yeah—I got two tonight!" I knew that would impress him.

"Young Harry Leppington was over here last weekend," Mickey remarked momentarily. "He apparently shot seventy-five!"

My final hunting excursion of that season began like its predecessors: walking parallel to the creek until it exited our property, then back along the line fence that extended to the maple bush at the northern boundary of our farm. It had been an unbearably hot, humid day and although well past seven o'clock, the sultry air was still oppressive. Therefore the mountain ash halfway between the creek and bush seemed to offer an ideal respite.

I sat down, leaning my head against its gnarled trunk, with the gun on my lap. I tried to imagine how different life must have been when Dad was my age and held this very rifle. Picking it up as though observing it for the first time, I marvelled at the weapon's uncomplicated mechanism. The firing pin hits the cartridge, heats and explodes the powder within the bullet, then sends the bullet charging down the barrel. Ignition, expansion, explosion, and expulsion.

I stared down the barrel—don't ask why. Let's blame it on the humidity—or perhaps stupidity. I certainly knew better, as I'd endured more than enough instruction from Dad. Witnessing such a flagrant disregard for firearm safety, he'd have taken the rifle from me for good. But here I was with my eye tight against the barrel, straining to capture what mysteries lay within. I could see only partway, but perceived enough to substantiate Dad's claim that a rifle barrel was indeed spiralled on its interior surface. "That gives the bullet its velocity," he said, "and sends it in a straight line."

I was approaching the edge of the bush about fifteen minutes later, when I spied a groundhog about seventy-five feet away. I'd been practicing extensively the previous week, so with an air of renewed confidence, reached slowly into my shirt pocket and retrieved a bullet. I guided it toward the chamber, not diverting my eyes from the target. For some stupid reason, it wouldn't insert, and I cursed under my breath. Any second my intended victim could catch my scent and retreat. I glanced down at the rifle, irritated with the delay—then noticed that there was already a bullet in the chamber!

I don't know when, why, or how I happened to leave a live shell in that rifle, but the incident certainly quelled my appetite for hunting that evening. And it provided plenty of food for thought during the long walk home.

"How many did you get?" Dad asked upon my return. "None," I answered—honestly, for once. "Well, there's always another day, and another groundhog."

"Yeah, I guess."

That was over fifty years ago—and I don't believe I've held a gun since, until today.

The House on Hickson

A FEW YEARS AGO, MY BROTHERS AND SISTER AND I WERE DRIVing through an area of downtown Toronto when we found ourselves in familiar surroundings. Just off Dundas Street, at Brock Avenue between the arteries of Dufferin and Landsdowne, is Hickson—a tiny street where my maternal grandparents lived for forty years.

Time had seemingly stood still at No. 8 Hickson. As I stood across from the house, I could easily imagine my grandfather Will Carruthers sitting on the front porch working a crossword puzzle, a cigarette clenched between his fingers. Originally he hand-rolled his smokes, but later on someone gave him a cigarette-rolling machine. To a five- or six-year-old, that was the greatest invention in the world. My brothers and I used to practice "coughing like Grandpa." Neither our mother nor our grandmother was particularly amused, as I recall.

If he wasn't doing a crossword, Grandpa would be

reading the sports pages of the *Toronto Star*. Because he always made such a shamble of the paper—pages turned inside out and upside down—Grandma grabbed the newspaper first, giving him the sports section while she read the rest. Once she was finished, he could do what he wanted with it. Grandpa was an avid sports fan all his life...and he was critical. There were two or three members on the Detroit Red Wings hockey team for which he had a dislike, and he hated the New York Rangers in general. During baseball season, he directed his emotions toward the Yankees.

Standing there reminded me of the important role a front porch served so many decades ago. Porches were the focal point of every neighbourhood—a community lifeline of sorts, where news and gossip could be exchanged freely, as easily as the telephone party line did for the rural population. On summer evenings, my grandmother would scurry to get the supper dishes washed and put away so she could be first out on the front porch. One reason was that she simply didn't want to miss anything. More importantly, an early appearance signalled a silent message to the neighbourhood of household efficiency. If someone did beat her, Grandma would grouse, "There's no way so-and-so could have all their chores done this soon!"

Because No. 8 Hickson was a duplex, its dimensions at first glance were deceiving. In reality, it was simply a small house with small rooms. But perhaps that's why it entertained a sort of coziness, apparent the moment you stepped through the door. The whole of Hickson Street was cozy for that matter—all the dwellings seemingly snuggled up to one another. No driveway existed—the little house sat practically on the sidewalk, and a narrow passageway, just wide enough to walk through, led to a handkerchief-sized back yard.

Toronto was about an hour's train ride from our hometown of Bradford. The giant steamer arrived without fail at Union Station, just at rush hour. Streetcars would be jammed with commuters heading home. So as not to lose us in the crush, Mom often elected to do some shopping at Eaton's department store until the crowd thinned out. Following an hour's stay, we'd finally be on our way via the city's familiar red-and-yellow trolleys.

Once off the streetcar at Brock Avenue, it was just a matter of yards to my grandparent's home. There was a store on the corner of Dundas and Brock, and right next to it, bordering Brock and Hickson, a junky old lot that customarily contained little more than used tires and scrap wood, which oddly enough had a habit of regularly catching fire.

This phenomenon seemed to occur despite my grandfather's constant vigil. The sight of any youngsters hanging around the lot would trigger a generous amount of hollering and cane waving until the offenders retreated. Despite these frequent outbursts, my grandfather harboured no specific grudge towards children, provided they remained in the street and minded their own business. This was unlike the gentleman across the street, who installed an electrically charged wire atop his board fence.

Continuing to stare at the house with so many memories, I could visualize my apron-clad grandmother baking in the tiny kitchen, the blue flame from the gas stove providing the room with a homey atmosphere. It's interesting to consider those memories clearly remembered and those that become discarded with time, but that blue flame is what leaps into my mind when reminded of that kitchen. One was barely through the door when Grandma would have the kettle on for tea. She must have boiled a million cups in her day. Everyone expected and received a cup of tea.

Another fond remembrance was sleeping overnight at my grandparent's home. The frequency and variety of sound were very different from the stillness of our farm back home. The rumble of trucks and rattle of streetcars seemed to go on indefinitely. These distractions were occasionally upstaged by a fire truck's wail, as it sped off into the neon night. The fire hall was just around the corner, so one heard every call. Mixed with the outside clamour was the chiming of the mantle clock. As a kid, I figured that clock to be the most wonderful object in the world. I enjoyed lying in the semi-darkness of my bed, waiting for the regular quarter-hour concert of the Westminster chimes.

Even at such a young age I was a lover of automobiles, and the bumper-to-bumper traffic on Dundas Street just a short block north of my grandparents' house was a constant source of entertainment. Mom wouldn't allow me to go alone, but if my older brother Richard was there, she'd relent, provided we remained at the corner of the intersection, well back from the curb.

On the corner in front of the variety store, Richard and I on one occasion discovered a bubble gum machine. We stared for the longest time at the colourful assortment within the glass bowl until suddenly I remembered I had a penny in my pocket. I'd found it on the floor at home the previous day and slipped it in my jeans. It had made me feel quite rich at the time, but until now, had been forgotten. Since it was mine to invest, I had the honour of inserting the coin into the machine and rotating the chrome handle. I don't remember how we planned to share one gumball... but we didn't have to. When I turned the handle, two tumbled out! If we had won the lottery that day, we'd probably have been no more excited. Of course we had to face the third degree from Mom when we returned; she wanted to know where we had gotten all that money to buy the gum we were so proudly chewing.

When I was older Mom would let me walk up to the busy intersection myself. I especially enjoyed it on an early summer's morning, when the air was still cool and fresh and the streets had been swept clean. Wind direction, if any, could always be determined quickly. A southwest breeze funnelled in the smell of the Guttapercha Rubber plant from Toronto's Parkdale District. A northwest breeze signalled the distinctive odour of the Ontario Stockyards at Keele and St. Clair. A north-easterly flow brought an improvement in aroma, via the Neilson Chocolate factory on Gladstone Avenue.

The local shopkeepers would be sweeping the sidewalks in front of their establishments and cranking down the awnings in preparation for another day's business. From my corner vantage point, I'd observe the fruit-and-vegetable trucks delivering their goods to those small stores so prevalent along Dundas Street in the 1950s. The produce appeared as fresh as our own garden's bounty that hour of the day—how I longed for a few pennies to buy a succulent peach or delicious red apple! The milkman would be finishing up his rounds at this point, delivering the glass bottles in those little snub-nosed vans so common in that era. And of course there was the bakery truck—one could almost taste those pastries as it passed by. It was an absolutely unforgettable and wonderful time of day!

Most of the families living on Hickson Street had been there as long as my grandparents, but during the 1950s, a major cultural shift emerged. The mammoth building boom that took place in cities all across Canada in the years following the Second World War was no more apparent than in Toronto. Between the Yonge Street subway, new office buildings and thousands of new homes springing up in the suburbs, plenty of opportunity awaited ambitious labourers. And few were more qualified or dedicated when it came to construction than the Europeans.

My grandparents began to feel like strangers, as old friends and neighbours one by one passed on or moved away and new Canadians took their place. Meat markets and fruit and vegetable stores they'd known for decades took on strange new names and cuisine. These new neighbours were friendly enough, but with their customs brought from home, they naturally had a different way of doing things. For the "Anglos" who'd lived most or all of their lives there, it simply took some getting used to.

By the summer of 1958, Grandpa and Grandma, both now in their mid-70s, finally, but not without some reluctance, decided the time was right to put the house with so many memories up for sale. In the seller's market of the 1950s, it sold in a matter of days.

Toronto's West End found appeal, and before long the real estate agent was driving them through the tree-lined avenues of the borough of Etobicoke. A bungalow just off Royal York Road beckoned, and a few days later a new deed was signed, and my grandparents relinquished control of 8 Hickson. After forty years, the house now belonged to someone else.

"Well, we'd better be going," Richard interrupted, bringing my mind back to the present. At that point I realized everyone was in the car. I climbed into the seat beside my brother, and we slowly threaded our way back through the seemingly endless blocks of red lights, traffic and pedestrian congestion, horn blowing, and hand gestures courtesy of Toronto's drivers. But in my mind, I was still sitting at the kitchen table of a cozy Hickson Street duplex, while the blue flame from an old gas stove boiled up yet another pot of tea.

Meet Me at the Coffee Shop

It was Christmas Day 2013. While driving by a church on the way home from family festivities, I noticed a sign out front. "Friendship is no big thing," it said. "It's a million little things."

The message reminded me of a close friend of mine. In fact, it was ten years to the day since he'd passed away and perhaps the reason those printed words had evoked his memory.

I never have been "one of the guys"…one of a group that enjoys fishing or hunting or golfing, or a pub night, or whatever else "normal" guys do. I was simply never comfortable in that setting. I was more of a one-on-one type person. That's probably one of the reasons Doug Hamilton's friendship meant so much to me. He inspired a wealth of memorable anecdotes that I have recorded over a span of three books.

Although he was fifteen years my senior, I always felt we were more like school buddies who'd grown up together.

I first met Doug when I was nine years old, when he hired Dad, a couple of my brothers, and I to help pick stones on his Perth County farm. That Saturday morning in 1958 began a relationship—and more importantly a friendship—that would survive 45 years.

Doug had come a long way from walking behind a team of horses and a single furrow plow on his father's farm. He envisioned the day he'd own his own farm, and that vision contained one predominant feature: a new John Deere tractor. The foundation of his dream began in 1956 with the purchase of his first tractor—and fourteen shiny new John Deeres would follow in the years to come. Meanwhile, his parents' 100-acre farm evolved to embrace 1100 acres.

But for all of Doug's accomplishments over that half century, it wasn't the farms or the trucks or the Oldsmobiles or long line of green equipment I recalled. It was the man—the loyal friend. Through all the years I knew him, not once...not *ever*, was an angry word exchanged between us. Not even the occasion he specifically warned me about crossing a steep side hill with the forage harvester and a loaded wagon of corn silage.

I didn't deliberately disobey him—I was into the situation before realizing it—but the result was an upside-down wagon in the field behind the harvester. We were forced to manually unload the wagon one forkful at a time before the wagon could be righted...and no one worked with more passion than I! We pulled the wagon back onto its wheels, and the damage proved minimal. Doug merely commented, "Don't be too hard on yourself. These things happen."

When Doug was operating his Mack tractor-trailer on a regular basis throughout the 1970s, 80s, and 90s, I often rode with him. Two daily loads of livestock were the norm. His co-driver Bob Scott took the first run, and Doug took the second. I got home from my courier route by 4 p.m., so about once every month or so I'd join Doug and we'd head out.

Once the load was delivered we'd have supper and arrive back home around midnight...sometimes long after midnight. "Bob can do this route a lot quicker than me because he doesn't spend as much time talking," Doug said.

When Doug passed the milestone of his fiftieth birthday, he wanted to prove (at least to himself) that he was still a youngster at heart, and ordered a new red Pontiac Fiero, a mid-engine, composite-plastic, two-seater coupe introduced just the previous year. He considered getting a Corvette but figured they were somewhat expensive, "for a toy."

It was during this period of the 1980s that Doug discovered flying, something of which he'd been forever fearful. This change in attitude began with a flight to Vancouver to his nephew's wedding, followed by a couple of trips to Calgary. Then came the holidays to England and Scotland, plus a whole series of winter excursions to Hawaii. Following these Hawaiian tours, Doug would have a brand-new batch of stories about banana farms and pineapple plantations; or perhaps just some character he'd met on the plane. Few could relate a story as Doug could—even if you heard the same account a dozen times!

In 1999, Doug was diagnosed with a disease that I and most everyone else had never heard of: Myasthenia Gravis. This disease breaks down communication between muscles and nerves, affecting the immune system as well. Side effects and symptoms included difficulty in swallowing, chewing, and even breathing. About that time Doug was also afflicted with various eye issues. His doctors thought this was another symptom. But at this point no one seemed certain about anything.

Trips to London (Ontario) for eye tests, blood tests, and transfusions became routine, while the medical field tried to figure what course to take. One specialist promised "a full cure within six months." Another claimed the disease had no known cure, that medication and a strict diet provided the best chance for a normal life.

And Doug was by no means a cooperative patient. With so many differing opinions concerning medication, therapy, exercise, diet, and lifestyle, he felt frustrated and helpless. Knowing only excellent health for sixty-five years, regimented adjustment was simply not easy to accept.

This medical saga continued for four years. There were low periods but also extreme highs when some prescribed combination of medication would appear to be the cure for which everyone was striving. Then, just as quickly, Doug's system would reject the new drug, and all concerned would be forced to regroup. Despite these peaks and valleys, Doug tried to maintain a sense of normalcy and routine. For the most part he succeeded—until the autumn of 2002.

During the final three months of that year, Doug spent more than half his time at the Health Sciences Centre in London. I visited as often as practical, helping him pass the time.

"I really enjoy your visits," he mentioned one day, "but you drive enough without another hour-and-a-half coming down here." I told him he was my best friend and that I had to make sure he was being treated right.

On the way home it occurred to me that was the only time I had told him that he was my best friend, or how much I cared. I know I was *his* best friend as well, but it was just something we never mentioned...it wasn't a "guy thing." Not stating how we feel about somebody is one of the shortcomings of human nature I guess.

That prolonged stay in London seemed to have a positive effect on Doug, and to his credit, he made an honest effort concerning diet and medication when returning home.

When the Ministry of Transport confiscated his tractor-trailer license due to recurring eye problems, it was difficult at first, but he confided to me he could live with it. Neither of us liked the fact we didn't get our trucking trips now that he was restricted from driving. He'd phone and say, "We haven't seen each other for a while; we've got some catching up to do."

Despite his comments to the contrary, I realized this restriction from driving was a difficult adjustment. "We don't have to be away in the truck to have a good visit," I mentioned one day. "How about we make a point of having coffee once or twice a month?" As time passed, our coffee breaks became more frequent.

Doug would pick me up, and during the growing season, and if weather conditions favoured, we'd begin with a thorough crop check: monitoring maturity, population stand, and herbicide effectiveness on his corn, beans, wheat, and canola crops. As well, any soil structure or drainage problems needing to be addressed would be monitored for future analysis. Only then would we head for Tim Horton's.

These coffee breaks followed a familiar format. We'd catch up on the local news and gossip we'd gleaned since the last visit, then spend the remaining hour or so swapping lies and tall tales and reliving stories we'd both heard a hundred times over five decades.

During the last month or so of 2003, Doug's eyesight wasn't conducive to night driving, so I would pick him up then head for coffee. The Sunday before Christmas, as he walked toward my van, I couldn't help but notice how carefully he moved—a marked difference from our last visit. He mentioned he'd been having some breathing complications. But by the time we reached Listowel he seemed his old self.

We discussed his 700 cattle, and although that autumn's replacements were bargain-priced compared to a year earlier, Doug still wondered whether it had been prudent to have such a high number with the market in such disarray. Seven months earlier, the US border had been closed to Canadian beef, due to a positive BSE confirmation on an Alberta ranch.

On other subjects, Doug mentioned that he'd taken advantage of the early discount for next season's corn seed, and described the squabble he'd had with his fuel supplier over the exorbitant cost of a replacement furnace tank. He'd had yet another battle with his insurance agent and was looking for a new company. This particular fight began when the insurance company with which he'd dealt for decades doubled the rate on his automotive premium because of his compromised vision. We discussed the outrageous price of new machinery and whether I thought the old sprayer would hang together for another season.

I dropped him at his home a couple of hours later, and as he exited the van he turned to me, asking, "So, do you think I'm looking better?" He'd endured a pretty tough period, and physically it showed. I answered simply, "You look better than you have for quite a while!"

I don't know if Doug believed me, but he laughed and said, "Well, David, I always feel better after a visit with you." He then wished me a Merry Christmas and we agreed to meet immediately following New Years'.

Three days later, on Christmas Eve, he suffered a mild stroke, and was admitted to Listowel Hospital, where he was also diagnosed with pneumonia. At 5 a.m. the next morning he was gone. The stroke, the pneumonia, and an immune system that couldn't fight anymore had proved too much.

Few days that go by that I'm not reminded of Doug in some way, especially in summer, when I'm driving his Fiero, which his family presented to me as a gift—although my wife and I smile when the word "gift" is mentioned.

Because of Doug's deteriorating health the little car sat basically unused the last two or three years of Doug's life, and was in need of some tender restoration. Brakes, exhaust, body work, and air-conditioning issues all needed addressing. The retractable headlights wouldn't—until expensive and elusive vacuum-electric motors were located. A major crack in the frame absorbed plenty of hours and dollars. During those first two or three years, Mary simply referred to the Fiero as "the gift that keeps on taking."

But it has been worth it. Sometimes, when I'm driving, I sense Doug is in the seat beside me. In my mind I can hear him relating one of his well-worn stories, and I can picture that infectious smile. When Doug smiled, his eyes crinkled and his entire face smiled.

Six decades of memories...in some other world now, Doug is probably sitting around a table telling old stories to new audiences. Perhaps we'll meet someday at that great Tim Horton's in the sky. "Well, David," he'll smile as I walk in. "We haven't seen each other for a while...we have a lot of catching up to do."

Beyond the Silver Moon

Nostalgia can be a great motivator...even if it takes a while, as in my case. For twenty-five years, I'd attentively listened to details of my heritage passed from generations before, collectively processing and storing these accounts for...well, I didn't know why.

I asked myself, why am I remembering all this information? What am I expected to do with it? Is there some reason I have this jumble of anecdotes, reminiscences, and recollections clogging my brain? What's the fascination with these old photographs scattered around the house? Why do I continually pelt my parents with questions pertaining to their past?

Something I realized early was when my parents and grandparents reminisced and reflected, it was with spirit and excitement. Their voices were governed by passion when describing the challenge of hacking farmland out of rocks and wilderness, felling trees by axe, hand-sawing lumber, even fabricating the tools to construct a homestead. A dozen decades beyond, many of these buildings remain—a memorial not only to their workmanship, but also to their pioneering spirit.

Or the urban side of the coin was my mother, who related stories about growing up in Toronto in the wake of the Great War; or the flu epidemic that followed; or the economic depression of the 1930s, when every third person was without a job. The latter was a period when the affluent struggled, the middle class became the poor, and the poor simply became society's outcasts...forgotten, neglected, and relegated to the status of thieves and beggars.

These true-life accounts sparked my interest. They reminded me that those scattered photos hidden away in bureau drawers were snapshots of my ancestral roots...individuals who fought and sacrificed to make a living for their families, at times under seemingly impossible odds.

For years I accumulated stories strictly within my mind. Fearing these recollections might become lost, I began recording them. My office desk became crammed with half-written stories, as well as endless post-it notes scribbled with reflections and musings—not just of my ancestors, but also of personal reflections of growing up in the last half of the twentieth century.

The spark that turned "someday" into "today" for me was *Grey with a Silver Lining*...a title Dad had chosen for the book he planned to write "someday" about growing up in Grey County. Although the spirit persisted, the book never progressed beyond the clever title. Convinced by now that I'd accumulated enough information to attract an audience with these stories—and since Dad had concluded that talking and doing were two different matters entirely—I decided to embark on the challenge.

During the winter of 1987 I finally put pen to paper and *Beyond the Moon* was born; the title courtesy a sign that hung from the door of our implement shed for fifty years. The metal sign was there when we moved to our Perth County farm in 1957, as it was when the previous owner purchased the farm a quarter-century earlier. Searching for a definition of our farm's character and heritage, the sign's mysterious origin and message seemed appropriate.

From the outset it had never been my intention to write an arid account of facts about who married and who died. The imagery long simmering in my mind was a complete narrative written in novel form, containing the stories and anecdotes I'd gathered, while utilizing local and world events as a backdrop.

Could I mention a company in which two generations of my ancestors laboured for a combined total of eighty years and not make some note of its history? How could I remark on my family's contributions to two world wars and not focus on some of the causes and repercussions of those global battles? Could I explain the personal excitement of being raised alongside Canada's busiest highway and not relay the integral magic of the 1950s automotive scene? And no narrative from our historical archives could ignore the romantic scandal that threatened to tear the limbs from our family tree!

Like my father, I realized that there is a big difference between a mere collection of thoughts and a book in which those thoughts are molded into cohesive form. Motivation is one thing...but more importantly, did I have the commitment? It turns out I did; working mostly through the winter months for seven years. "Work" was the definitive word. I recall an adaptation of Thomas Edison's comment that "writing is 10 percent inspiration and 90 percent perspiration."

I kept rewriting, revising, rewriting, and revising, until my brother Don, who'd been following my progress and offering encouragement, stated, "You've got to put it to bed. You're never going to be 100 percent satisfied."

Don then presented a dash of psychology...or was it patronization? "Are you aware that only about one person in a thousand who dreams of writing a book ever completes it? So even if it's a literary disaster, at least you tried!"

With some amusement, he remarked on a movie he had recently seen. "This guy takes his completed manuscript to a publisher for editing," he explained, "and after reading what he'd sweated five years to write, the publisher tosses the entire manuscript into the trash can and says, 'There... it's edited!'"

When learning that my book (even in its edited form) was approaching 700 pages, Don voiced the opinion he'd maybe "wait for the movie."

My father played an important role in assuring accuracy in the stories I was recreating. His attention to detail and his recollections of events both extraordinary and trivial proved priceless. It seemed forever I'd been listening to his ramblings, and was intent on reproducing them in the spirit told. I'm thankful Dad paid no attention to Mom when she'd say, "Oh Harold, we've heard that story a hundred times!"

Beyond the Moon was a highly exclusive endeavour of perhaps two dozen copies, total: parents, siblings, first cousins, and aunts and uncles. Families are poor barometers of honest criticism, but their support was nonetheless gratifying. It was my parent's enthusiasm I most appreciated; to a large degree it was their story, and I'm thankful they lived to see the result.

Dad was taken almost to the point of fanaticism. I believe he read it four times...all 700 pages! "After reading your book," he'd say, "I just can't get interested in anything else."

One day he was trailing on about my book and what a great writer I was. Mom, whose literary memory bank of consumed books numbered in the tens of thousands, was tolerant to the extreme with his ramblings, but had finally endured enough when he proclaimed that I was "better than Pierre Berton." "Okay, Harold," she replied. "Now you're beginning to sound foolish!"

Three or four years passed when the co-owner of our local bookstore heard about my endeavour and suggested publication. The first thing Danielle suggested—insisted—was that I shorten the book to 450 pages. So for the next two years I addressed what Danielle claimed were the three most important components of publishing: editing, editing, and editing.

Danielle provided me with names and addresses of publishers and places I might apply for literary grants; offered tips and instructions on submitting a manuscript; gave me direction on copyrighting, printing fonts, binding options, photo inclusion, prologues, and epilogues...all the while fueling me with elaborate conceptions of a best seller. (I was reminded of the writer claiming his book was a million seller, when actually he had a million books in the cellar.)

"You are every bit as good as Dan Needles or Marsha Boulton," Danielle said. (She didn't include Pierre Berton.) "Your book could be purchased by a local theatre for a play. The Huron County Theatre in Blyth is always looking for new Canadian playwrights. A piece of Canadiana such as yours would be perfect! Or the CBC...they love historical drama; maybe even a televised miniseries!"

I'm not exaggerating...that's what she said! I was beginning to have doubts about Danielle's enthusiasm but her alluring accent and not-so-subtle flirtations prevented me from recognizing the fact. At this point she could have convinced me birds flew south in the spring and the sun rose in the west.

The bubble burst when Danielle confessed that she and her husband were parting ways and selling the store. Long story short...Danielle split for Montreal, and I was left holding the book.

Without the distraction of Danielle's charms, I returned to job one: finding a publisher. Not inclined to discard the knowledge she had provided, I sent various samples of my manuscript to a dozen publishers. Danielle had emphasized that by utilizing a wide range of publishing options it would simply be a matter of picking the best offer! I wasn't long hurtling back to earth as the rejection slips poured in. In some cases, the publishers simply didn't bother replying.

With that avenue going nowhere, I adjusted my creative talent, writing stories for magazine and newspapers that specialized in nostalgia. Some paid for submissions, some didn't. The "freebies" I simply considered good practice. The challenge of commercial writing was confining to a certain size...generally 1000-1500 words. I was used to telling a story and utilizing whatever timeframe was necessary.

Since storytelling was my preferred genre, my wife Mary suggested I do just that.

"What kind of stories?" I asked.

"Short stories," she answered. "That novel you wrote is filled with hundreds of short stories!"

It made perfect sense...except to me.

Mary repeated her short story idea two or three times over the following couple of years, but that mass of nerve tissue known as the male brain can be a very non-receptive conductor, especially concerning spousal advice.

But finally it sunk in. Short stories...hmm...she's absolutely right! *Beyond the Moon* contained a treasure trove of reflections perfectly suited for what qualified as a short story! What a great idea! I'm sure it would only have been a matter of time before I thought of it myself.

With renewed zeal I began adapting *Beyond the Moon* into a series of short stories. Just because I (or more accurately Mary) had discovered a new focus for my writing abilities, that by no means guaranteed publication. Book publishing is in a despondent state. Dozens of North American publishers have declared bankruptcy or simply shuttered their doors during the past few years. Many retained bestselling authors on their roster, but still couldn't compete with Chapters/Indigo mega-giants. Similar to the recording industry, book publishing is immersed in a top forty mindset, and I guess short story reminiscences become somewhat invisible.

Then I decided to travel the route many authors choose...self-publication. Utilizing that extraordinary information resource, Google, I searched for Canadian companies offering self-publication services, becoming increasingly frustrated by web pages, whereby checking appropriate boxes was the only means of advancement to successive questions.

"What is your book about?"

"A group of short stories" would have been the correct

answer, but that wasn't one of the options. "You must check an appropriate box," the website responded. "Please try again!"

Next, they wanted a brief description of the manuscript.

"It's a group of short stories," I wrote.

"That is not an appropriate response," came the stock answer once more. "Please try again!"

Next, they wanted to know what category best described my book. Two dozen options followed, but none referred to short stories. I clicked "biography" in an attempt to move things along.

Then they wanted to know who the biography was about. The answer of course was that it wasn't really one individual, but a cross section of people.

"This is not an appropriate response...please try again!"

Throughout this maze of publication jargon, one website continued to surface: Inkwater Press. I checked the phone number and learned it was an American organization based in Portland, Oregon. Although feeling guilty for not supporting local commerce, compared to what I had endured it was a breath of spring air. Every question concerning self-publication had a clear answer. Instead of clicking obscure boxes, this site invited actual typed answers, allowing each individual to define their particular focus.

It's a common misconception that self-publishing companies will accept anything because the author is financing the project. But self-publishing or otherwise, standards have to be met. I was referred to the company's acquisition director suggesting a submission for evaluation and consideration.

I sent six stories and received an immediate e-mail of when I could expect an answer; a timeline of three or four weeks if I recall. I received a response that they liked what they read, mentioning a couple of stories in particular. I was encouraged when asked to submit several more. Then I received acknowledgment that they wished to proceed with an entire manuscript (although I wrote short stories, officially all books are referred to as a "manuscripts").

Editing is a key factor when publishing a book. Two cents a word adds up! Because my manuscript was already "well edited" in their words (I hadn't forgotten Danielle's advice), I received a 25 percent discount. Despite my diligence, the procedure still dictated a complete edit, including minor grammatical errors, but most importantly story errors, where certain facts needed redefining, or a particular event or character needed clarification.

Digital printing has been one of the most important advances in self-publishing, as "print-on-demand" allows any number of books to be printed. In the pre-digital world, 1000 books was a minimum print-off or else costs were prohibitive; with POD capabilities, whether ten or two hundred, the price per book is the same.

Following editing, the process transfers to the graphics department, where photos and captions are inserted and the pages and chapters are formatted the way they will actually appear in the finished book. Front and back covers are designed and approved and back-page text added.

It's difficult to describe the sensation when receiving that first shipment of books and holding an actual copy in my hand. On the road as a courier for forty years, I'd gained a lot of friends and had subtly mentioned that I had a book available. My first sale was to Diane, a laboratory technologist at Listowel Hospital. I wrote on the inside cover something to the effect that she had purchased the very first copy and no doubt this book would be rare and valuable some day when I was a world-renowned author!

So here I am two years later with my second volume (*Yesterday...the Search Continues*) on the market and preparing and organizing the final edit for volume three... that which you are holding in your hands. In an attempt to market the books as a trilogy and trying to retain both the spirit and theme of the first two, *Yesterday's Moments... Today's Memories* seemed to capture the intent.

Just coming up with a title for an individual story is challenging. Sometimes an idea will surface in my subconscious and I'll write a story utilizing that thought. Or I'll use a working title to launch a new story, then substitute a more appropriate designation as the story unfolds. The working title for the story before you was *How to Write a Book...No Easy Steps*. In time, *Beyond the Silver Moon* was chosen, a reference to the book that started it all, and my father's still-born rendering (*Grey with a Silver Lining*).

I've never considered myself a writer. My talent was the capacity to absorb and package what I'd heard, then re-establish and reconstruct those remembrances at a later date—not just for my family, but hopefully for a wider audience as well. I'd like to make another attempt at a traditional publisher that could promote my books throughout North America. Whether that transpires, I guess history will be the ultimate judge.

In the meantime what I find the most rewarding is someone simply relating how much they enjoy my writing.

"I planned on reading just a story or two one evening but instead read the book in two days!"

"You have no idea how many of the stories reminded me of my own family...I loved it!"

"I was so disappointed when the book was done. I can't wait for the next one!"

"Laughter, tears and every emotion in between...what a great read!"

Then there's my friend Dirk, from Oxford County, who tracked me down through an advertisement for an auction sale. Someone had given him a copy of my book; he so thoroughly enjoyed it he wanted to meet me and get an autographed copy of his own. When the second book became available, we met over coffee in Stratford for another exchange. When mentioning the third book should be ready by November 2015, Dirk's comment was, "November can't come soon enough." Support of that stature is priceless!

A while ago I was talking to my friend Gail, whom I've known since...forever. In her unhurried style, Gail expressed how she had finished my first book and was looking forward to the second.

"I sure enjoyed the first one," she said. "You are one talented writer! You know...I bought a book by that Wingham lady who won that big prize...I forget her name..."

"Alice Monroe."

"Yeah, that's the name. Well, I started reading, and I know she's supposed to be an important writer...and maybe it's just me...but I just couldn't get into it."

Being so far removed from Miss Monroe's world I couldn't help but laugh.

"That prize," I answered, "was the Nobel Prize for Literature—the highest honour in the world."

Gail merely shrugged her shoulders.

Enjoying the moment, I added, "Actually, if you want to know the truth, Gail...I was a runner-up."

"Well," Gail drawled, "in my opinion you should have been first!"

Somewhere from beyond the mists of time I expected

this glowing moment to be shattered by the echo of my mother's voice...

"Okay Gail—now you're beginning to sound foolish!"

Wedding Bell Blues

It's an early Saturday morning, but the sun is already streaming through the bedroom window, promising a beautiful summer's day...until I'm reminded I have a wedding to attend this afternoon. So much for the beautiful Saturday. The wedding is a daughter of a friend of ours, I believe...or is it my niece? Maybe it's our neighbour's daughter. We have three weddings to attend this summer, so forgive me for not remembering which one is which. It doesn't really matter—the basic script and ceremony are identical from wedding to wedding and from year to year, with only the characters changing.

I'll be perfectly honest. I hate going to weddings...or more accurately it's the reception rather than the wedding that I dislike. First there's the long boring wait following the ceremony, trying to make conversation with people who have nothing to say. Then there's the return of the wedding party from the photo session, which only signals the beginning of another ritual...inching your way forward in the reception line for an hour to say something profound like, "You sure picked a nice day."

It doesn't seem to matter where I get seated at the reception, you can be assured it will be the last table called to the buffet. And let's not forget the toasts and personal stories directed towards the bride and groom by various intoxicated friends and relatives. Alcohol is not really my thing, and dancing even less—plus the music is always so loud that even if you are fortunate enough to find someone interesting at your table, it's impossible to carry on any semblance of conversation.

I referred to my aversion to dancing in an earlier account. My explanation at the time was that some disaster on the dance floor must have occurred in a former life. I recall a recurring dream where I'm walking past a group of dancers when a giant tentacle reaches out, drawing me into this revolving maelstrom of writhing, rotating bodies, spinning me continuously faster and faster until I'm unable to breathe. These nightmares were almost as scary as my disorder concerning the peanut man.

My animosity, objection, indifference—call it what you will—to these social engagements is deep-rooted. It began in 1955, I think, when Mom and Dad were getting ready to attend a wedding. I didn't want them to go, for whatever reason, and I methodically plugged the tailpipe of our Pontiac with dry leaves, hoping to incapacitate the car. Dad started the engine, and the Pontiac simply and unceremoniously farted the leaves onto the driveway, and away drove my parents. In hindsight, it was a poorly executed plan, but I was only six years old.

I recall Dad telling a story of when he was in public

school and how he and some classmates had rammed a potato up the exhaust pipe of their teacher's Essex so it wouldn't start when she left to go home. So snug was the fit, the backfire blew the exhaust system completely off the car. When the cause was discovered, there was hell to pay for the instigators, but Dad claimed the spectacle was well worth the repercussions that followed.

The first traditional wedding in our family—involving bridesmaids, ushers, an organist, and confetti—was my brother Richard marrying Peggy Gibson. It was held on July 1, 1967—Canada's centennial birthday. I was eighteen by this time, and old enough to inform Mom that I would *not* be attending. Mom informed me in no uncertain terms that I *would* be attending!

Just three quarters of an hour before the wedding ceremony was to begin, Dad was still out in the front field cutting hay. He wanted to finish the field so it would cure and be ready for baling the following Monday. No one paid any attention when I volunteered to stay home and complete the job while the rest went to the wedding. As fate would have it, Dad didn't finish either, as a front wheel of the Allis-Chalmers dropped into a hole created by a broken irrigation tile. Again I volunteered to stay behind, pull the tractor out then finish mowing the hay...but again my argument fell on deaf ears.

Following the ceremony, while the wedding party were away getting their pictures taken, Brian and I decorated Richard's Pontiac with cotton balls and streamers. Although commissioned by Richard himself for this task, Brian and I were all-too-familiar with his history of retaliation towards anyone messing with his car, and remarked what a strange feeling it was not to be getting punched out.

There was no music or dancing or booze at the reception—just a nice supper in the church basement. Following the meal I went home to milk the cows, but apparently missed the best part, according to those in attendance. I guess the wedding party and their guests had retreated to Peggy's parents' place to admire the gifts. My brother Bill, Richard's attendant, had been advised, not surprisingly, to protect the car. Bill by no means took his responsibility lightly, so when three "good ole boys" tried to commandeer the vehicle, he had no intention of backing down. A scuffle ensued, and my brother, who was outnumbered, ended up on the ground.

One of the assailants, with great ceremony, then proceeded to pour a five-gallon pail of oats from the Gibson granary onto the front seat of Richard's Pontiac. Peggy's mother became agitated at the prospect of what this juvenile act would do to her daughter's hay fever allergy. At that moment, Peggy's father, who had disappeared momentarily, returned with a pail of grain of his own.

"Is this your car, Dave?" Blake Gibson asked the trio's ringleader. Those gathered looked towards the new Chrysler. "I thought so," Blake said, and with equal formality dumped the contents onto the black vinyl interior. That ended the fun. Peggy's father vacuumed out the Pontiac, the crowd dispersed, and the newlyweds left for Niagara.

The next family wedding was two years later, when Bill married Donna Hurlbut. Bill asked Richard to be his best man, but as the wedding was held on a Friday, and as he'd just been transferred by his employer to Toronto, Richard didn't feel justified asking for the day off.

I was second choice, and I also declined, although I didn't need a reason. I'd been just warming up at Richard's wedding, but was now in full protest mode. Even the chance to chauffeur the prospective wedding party in Donna's sporty red Acadian—bucket seats, floor shift, and all—failed to sway my position.

"I never thought it would be so difficult to find a best man!" Bill complained, in obvious frustration. He then asked Brian, who accepted without second thought. There's some controversy to this day as to the legality of the marriage, as Brian was three weeks short of his eighteenth birthday when he signed the register as witness. I suppose after close to fifty years, it doesn't really matter.

I not only refused be part of the official ceremony—I didn't even attend the wedding. I'd purchased a brand new manure spreader the previous day and wanted to try it out. So while the rest of the family joined Bill and Donna on their special day, I hauled manure. About a dozen loads as I recall. The spreader performed flawlessly.

Two years later, when my cousin and best friend Doug Watt took the matrimonial plunge, my feelings hadn't changed. After I turned down the top job, Doug tried another approach. "What about an usher?"

"Sorry." Sheer stubbornness was in command now! So while Doug and Judy spoke their wedding vows, I was home swathing grain.

There seemed no end to weddings…in the early spring of 1974, my soon-to-be sister-in-law Judy Scott asked if I would consider being best man for my brother Brian. A year earlier, my answer would have been a rude and inconsiderate "no"—after all, my record was legendary.

"It'll just be a small wedding," Brian's fiancée explained. Brian reiterated this point by adding that it would be just brothers and sisters.

"You won't have to make speeches or conduct toasts or anything like that," continued Judy.

"Are you having a big reception and dance?"

Judy explained that this was not the case. "After the wedding, we're just going to entertain the two families back at our apartment for a snack."

"Well, I suppose..."

Their wedding took place on an unseasonably hot, muggy mid-May Friday evening, in a little village near London. When arriving at the church, I noticed the "brothers and sisters only" rule had been relaxed, as Doug and Judy Watt were among the small knot of guests milling about the sidewalk. But then Doug had always seemed more like a brother to us anyway. While waiting for the ceremony to commence, those gathered stood around and chatted about the unseasonably hot weather.

The strains of an organ solo filtered through the walls of the Minister's study, where the four of us stood waiting for our cue. Brian and I were sweating like workhorses—partly from nervousness, partly from the unseasonably hot weather. Barb, Judy's "best girl," proved to be an easygoing person with an infectious personality, and helped put me at ease—enough that I managed to stand through the service, hand over the ring without dropping it, sign the paperwork, and walk down the aisle and out of the church, all without fainting (or worse).

Once we were outside, somebody threw the traditional bag of rice. Cameras clicked and the assembly broke off into discussion groups, the main subject being the unseasonably hot weather. The unfortunate highlight of this portion of the festivities occurred when Judy Watt was backing up in order to get the proper angle for the photo she was about to shoot, and her heel caught in a crack in the sidewalk, causing her to fall fanny-first into the flower bed.

By the time I delivered the wedding party to Brian and Judy's apartment, the gathering was moving along nicely. Judy's mother and aunt had prepared sandwiches, and everyone was busy eating and talking about the unseasonably hot weather. Brian and Judy had a fine big balcony, its fifteenth floor vantage point affording an unobstructed view of downtown London.

It felt like a hundred degrees in the living room of their apartment, so the balcony proved to be a popular haven throughout the evening. Even when it came time to open the gifts—and despite Judy Watt's insistence that it was part of the best man's job to be in attendance—I stayed on that balcony. As far as I was concerned, my job was completed.

That wedding pretty much took care of my brothers. Then came the assault of weddings for my nieces and nephews and daughters-of-friends and sons-of-neighbours and…and…and…

And now, there just didn't seem to be any feasible excuse to escape this particular wedding, which was only a few hours away.

However, as I was washing the car, I suddenly had an idea—granted, one born of desperation. Suppose I was to discreetly slip into the pantry and locate the perfect-sized spud? Surely after sixty years it's worth another try!

Lest I Forget

While travelling through Midwestern Ontario during my career as a medical courier, I always made a point of pulling off to the side of the road as the eleven o'clock hour approached on Remembrance Day. That two minutes of relative silence gave me a chance to collect my thoughts and try to comprehend what it meant to actually go to war. After several years I deduced it couldn't be done.

I therefore decided that those of us who have not experienced war firsthand must discover our own ways of commemorating this special day. Of course it's not as if Canadians are completely free of war. Anyone who has lost a family member in Afghanistan or some other corner of the world where our troops are trying to neutralize conflict knows war's sacrifice all too well. But the scope and magnitude of the two world wars is almost unimaginable to me and my generation.

During World War One, my grandfather, Sergeant-Major Will Carruthers, trained new army recruits for overseas duty from the Armed Forces site at Camp Borden, Ontario. Now here was a war that few really understood! Several East European countries had been squabbling for decades over land claims of one form or another, but on June 28, 1914, some guy who was the apparent heir to the throne of Austria-Hungary was assassinated. Events continued to worsen over the next month, as blame was assigned and countries picked their partners. In the beginning, it was basically Austria-Hungary, Turkey, and Germany (under Emperor Kaiser Wilhelm) against Russia, France, and Belgium. Great Britain had little choice but to defend its French and Belgium neighbours just across the English Channel. On August 4, Great Britain declared war on the German Empire. Because of Great Britain's mighty geographical empire at the time, it now truly was a "world war."

Patriotism was paramount in 1914. "If Great Britain is at war, Canada is at war!" was the rallying cry in the Canadian parliament. Young men lined up by the thousands at enlistment offices, many lying about their age just to get a chance to join in the excitement of a good battle. Although most had regular jobs, they assumed there'd be nothing wrong with a few months off. A dollar a day and free board would be a nice change from routine. Most were familiar only with the perceived nobility of war anyway.

Even England had no idea of the sacrifices of a global war. It had always fought wars...if you could call them that. For centuries, whenever life at home became boring, British Armed Forces personnel would recruit the farmers and townspeople to capture or recapture some useless plot of ground. If the "war" was consuming too much time and harvest time was nearing, the "soldiers" would simply return home, take care of the crops, and resume hostilities at a more convenient time.

Most Canadian soldiers naively believed they'd "kick the Kaiser's ass" and be home by Christmas, or by spring at the latest. Reality dictated that most didn't even leave England for France until February 1915, where they joined a struggle that had already settled into a monotonous pattern that would change little until war's end. From flooded, muddy, rat-infested trenches, tens of thousands of soldiers fought a continuous series of skirmishes with the same piece of ground being captured and recaptured, with nothing but dead and wounded soldiers to show for it.

The sacrifices were almost unimaginable. At Vimy Ridge, France, in April 1917, 3600 men died in four days, and nearly 10,000 were wounded. In Passenchendaele, Belguim, between October 26 and November 7 of the same year, more than 15,000 out of a regiment of 20,000 Canadians died or were wounded in order to capture the German held city. To put the Passchendaele loss into perspective, and perhaps parallel something we might understand, it would be as if the Grey County city of Owen Sound through which I travelled for forty years was hit by some super virus or environmental disaster that over a period of twelve days struck down three quarters of its 20,000 population!

It would be to this European hell my grandfather and hundreds of recruiters like him would be sending waves of platoons. 60,000 Canadians would lose their lives in that war...10,000 who were residents of my grandfather's hometown of Toronto. It's probably a good thing he had little idea what awaited these innocent lads in the "war to end wars."

Then came September 1939 and another world war. At

least this one was easier to understand. A crackpot dictator, Adolf Hitler, was threatening to take control of the world with a Nazi regime that would, in his words, "last one thousand years." When Canada declared war on Germany, every city, town, and village immediately opened temporary registration offices. Everyone of voting age received a number, and was asked general questions concerning the segment of the armed forces they were interested in, and also if they had any special skills. The questionnaire basically served to find out who was who and where you lived. If and when a draft notice was issued, a more thorough report would be completed. By Christmas 1939, more than 50,000 new recruits were being trained at various bases across Canada. This time there wasn't the carefree, can't-wait-to-fight stampede. Memories of World War One were too vivid.

At this time, my parents were living in Artemesia Township, in Grey County, just a couple of miles from the Eugenia hydro power station. The very week war was declared, huge spotlights were erected at the dam site, in an effort to thwart any acts of sabotage by infiltrating German armies. Supposedly, dams were the first items blown up during occupation. The intense lighting of the dam and power station caused mixed feelings among the locals, who figured illumination only made the site easier to locate. Over time, Eugenia was spared from attack, but among any gathering of those in close proximity to the dam, rumours were rampant of German sightings. One account explained how Germans were capable of parachuting from the sky with folding bicycles, which with just a few seconds preparation could be ready to pedal off in any direction to create chaos and destruction.

My uncle Verdun "Mac" McIsaac, a Toronto native, was

drafted in early 1942, and by November of that year was part of the Allied Forces North African campaign. Through the fierce desert heat of Algeria, Morocco, Ethiopia, Libya, and Egypt, went my uncle and a hundred thousand more, inching their way forward by day and pitching tents at night. Then followed the arduous struggle up the Italian Peninsula, where soldiers faced winter rain, mud, and treacherous terrain, not to mention a hardened German army every mile of the way. In one incident, a shell explosion knocked Mac from his motorcycle while he was on night convoy duty, fracturing his shoulder. Another time a mortar shell hit the tank in which he was riding, cracking both eardrums—but the tank's steel walls prevented more serious injury.

On Christmas Day, 1943, while Allied troops which included my uncle were preparing to attack Rome, a leading Canadian magazine, in an effort to bolster sagging spirits, featured in its December issue a picture of a soldier leaning against a fireplace, chatting warmly with family members. Above the photograph, a caption read: "Home for Christmas." The model soldier featured was Mac McIsaac.

Back home, his wife waited...one year, two years, three years. Like all servicemen's wives, my aunt lived from one letter to the next. Always relieved to find the letter with the familiar handwriting in the mailbox, but forever afraid to discover an official letter disclosing contents you dared not even imagine. Every day the war casualties were listed in the newspaper—and just as regularly, one of those names was someone you knew. No one was immune from this conflict. An even more dramatic visual, if one were needed, was the practice of placing stars in the windows of homes to inform or remind passersby how that particular household had lost a family member in the ongoing war.

Finally came that day in the late summer of 1945, at Toronto's Union Station...the same station from which my uncle had departed forty-two months earlier. Disembarking from the train and into the welcoming throng, Mac McIsaac, although somewhat thinner, appeared as handsome as ever in his uniform. However, like all arrivals, the years of combat showed, no matter how wide the grin. Like the tens of thousands who preceded or followed him home, the transition back to normalcy would be difficult. On a daily basis, these soldiers had existed in a world filled only with fear and uncertainty and chilling visions of war's insanity. One moment you were fighting side-by-side with your best friend...the next his body was scattered to bits by a shell and left behind in the mud. Small wonder some returning soldiers would have nightmares to last a lifetime.

One last thought...Ted Edwards, a Simcoe County neighbour of ours. I was only six or seven, but recall him telling my father on one occasion of how terrified he'd been each evening on the regular bombing runs over Germany during World War Two. Ted was a tail-gunner on a Lancaster bomber, and each night his squadron would fly off into the inky blackness, and each morning without fail at least two or three planes would be missing. These men were well aware of the odds facing them every mission, realizing each night's exercise might be their last. They knew it would be, for someone. One evening it was the bomber in which Ted's brother rode that never returned.

I'm not sure why I remember that particular conversation. When I was a child in the mid-1950s, I had heard adults occasionally relate stories of their days in the armed forces. Uncle Mac from time to time would mention something about his war years...but then, he came back. I guess I just figured everybody did.

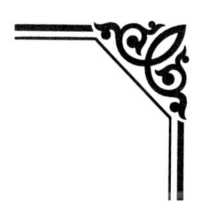

World Through a Windshield

THIS WORLD IS FULL OF PERSONAL DECISIONS. SOME MAY SEEM trivial and inconsequential—whether to add milk or cream to your coffee, pepper to your soup, or ice cubes to your glass of water. Others have more impact and become turning points in our lives. These are sometimes referred to as "crossroad" decisions.

One "crossroad" decision for me began simply enough, with an advertisement in our local newspaper, in late October 1973. "Wanted," the ad said. "Someone to drive daily courier route to Owen Sound...apply Don's Taxi."

Who would have thought that two-lined announcement would provide a career change that would span five decades? I'd grown up on a farm, and agriculture had been the only venue I'd known.

But the preceding years had spawned a succession of farming challenges. Whether the stated commodity was corn, beans or pork, the bottom line had been the same...a financial disaster. I think it was Einstein who defined insanity as doing relatively the same thing over and over and somehow expecting different results.

It was actually my father who brought the newspaper ad to my attention, figuring it would be a good interim job while I considered my future in agriculture. But the start date for this position coincided with a pre-planned Florida getaway with a girl I'd recently met, so I decided to pass—this despite my limited income, mailboxes full of overdue bills, and a stream of phone calls from collection agencies and finance companies!

Sometimes we can glance backward and observe all the missed opportunities in life. Well, I did my best to screw that one up, but received a second chance in spite of myself...thanks to Dad, who covered for me the two weeks I ran off to the Sunshine State. In return, I promised Dad I'd give the job a try for the winter.

Years later I recall relating this incident to a good friend of mine. "Let me get this straight," she began. "You had no money, no job, no career, no credit, owed everybody, and your father already had a full time job. However, you chose to let him perform two jobs, just so you could run off to Florida with this girl...talk about immature!"

Don Ganner, who offered the position, was Palmerston's premier entrepreneur at the time. He and his partner Helen Woods owned a couple of taxis, provided an airport service to cities in Ontario and across the border, had a contract for delivering newspapers for the Kitchener-Waterloo Record, and owned a tour bus. Don would bid on anything needing a vehicle, and was successful bidder for two medical courier contracts: one to Guelph, and the other to Owen Sound. Both routes originated from the Ontario Ministry of

Health's Palmerston laboratory facility, just minutes from where I lived.

Change being the only constant, the route underwent both gradual and accelerated alterations and transformations over the years, with stops being added and deleted depending upon shifting demographics. Milk samples were an integral part of Ministry of Health testing in those early days. At Walkerton I'd meet up with one of the inspectors for the Grey-Bruce area, who'd often have as many as three or four coolers of milk samples. I drove small cars in those days—a Chevrolet Vega and a Ford Pinto—and I wonder now how I managed to fit everything in.

I recall how that brand-new Vega was practically rusted out after one year on the road. It also entertained an unhealthy appetite for oil, consuming two quarts a day. And that Pinto had to be the slowest accelerating car I'd driven to date. The introduction of these medical route contracts coincided exactly with the first OPEC oil embargo and subsequent spike in fuel prices, so Ganner purchased small cars for their economic advantage. He certainly wasn't a proponent, however. In reference to the Pinto, Don noted he could "walk faster than that piece of junk!" He generally referred to the entire category of compact vehicles of that era as nothing more than "mouse-motored shit-boxes."

I recall some of the winters from the 1970s, when Highway 21, which parallels the eastern shore of Lake Huron, was like driving through a canyon made of banks of snow that towered twelve feet high.

On this artery one day in January 1977, while driving through continuous snow squalls, a pair of headlights suddenly appeared on my side of the road. Naturally neither of us was travelling with much speed, but the impact certainly scattered everything that was within the car. Coolers, boxes, x-rays, mail…all went flying.

Don Ganner had recently upgraded me to a 1976 Meteor, a virtual land-yacht by today's standards. Its bulk was definitely a plus. The other car involved in the collision was a full-sized Chevy so neither of us sustained any personal injuries. Ganner had given up on small cars by this point, figuring that what he saved on fuel he spent on repairs. Unlike today, small cars of that period seemed totally ill-equipped for daily high-mileage usage.

Despite their heft, both cars sustained enough damage to be non-driveable. We spent nearly two hours following the accident in the front seat of the tow truck, waiting for the police to arrive, as they had so many accidents to investigate that morning. The Meteor was finally towed to a garage in Underwood, and by this time the road was officially closed.

Because of weather conditions, accommodations were scarce. I managed to find a room above a restaurant in Tiverton, a few kilometres south of the accident scene. There I spent the next twenty-four hours, until I could get the car towed back to Palmerston. Stuck with a cot whose mattress sank to floor level, and only a scratchy wool blanket for warmth, I didn't sleep well. At one point I recall someone throwing up in the hallway outside my door. Vomit was still splattered against the door the next morning.

In Kincardine a few days later I was relating my experience when one of my "route girls" spoke up. "I live in Tiverton…I wish I'd known. I would have invited you to my place. My husband was working the night shift and was storm-stayed himself!"

That incident proved to be my only physical contact

with another vehicle. Despite all the snow and slush that passed beneath my wheels in those forty years I never once had to be extracted from a ditch. And I've only had a few encounters with police radar—most memorably when I received two speeding tickets in one day!

I'd gotten behind schedule for some reason when a Wiarton cop nailed me. An hour later, while making up time for that delay, another caught me in Owen Sound. When the officer gave me that spiel asking whether I wanted to dispute this ticket, I was tempted to answer, "Yeah, yeah—I heard all this an hour ago!"

One thing I discovered throughout these many years, and have never taken for granted, is the loyalty of the people on my route. Even if I messed up, those involved were able to find every excuse why it was their fault, or the labelling wasn't clear, or there was a communication deficiency, or it really wasn't that important anyway, or…or…or.

Decades ago, when I had all the energy in the world and fourteen- or fifteen-hour days were no big deal, along with my Owen Sound route I drove a Stratford route, for what was then MDS Laboratories (now LifeLabs). One night I forgot to leave some specimens at the Stratford lab and it wasn't until my return to Listowel that I realized my mistake. Mary, my wife, was head technologist at the MDS Listowel lab at the time, so I called her to relate the sad tale. It was about 10:00 p.m. by this time. Mary had no recourse but to drive to Listowel, and sort, spin, and refrigerate the blood cultures—otherwise they would have been worthless the next day. By the time she finished, it was midnight.

The next morning, Mary phoned Stratford and explained how "the courier" had screwed up, describing what she'd done and promising to send the paperwork down to Stratford on today's run. The receptionist made no comment whatsoever about Mary having to work so late, but merely stated, "Don't you say anything bad about David...he's just so sweet!"

As I write this, so many memories return. There was the time I was sent to an address in Owen Sound to pick up a water sample. Perhaps the storefront sign, Fantasyland, should have tipped me off, but I had been informed that it was a travel agency. It was not until I had stood embarrassed for several minutes among the X-rated videos and cards, sex toys, anatomically correct inflatable dolls, "love lube," vibrators, and edible underwear, that it finally occurred to me that it was April 1.

Over a forty-year period, change is unremitting. The most significant came in 1998, when the Palmerston Public Health Laboratory closed as part of the provincial government's deficit-reducing program. Everyone knew it was coming, as the previous two years had been rampant with rumours. Downsizing, downscaling, rightsizing, streamlining, wage freezes, alignment, amalgamation, takeovers, job cuts, voluntary retirement, involuntary retirement, transfers...the rhetoric was unending.

Someone at the time used the analogy that it was "like waiting for a terminal illness to take a friend. You want the waiting to end...yet it's so hard to actually let go."

A couple days after the final announcement, someone said to me, "It's sure going to be different for you as well, not stopping here every day."

That was certainly true. For twenty-five years the Palmerston Public Health Laboratory had been the nucleus of my entire route—the centre point of each day's operation. For twenty-five years, every parcel, envelope, cooler, and container originated from, transferred from, headed to, or was transferred through that lab.

Because it was such an important component of my job for so long, a certain part of me has remained in that building out on Highway 23. I guess it takes more than the closing of a door and an official government statement to erase a quarter century of memories. It's difficult to pick a particular recollection. One highlight was discussing my writing endeavours with the office secretary. I was just beginning to submit stories to local magazines, and had recently completed a family history. Pamela was always accommodating in her reviews, whether warranted or not. She was a voracious reader and aspiring poet, and together we shared a common goal of searching for new ways to keep alive our artistic desires. I lost track of her recently, so whether she continued her pursuit, I don't know.

Following the closure of the Palmerston Lab, all specimens were re-routed to the laboratory in London. Another major transformation was the reduction in county health units. I think there were nine offices scattered throughout the towns and villages of Grey and Bruce Counties when I began. On my final day, there was but one.

Water testing had always been a major component of this route from the outset. But during summer, due to the influx of tourists flocking to the beaches of Lake Huron and Georgian Bay, water testing by public health personnel increased dramatically. However, nothing prepared us for what developed Victoria Day weekend, 2000.

It began with more than a normal number of intestinal disorder complaints at the Walkerton Hospital emergency area, and gradually expanded as the weekend progressed. When E. Coli 0157—a deadly virus—was confirmed, the

Medical Officer of Health was informed. Food poisoning is always the first suspect—but as new cases were diagnosed with such rapidity, it was determined that water must be the source.

According to Walkerton Public Utilities Commission officials, everything was fine with the water system. Valuable time was wasted as other causes were investigated, but because of the number as well as the severity of emergency cases, Walkerton's water system again came under scrutiny...this time more closely. What was discovered was a chlorinating system ineffective for months but no reports filed. Unsafe drinking water results had been coming into the Walkerton office but were either ignored or altered. By the time contaminated water from a farm just outside of town was pinpointed, seven people were dead and several hundred were severely ill.

What followed can only be described as a nightmare, as journalists from every TV station in Ontario converged on the scene. Phone calls came from every province in Canada, and several sites in the United States. Two men basically in charge of Walkerton's PUC, and to whom practically all the anger had been directed, were in police custody in order to protect them from the general populace, who were in "lynch mode." Anyone even remotely involved could hardly move around Walkerton those next few weeks without running into media. Everyone, including myself, was told not to make any comments to the media without direct clearance from the Medical Officer of Health office. I had TV zealots stick their microphones right into the van for "comment on the situation."

Prior to that May weekend, three or four moderately-sized picnic coolers full of water samples would be considered normal for one day's pickup. On one particular day at the peak of the crisis, sixteen coolers were sent to the London Public Health Laboratory. Panic erupted. It seemed everybody within a one-hundred-kilometre radius of Walkerton wanted their water tested.

I'll never forget the atmosphere around Walkerton during those dark days when the epidemic was still spreading with no end in sight. It reminded me of a war zone. Air ambulance helicopters carried the most critically ill, while land ambulances continually transferred less acute (but still serious) cases to other hospital sites, hoping to ease the burden on Walkerton's overtaxed emergency system.

Some have estimated that 2500 people were affected. I travelled to London seven days a week, for three weeks, and it took another three weeks before any semblance of normality returned to my route. When I retired in 2014, fourteen years had passed since that disaster, but any time there was an abnormally heavy rainfall causing flooding conditions, or a "boil water" advisory, no matter how isolated, the number of water testing samples from surrounding counties escalated dramatically.

Once the crisis was brought under control, the political and legal investigations began. Those at the centre of the tragedy claimed they weren't adequately trained to recognize the danger signs associated with poor water reports. Other PUC officials blamed public health inspectors for not monitoring water results more closely and failing to check up on personnel in charge. Inspectors blamed the provincial government, claiming that cutbacks had made it difficult to carry out their responsibilities adequately. Even the farm from which the contaminated water had supposedly leached was sued. It was a terrible and unsettling ordeal from the start.

And it's not over...nor will it ever be for those who lost loved ones, or those who still suffer with the medical repercussions on a regular basis. Children particularly could experience the effects for life. Clean, safe, fresh drinking water was something Ontario simply took for granted until that weekend in May 2000.

Then there was September 11, 2001. Everyone was seeing terrorists in their rear-view mirrors after that—and security programs, if they existed at all, were instigated, reviewed, or updated as the situation warranted. People freaked out at the sight of icing sugar or flour, as radio and TV media warned of an upcoming anthrax pandemic. Twice in the aftermath of 9/11, the Owen Sound Health Unit was shut down and personnel decontaminated while various "suspicious" white powdered materials were investigated by police.

Then there was the SARS (Severe Acute Respiratory Syndrome) virus outbreak in 2002, where mandatory screening was paramount before entering any hospital, health unit, medical clinic, or retirement home. From many sites, all delivery personnel were barred, necessitating all medical specimens from within the site be delivered to an outside entrance door.

That was the beginning of the sanitation dispensers that to this day one sees at every medical associated institution in Ontario, in a supposed effort to curb another outbreak or similar virus. Despite the almost fanatical use of these dispensers, to date no scientific data has actually confirmed they make any difference, except to generate huge profits for their manufacturers.

After forty years behind the wheel, the most-asked

question about my job was always, "How do you stand driving the same route day after day after day?"

I guess there's a certain amount of repetition with any job, but really it wasn't the same. It may have appeared so, but looking through that windshield, I'd observe what was barren farmland one week, sprouting a multitude of different crops the next. I'd watch these crops grow and mature until gobbled by harvesting equipment with the arrival of autumn, before the earth was plowed to rest beneath the snow until the cycle repeated.

Over that forty-year period, I witnessed new houses and business establishments built; old ones renovated; new barns erected; and old ones torn down, burned down, or simply allowed to deteriorate. I watched the transition of metal to plastic in automobiles, the coming and going of bumper sticker messages, and the phenomenal rise of the SUV market and $50,000 pickup trucks. I experienced gas hikes, gas wars, "idiot" drivers, campers, boats, bicycles, motorcycles, and joggers—plus never-ending road construction. I felt the entire spectrum of weather—from snowstorms to thunderstorms, from thirty-five degree summer heat to minus-thirty-five degree wind chills, from the greenery of spring to the breathtaking colours of autumn.

I think a ribbon of film is an accurate analogy of my daily route through the years, with each frame recording and representing a single day. Individually, it might appear as if nothing was happening—but once you place the frames in a continuous sequence, a complete story unfolds.

I estimate I drove in the realm of seven million kilometres and gave 10,000 road reports during my career—even if I wasn't always believed. I recall a girl on my route once said, "If Dave says the weather is not too bad, that means it's really bad…and if he says it's not too good, it's terrible!"

As mentioned earlier, what has made those forty-plus years so enjoyable and entertaining were the people…"my girls," as I referred to them. I realize there were a few guys in the mix, but 95 percent of those with whom I was in contact each day were women. It's a tough job but…

Because there was such a disproportionate ratio in favour of the fairer sex, I guess it should be no surprise that a few would fall into that "special" category. On my last day, hugs, kisses, tears, and fond farewells abounded; I'd been the recipient of some great hugs by one particular girl throughout the years, and that final Friday she left no emotion hidden, with a farewell that stretched far beyond any description of "hug." As the next girl in line offered her goodbye, she whispered, "I can't top that…at least with my clothes on."

I recall with fondness one girl who'd often carry water samples or mail out to my van in order to, in her words, "save you a few steps." "You're running late," she'd say sometimes, or "I needed some fresh air." Whatever the reason or excuse, she made even the average days special—we had some great parking lot chats over the years. She was blessed with an aptitude for discovering Christmas and birthday card messages that seemed personally written. When my mother passed away in 2000, she gave me a wind chime. Its melodic tones not only keep Mom's memory alive…but continue to provide a constant reminder of the warmth and kindness of the one who offered it.

Thinking back, I remember many of the seemingly trivial things. Entering the different hospital labs each day and overhearing a multitude of topics under debate—the upcoming weekend or holiday, sports in which their kids were involved, where their kids were working, or what university or college they were attending. Pets, husbands, weather, crops, restaurant reviews, TV shows, "goddam computers," and of course management, were discussed with regularity. And of course the occasional frantic look at the clock upon my arrival, followed generally with something like, "Dave...oh shit...I forgot all about you!"

I consider myself very fortunate to have been able to do something I thoroughly enjoyed for so long. It's unbelievable and almost sad, the number of people who simply live for Friday and hate the thought of another Monday. I once heard someone say "the person who has a job they love has it made."

In that respect, I'm wealthy beyond measure. That tiny ad in our local newspaper was a "crossroad" decision to be sure. Forty years of trust, faith, appreciation, love, and friendship...Could a person ask any more?

Treasured Memories

DIFFERENT TIMES THROUGHOUT OUR LIVES, ESPECIALLY AS WE grow older, we realize just how quickly the years have passed. An event clearly illustrating this time flight was our parents' fiftieth wedding anniversary, in May 1989.

As that historic occasion approached, our family debated on how best to celebrate. Mom and Dad had been very clear they wanted no part of a "big anniversary party." "If you must have something," we were told, "then just immediate family." Some thought we should abide by their wishes, but after lengthy discussion, a "big anniversary party" won the vote. We'd never paid much attention to what our parents had said in the past...why change now!

Once decided, the next question was: where? Different locations were discussed, explored, and discarded. Finally the Palmerston Presbyterian church basement was selected as most suitable, because it was familiar, comfortable, and compact.

I was selected to broach the subject. "Now, about your

anniversary," I began over a cup of tea two or three days later. I was instantly interrupted, as Mom and Dad reiterated their earlier stand.

"Well, I recognize your position, but you have to agree that fifty years is a significant milestone." I was met with silence.

"We sort of have to do something," I added, hoping for some response at least.

Under continued silence, I pressed on. "We thought we'd have supper at Ranton Place"—this was a favourite local eating establishment of theirs—"just family." I emphasized "family," figuring they could learn of their brothers, sisters, cousins, nephews, nieces, grandchildren, neighbours, and close friends later.

"Now, before the meal, we thought we'd have a small open house at the church"—(I emphasized "small")—"just on the off chance someone wants to drop by and say hello."

Mom asked a couple of general questions, and Dad repeated his "no party" stand, but otherwise the exchange was heavily one-sided, and I gladly switched to a different topic. Over the next few weeks, I guess Dad continually grumbled and complained to Mom about how he wished we'd just forget the entire episode. Mom had retreated somewhat by this point, stating that "if the kids think enough of us to go to all this trouble, the least we can do is try to show our appreciation."

The designated Sunday arrived, and shortly before 2 p.m., the celebrated couple did as well—Dad appearing not to have been dragged too far. The previous hour, we'd strung streamers, inflated balloons, set up chairs and tables, and organized a table to accept cards and gifts—despite the "no gifts" announcement.

Mom and Dad were visibly impressed with our preparations, especially the wedding photos we'd enlarged and displayed along with a copy of their marriage license. Other photos provided a snapshot of their fifty years together. On a blackboard, Richard had sketched a drawing of a 1930 Chevrolet (their honeymoon car), printing "JUST MARRIED" on the front bumper. Other items of interest included a congratulatory letter from then-Prime Minister Brian Mulroney—although since she was a lifelong supporter of the Liberal Party, Mom probably paid little attention to the Conservative PM's message. She showed more enthusiasm for Ontario Liberal Premier David Petersen's remarks pertaining to their special day.

So far removed from the world of reality, I was under the impression these messages were automatically dispersed by some governmental department entirely devoted to recognizing celebratory occasions. (Apparently there is a department dedicated to this purpose, but one must fill out an application with all the required information.) Somewhere in this administration process, the application from Vivien Cober (my sister) commemorating the golden anniversary of HAROLD and EVELYN TURNER was transformed by a governmental official into a handsome, leather-bound, gilt-edged congratulatory greeting for HAROLD and EVELYN COBER.

Well-wishers began arriving within minutes of the 2:00 p.m. posting and never ceased. It seemed the entire Presbyterian Church congregation and half the town's population was in attendance at some point. School chums, friends, relatives, and neighbours from a large geographical expanse kept the church basement full, convenors rushing, and our parents occupied.

Probably the most satisfying moment was listening to our parents expound on the glorious afternoon they'd enjoyed.

"I'm so glad you didn't listen to us," commented Mom. "It was such a delight seeing so many people we hadn't seen in years."

Fifty years...such changes they'd seen. When our parents spoke their vows that afternoon back in 1939, North America had just endured the longest and most devastating economic upheaval in history, and the world was perched on the brink of war. One hundred days later, that fear became reality—then followed six years of shortages, rationing, and gloomy news reports from far-off places, where the Allies were fighting for their lives as well as world freedom. It was a challenge reading the lengthy casualty lists in the daily newspaper, and praying that you wouldn't recognize a name. But that was only a dream—no one was left untouched in this world battle.

Then came the postwar economic boom, when job opportunities were high and unemployment numbers low, and when practically anyone could buy a new car, new appliances, or any number of electronic gadgets, using something called credit. Our parents witnessed the end of the "golden age of radio" and marvelled at a new medium...television.

They saw the end of the pain and suffering of polio and the dawning of the "wonder drug" penicillin. "Iron Curtain" and "Cold War" became regularly used phrases. They tried to grasp the magnitude of the atomic age, holding their breath when events would push the nuclear threat to the extreme. They stood fascinated as Sputnik circled the earth, and twelve years later watched Neil Armstrong step from his spacecraft onto the rocky surface of the moon.

During that fifty-year span, the Berlin Wall came and

went, seven Canadian Prime Ministers and ten US Presidents came and went, and Canada's national flag—the "Red Ensign"—simply went.

Automobile colours changed from mostly black to dual- and even triple-toned colour schemes, with V8 engines seemingly powerful enough to propel rockets...before a politically motivated group of oil producing countries in the Middle East figured out the concept of supply and demand, and turned off the tap. Dozens of well-known and respected marques disappeared from the North American automotive landscape, replaced by strange nameplates from Japan. My parents had also witnessed the birth of a German car, which at the outset seemed little more than a joke, but evolved into a world sales phenomenon.

Through all this change, our parents struggled to provide the physical necessities for six children, as well as the more abstract qualities of human values and principles that would shape our lives in the years to come. From Chalmers Presbyterian Church in Toronto in 1939, they would follow a road of twists and turns that would lead them...not always smoothly...through the counties of Grey, Peel, Simcoe, and Perth.

As I watched Mom and Dad chatting with old friends and renewing acquaintances from decades ago, it occurred to me how people of my generation and before often dwell on events of the past, particularly childhood, as the greatest times of their lives. I'm certain my parents' generation was no different. They no doubt had plenty of good times—yet I was struck by the worry, suffering, sickness, and tragedy that were part of everyday life. Diseases such as diphtheria, polio, and tuberculosis, which attacked without warning and without cure; global outbreaks, like the influenza epidemic; two world wars of unbelievable carnage; stock market crashes; a crippling economic depression lasting a decade...I wonder if these were indeed the "good old days."

When my parents moved off the farm and into town in 1979, Dad retired, while Mom continued her job as head librarian at the Palmerston branch for three more years before retiring at age seventy. Dad might have withdrawn from the workforce, but he became a regular fixture on Palmerston's main street. Whether the drug store, variety store, post office, or grocery store, Dad was there. Groceries were a particular obsession—if a commodity was on sale, into the cart it went. At one point I recall close to forty cans of Aylmer tomato soup on their pantry shelf, and when wheat prices began to rise, Dad stocked up on Cream of Wheat porridge. It was the same story when a severe frost in Brazil threatened to send coffee prices spiralling.

Early in 1996, at 82 years of age, Dad was diagnosed with bowel cancer, and although he refused treatment at the outset ("I've had a good life"), he relented when facing strong family opposition. A month later, he was back on Palmerston's downtown street, resuming his shopping schedule.

Next to the L & M grocery store, Dad's most popular location remained the post office. Anyone who knew Dad well during the last ten years of his life realized he was a compulsive letter writer. Cousins, siblings, children, grandchildren, nephews, and nieces were all recipients of Dad's lengthy letters.

Actually "letter" was a misnomer...historical essays would be a more accurate description, as Dad's missives often encompassed a half-dozen pages. He'd compose as many as six a week, and all had to be posted Monday morning, come thunderstorm, blizzard, or any extreme of temperature—no exceptions! Mom would plead for him to reconsider, but to no avail. "Hazel will be expecting my letter on Wednesday," he'd say, and off he'd head into whatever Mother Nature might offer.

An event that captured Dad's character fully at this time was the death of his sister Evelyn. Dad made it clear he would not attend the funeral or visitation.

"I want my memories to be of the good times we knew, and remember what a wonderful and loyal sister she was...not displayed in a casket as in some pagan ritual for everyone to stare at!"

This declaration was no idiosyncrasy, but rather a flash-back to that terrible day nearly seventy years earlier when his mother lay in state in their family living room. That disturbing scene remained embedded in his subconscious and haunted him for life.

During the summer of 1997, Dad's cancer returned, spreading to his kidneys...and this time there were no options. Following a week at Stratford, Dad returned to Palmerston, making it much easier for Mom, since the hospital was just two blocks away. It was convenient for me as well, and I visited every afternoon upon completion of my courier route.

During what proved to be one of my last visits, Dad asked if I'd say "a few words" at his memorial service. I hesitated, and not just because of the nature of the request, but more acutely because of the reality of the request! Two days later, with his family by his side, my father passed on, in search of whatever it was that lay ahead.

During the next few days we all spent time reliving our special moments. I recalled a comment made just a few days earlier. Dad was reminiscing about school days or something. "You know people are always talking about the good old days," he had said, "but it's not the good old days…it's the good old memories."

My memories are infinite. I recall his "women speeches." I'm sure all my brothers received a variation of this address at some point. The key ingredient was respect. It took a special sort of patience and understanding, Dad said, to coexist in this emotional topography better known as the world of women. I guess he figured through these talks that we would gain a better understanding and be better prepared for the male-female relationships that ultimately lay ahead.

Dad knew of which he spoke. In many instances, our mother will be remembered for her shyness. But just as easily, her ignitable personality could flare brightly and strongly at a moment's notice. With these ever-changing patterns and temperaments in mind, Dad obviously felt qualified to offer his experience in this complicated field.

A fond and personal memory of mine is a simple one: how Dad always wore a tie when I visited. Ever since my parents had moved to town eighteen years earlier, if at all possible I'd drop by on a once- or twice-a-week schedule. Over a cup of tea and a homemade biscuit or muffin, Dad and Mom would bring me up to date on the gossip around town, what our relatives were doing, what books they were reading, and so on. And no matter what shirt or sweater Dad might be wearing, it would be accented with a tie. I mentioned once he didn't need to dress up for me. He answered simply, "I like dressing up for company."

Personally, I seldom wear a tie…but as I stood at the Presbyterian Church lectern that October day in 1997, fulfilling my father's promise, you can bet I was wearing one!

It was 1935 when Dad first came to Toronto, so the end of a relationship of that duration took some adjustment. An incident Mom could have survived nicely without happened exactly two months to the day from Dad's death. Some spilled grease ignited by the stove quickly spread to the cupboards, very nearly destroying the entire kitchen. For the next two months, while the kitchen was being renovated and the rest of the house fumigated, Mom took up residence at Royal Terrace, a first-class retirement-and-nursing home just two blocks away.

Mom had suffered a couple of falls the previous winter, and with another winter season approaching, we secretly hoped this new environment, free of domestic chores, might become permanent. However, it was clear she wasn't ready for this step, and just wanted to get back home.

Back on Boulton Street, Mom again tried to adjust to life alone. She seldom missed church, and continued to make her twice-a-week trek to the library—but we could see that her energy level was decreasing as the months passed. Reading always consumed a large portion of each day—next to family, books had always remained the most significant aspect of her life.

Perhaps we didn't fully recognize the significance of this event at the time, but in 1999, the death of Mom's long-time friend Peggy Hayes hit hard. They'd met while attending college in Toronto in 1931, and had been the closest of friends ever since. Mom's grief was great enough without the painful circumstance of only learning about the death through her sister Alma, who lived in Toronto. Several days after the fact, Alma was catching up on her newspaper reading, and happened to recognize Peggy's name in the *Toronto Star* obituary column.

In December of that year, Mom took ill, and upon hospitalization it was confirmed she'd suffered a slight heart attack. "I have to be home by Christmas," she insisted. When it became apparent that that wasn't possible, New Years' became the target.

It had been Mom's wish for as long as I can remember to witness the arrival of the new century. There was a great deal of rhetorical comment and scare tactics employed in previous months about how the world would probably quit revolving when all the computers, whose internal clocks hadn't been designed for the millennium, shut down. I recall Mom's comment when I visited her the day after New Years'. "Well," she said, "that was a lot of fuss over nothing wasn't it?"

It almost seemed there was nothing left to live for when that milestone passed, and Mom grew steadily weaker in the following two weeks. When she no longer had the strength or will to read, we knew her time had run out.

The day following her passing, I was at the local hardware store in Listowel. My niece's husband was behind me in the checkout line, and he offered his condolences. In conversation, I mentioned how almost the entire time Mom was hospitalized, she never relinquished the hope that she would be returning to her little house on Boulton Street. George nodded, paused a few seconds, then added, "Well, now she's home."

In 2013, my sister-in-law Peggy compiled an absolutely delightful collection of photographs, captions, and historical footnotes into an eleven-by-fourteen-inch, twenty-page hardcover memorial booklet that depicts our family's history over the past century—particularly the fifty-year span Mom and Dad spent together. On the final page of this testament to our past are two photographs that, like all photographs, capture a tick of time that can never be recreated, but which will never be forgotten.

These two photos, snapped probably within a sixty-second timeframe, included a barely discernible Brantford Twine wall calendar that set the date as January 1, 1960. The first, taken by Mom, captures the entire family sitting at the kitchen table of our Wallace Township farmhouse. The second image is courtesy my brother Bill, and features the same scene and characters, but is shot from the opposite side of the room.

So many powerful childhood memories are re-established from those two photographs. Although they are in black and white, my mind can reconstruct the colour of every shirt and sweater my brothers and I were wearing, as well as the various shades of the heavily-patterned wallpaper and drapes. I recall the dark-stained wainscoting that practically surrounded the kitchen, its colour matched by solid oak doorframes that were embraced with intricate mouldings. I remember also the painted wooden chairs that continually changed colour in accordance with our mother's impulse and inclination.

In the forefront, Don, my youngest brother, is sitting on one of the good dining room chairs, as there were never enough kitchen chairs for everyone. The Universal refrigerator in the north-east corner; the cupboards Mom updated every half-dozen years or so in vibrant new tones such as yellow and turquoise; the kitchen's east wall, dominated by heavy winter apparel hanging on steel hooks; Mom's window-sill plants; our calendars; our lone candle-within-a-wreath Christmas decoration hanging in the kitchen's west window...are all etched in memory.

The kitchen table—complete with paint chips—was the nucleus of farm family life in the mid-twentieth century, and these photographs telegraph that atmosphere with absolute clarity. Gathered around that wooden structure, our parents appear youthful and ageless, and for an hour or two at least, seem detached from the outside-world problems of snow-clogged laneways, frozen water pipes, and financial obligations. And we kids seem to be still retaining the smiles and relaxed innocence of the magical season just passed. In the grand scheme of the world, these photographs represent but a moment in time...but what a special moment!

In conjunction with these keepsakes from another time, my sister-in-law printed an accompanying caption: "Ordinary photos at the time are treasures fifty years later."

In reality...those photos were treasures the second the camera shutter clicked.

Homestead on the Hill

The 8th concession of Artemesia Township, known now as the Municipality of Grey Highlands, originates at the southern extremity of the hamlet of Eugenia, heading east straight as an arrow some twenty-five kilometres to the Grey-Simcoe County border.

The first crossroads east of the village is the Rock Mills side road; the next is known simply as Side Road 35. Turn left at this intersection, and within a short distance you will approach a sharp incline. At the foot of this incline, an approximately four-by-one-foot blue sign with contrasting letters informs travellers they are about to ascend "Turner's Hill." Only recently was it designated as such, but for more than a century that was the unofficial title, used by anyone familiar with the area.

Proceed up the steep grade, and at the very apex on the right-hand side are a set of farm buildings—buildings now so overgrown that one must drive slowly to catch a glimpse of the large brick house hidden within the forested laneway, and a barn only visible through a narrow gap in the in the tree-lined roadway in front of the property.

For the greater part of a century, this farm was home to four generations of my family. In the early 1870s, Solomon Turner, my great grandfather, emigrated from Lincolnshire, England, living for a while in York Mills, where he meant his future wife, Martha, a Charlottetown PEI native. In 1888, Solomon and Martha relocated to Artemesia Township, purchasing 100 acres in the Beaver Valley near the village of Eugenia.

A few years later, with their family of five girls and three boys outgrowing the valley farm, they bought 200 acres of trees and rocks on Sideroad 35 between the 8th and 10th concessions of Artemesia. Clearing as many acres as was humanly possible over a period of a decade, and constructing a barn and house, my great-grandparents eventually sold the valley farm and moved into their new home. These are the buildings that now reside atop the steep grade known as Turner's Hill.

From the beginning, Turner's Hill was a formidable challenge for human and equine alike; whether hauling logs or hay, grain or gravel, the sharp ascent and equally abrupt descent became a yardstick by which travellers determined load volume, weight, and safety concerns. Early settlers to the area would boast of how many cords of wood or yards of gravel they were able to haul up Turner's Hill. And there were always stories of some unsecured load falling off halfway up the hill, or a wagon disconnecting and racing backwards down the steep slope.

When automobiles began appearing in the neighbourhood, they discovered the hill a trial as well. My grandfather on one occasion failed in his attempt to downshift as the family Chevrolet laboured up the incline. The result was a car stuck in neutral, rolling backwards down the hill until it bounced off a large rock located in the ditch before coming to rest against a rail fence.

During the last decade of the nineteenth century, when Solomon and Martha Turner set about designing the dimensions of their new home, the plan was that it be large enough that the entire family, including grandchildren, could gather on special occasions without feeling crowded (a chronic complaint in their original valley home).

But my great-grandparents were in their fifties by this time, with their children becoming scattered in the struggle to begin their own lives; hence that desire for their family to be united under one roof at some point never materialized.

Mary, the oldest child, had been the first to marry, and was living in Eugenia. She honoured Solomon and Martha with their first grandchild, but two other children died in infancy.

Belle moved to New Jersey, while both Reba and Eva relocated to Toronto. The youngest daughter, Ada, moved to a farm just outside the hamlet of Ceylon.

Solomon and Martha's oldest son, Edward, died of diphtheria at the age of 28—just two months after he was married. Isaac went west, to Winnipeg, where he remained for life.

The youngest of the Turner boys was Oliver (my grandfather). He married Janie Magee in 1910, and they took possession of the farm in 1918, when Solomon and Martha retired and moved to Eugenia. Janie passed away in 1924, while still in her thirties, leaving two children, Evelyn and Harold (my father).

Farming was a tough business a century ago when my grandfather, Oliver took over the family farm. Agriculture never capitalized on the economic buoyancy most business sectors enjoyed in the 1920s, and the Great Depression of the 1930s only magnified the challenge. Anywhere an extra dollar could be earned was welcome. Providing a team of horses and a wagon for the ongoing maintenance of township roads was one source of income. Another enterprise that helped pay the bills was logging.

There was good income from this source, but you worked for it! Every tree was felled, de-limbed, and cut into manageably-sized logs with only the aid of a crosscut saw and axe. While the snow still lay thickly on the ground, the logs were skidded from the bush by team and sleigh, and consequently hauled three miles to Rock Mills sawmill for final processing.

Throughout one winter, Oliver cut a considerable amount of timber, but the new season arrived early and he was unable to remove the logs before the snow melted. Although counting upon the income to pay that quarter's Township taxes, there was no choice but to leave the cut logs until next season's snowfall. The only good news was that the nine months extra seasoning would generate a premium at that time.

But there was also some not-so-good news, when a neighbour informed Oliver that the land on which he'd been cutting all winter was in truth not his.

Oliver realized his father had sold this particular piece of woodlot to Ontario Hydro when the Eugenia Dam was built, but had retained "cutting rights" for a specified number of years. After considerable discussion, the details became clear. There had been a leasing agreement, but it had expired, and unbeknownst to Oliver, a new lessee had assumed control.

Outwardly Oliver Turner was not one to show anger, inside it was a different story for simply allowing the lease to lapse without his knowledge. Most annoying was why his neighbour hadn't addressed this misunderstanding at the outset.

It then became clear that perhaps this had been the plan… let Oliver Turner perform the work, then, with the law on his side, step forward and collect the income for the lumber.

In a somewhat patronizing manner, the neighbour remarked he'd "allow" Oliver to retain any logs he could skid during the balance of the winter. With the calendar a full week into April and the ground bare, Oliver was well aware there would be no more log removal this season.

Oliver Turner was a deeply religious man, so he must have believed that God was on his side when three days later a heavy spring storm blanketed the area with more than a foot of snow, enabling every last log to be removed. Because of my grandfather's moral upbringing, his feeling would have been well-hidden, but I'll bet a smug satisfaction accompanied that last log as it was pulled from the bush.

At the beginning of this chapter I declared how four generations of my family have inhabited the property on Turner's Hill. Oliver was the second generation and Harold (my father) the third. When Solomon Turner retired from farming in 1918, Oliver moved his family to the original homestead on the hill, and for the next twenty-seven years, that was where my father lived.

The only exception occurred in the mid-1930s, when he left for Ontario's capital, in the hopes of making it in the business world. Thanks to the economic collapse of that period, this venture was short-lived, and within two years my father was back home.

Here he would spend the next five years—the first three for little more than free board, as the farm was barely surviving. With the arrival of the Second World War, labour markets decimated by the Depression began to open up, and when an opportunity for employment opened near Brampton Ontario in 1941, Dad left home for good.

Waiting in the wings were his two half-brothers. His father, Oliver, had married Mamie Magee in 1927. Doug was born a year later, and Eldon in 1934—the pair fourteen and twenty years younger than Harold, respectively.

Despite my father's claim that Doug and Eldon were the "two best brothers one could have," when his business venture failed and he was forced home, he made no attempt to hide his frustration...and it was often towards his brothers that he vented this frustration.

In his opinion, they weren't pulling their weight... especially Doug. There were plenty of chores a ten-year-old could perform. Oliver agreed, but Mamie argued there would be "plenty of time for work in the years ahead."

Thus Doug was allowed only to gather eggs—a "sissy" job, in Harold's mind. Occasionally, if the opportunity arose, Dad would wait until Doug entered the chicken house, then lock the door from the outside and simply walk away. "It offered satisfaction at the time," Dad recalled.

Although his involvement may have been restricted, that didn't mean Doug wasn't interested in the farm itself. He became enthusiastically involved in a school project whereby everyone planted a tree. Doug's venture consisted of planting a walnut tree in the front yard. Despite windstorms, ice storms, and other whims of nature, as well as my father backing over it (accidentally) with the car, the tree not only survived, but thrives eighty years later.

Doug and his father also undertook another ambitious project: the stone fence that paralleled the road in front of their property was pushed, pulled, dragged, hauled then reassembled on the opposite side of the road. Believing the relocated stone fence looked barren, Oliver dug up several cedar seedlings and planted them on top of the stone wall. Fred Wilkinson, long-time hired man and family friend, doubted this exercise. "You realize, Oliver, that you'll never live to see those trees grown!"

Well, old Fred was wrong. My grandfather was on this earth for another twenty years, by which time a fine thick row of cedar trees stretched high beyond the fence line.

Doug actually paid far more interest to the farm than to schooling. He attended just a single year of high school, riding to Flesherton with a neighbour friend, Earl Magee. Although classes didn't begin until nine, and it was but a ten-minute drive, Earl always arrived at the Turner house shortly after eight. This wouldn't have been a major deal, except that mornings weren't Doug's strong suit.

"Earl's here!" his mother would holler up the stairs. Not wanting Earl to know Doug was still in bed, Mamie would race upstairs, bowl of shredded wheat in hand. Doug could gobble down his cereal upstairs, then arrive downstairs ready to go and Earl none the wiser.

If Doug took little interest in higher education, Eldon took even less. Soon after Eldon began classes, the local 8th Line school closed for lack of enrollment, and Eldon was transferred to Rock Mills, adding another two miles to the daily trek. Not familiar with the kids and not enthused about school anyway, truancy proved to be his favourite subject.

For a six-year-old, Eldon was quite ingenious with his

excuses. Facial expressions that advertised absolute sincerity were almost a practiced art.

"The teacher's sick," he'd say. "There's no school today...I wasn't feeling well so the teacher sent me home... the teacher sent me home for a book I forgot..."

One day when Eldon failed to show up for classes, the teacher, familiar with his attendance record, phoned his home. When learning her little boy hadn't arrived, his mother imagined the worst. Harvest was in full force, and Dad and Oliver were busy in the fields, but they immediately stopped what they were doing and pushed the old Chevrolet into service. Along with Mamie, the three searched the concession all the way to Rock Mills, hollering Eldon's name out the window as they idled along.

"I just know something terrible has happened!" Mamie cried. "Poor little fellow probably got lost in the swamp and was eaten by a bear or wildcat!"

When the road search proved fruitless they began knocking on doors of neighbours; most were familiar with Eldon's academic record and agreed to keep watch for the young lad. One last time before returning home, the search party scoured the side road from the 8th concession all the way south to the Flesherton highway.

With no sign of the youngster, they plotted their next move. Mamie was understandably near hysterics by this point, so the plan was to return to base, regroup, and undertake a more thorough walking search, perhaps with the help of neighbours.

As they pulled into their laneway, they saw Eldon calmly sitting on the front steps. It seemed he hadn't been "in the mood" for school that day, so he simply hid out in a forested section of their farm, just a few hundred feet away. He later admitted that he'd found it quite entertaining watching the family Chevrolet drive up and down the side road, with everybody hanging out the window bawling out his name.

Before the car came to a full stop, Mamie was out of the car. Crying, she gave her son a big hug.

"I thought I'd never see you again!" she wailed. "You poor wee dear...you must be famished. You wait right here and I'll get you some lemonade and a sandwich." With that she disappeared into the house.

Reflecting on the matter years later, Dad commented, "After wasting more than two hours of a perfectly good harvest day...it certainly wouldn't have been a drink and sandwich I'd have given the little beggar!"

1950 proved a milestone for the family at the top of the hill. Commodity prices on agricultural products had at last witnessed some optimism and the Turners felt it was time to modernize. Prices were especially good for purebred cattle, and Oliver sold a couple of his prize Shorthorns. Eldon recalled that the transaction involved several hundred dollar bills. "I was sixteen," he later said, "but it was the first time I'd ever seen a hundred dollar bill."

True horsepower was traded for gasoline power with the purchase of a new Ford tractor and two-furrow plow. The twenty-year-old Chevrolet was finally retired, replaced by a two-year-old Chevy. Perhaps even more exciting was when hydro arrived on Turner's Hill.

Electric power had been a long time coming. Back in 1940, four neighbours had signed with Ontario Hydro, thus allowing the service to be extended from Eugenia east along the 8th concession. Whenever circumstances dictated the affordability of pole and wire installation to the hilltop, the

Turners would have it too; a decade would pass before this goal became reality.

By 1950 Oliver had reached the age of 70, so this major shift from the "horse age" was largely left to his sons. Four years later, Doug purchased his own farm near Shelburne, and Eldon became head of farm operations. In 1957, he and his wife Iowna officially took possession of the original two-lot homestead, as well as the farm directly across the road.

If one were to ask Eldon and Iowna to quantify their years of farming atop Turner's Hill into a single phrase, it would probably be "long hours, hard work, and little money." One might also add picking stones—a task that consumed not hours, or even days, but weeks each season. When Eldon's grandfather purchased this particular chunk of land, he realized it was prolific with stones; unfamiliar with the geology of the area, Solomon Turner surmised it would be a one-time endeavour. Was he—and every generation thereafter—in for a surprise!

In 1979 Eldon and Iowna sold the home farm and moved across the road to land that had been part of the Turner homestead since the beginning. Here my aunt and uncle severed a lot from the agricultural acreage and built the house in which they live today. Looking for a new challenge, Eldon undertook a salesman's role for the local Ford implement dealer before securing a job as custodian at Beavercrest Elementary School in Markdale, where he worked until retirement age.

At the same time, Iowna began a job at Grey Gables Retirement Home, also in Markdale, as a personal support worker. After retirement age, she worked as a volunteer for the retirement centre for another decade or more.

Move the calendar ahead to July, 2014. Lynne Turner, Eldon and Iowna's eldest daughter, was attending a funeral at Rock Mills Baptist church, and noted that during the minister's eulogy a couple of references were made to "Turner's Hill," where the recently departed had lived for many years. That reference, in conjunction with her Uncle Doug Turner's funeral just a week earlier, prompted Lynne to investigate the possibility of officially designating the hill as such.

As an added incentive, her parents would be celebrating their eightieth birthdays later that year, and their sixtieth wedding anniversary the following spring.

Unsure how to begin, Lynne sent a letter of intent to the local council. On July 28, a letter describing her proposal was presented to council, who in turn passed it on to the Legislative Services Department. Their task, in conjunction with the Artemesia Museum and Heritage Committee, was to provide the necessary research for the request, and report back to the council.

On August 27, Lynne was advised that her request was being reviewed by all interested parties, but because of an Ontario provincial election and summer recess to follow, it was anticipated to be late September before she would receive any updated information.

Lynne asked for a progress report in late October, but little transpired until February. At this time, the council stated they were finalizing their report, but needed assurance that all neighbours in the affected area had been properly notified and were aware of the proposal.

Lynne replied that she had accomplished that issue by verbally communicating with all concerned. The council then insisted that community consensus must be in writing, with all correspondence forwarded directly to them. Lynne was likewise advised that despite what council may have stated at the outset, the entire cost of the signage designation, including any replacement costs, must be borne by the applicant.

Despite the appearance of dragging its feet, the council did add that if their requests were fulfilled to their satisfaction, the application would be tabled for approval March 23, 2015, and through another reversal of policy stated the project would be financed after all through a reserve fund of the Township Heritage Committee.

Lynne had been hoping from the very start of her endeavour that everything could be legalized and designated by the time of her parent's anniversary on May 14, 2015. It was a close race; on May 8, two signs were installed at the base of both southern and northern extremities of the hill. The front page of the *Flesherton Advance* the following week featured a four-column account explaining both the history of the hill and the family for which it was designated. A photo of Eldon and Iowna posing beneath the newly erected sign graced the front page.

With or without the declaration of a sign, my memories remain vivid of the farm on Turner's Hill. When I was very young I was always somewhat nervous travelling north on the narrow tree-lined artery that led to my grandparent's farm. If I was sitting by one of the rear doors of our old Pontiac I made certain the window was wound up tight, half expecting any moment for a bear, wolf or some other wild creature to spring from the thick foliage. Even when the safety of their yard was reached, the stillness and silence was eerie. Unlike at home, not a neighbour was visible, and "traffic" consisted of a car idling by perhaps every two hours.

Yet there was something magical about the place...the

colourful Barred Rock and Rhode Island Red chickens that roamed free in the yard; the herd of Shorthorn cattle being milked in the huge barn (I would ask Doug or Eldon if I could rotate the crank to operate the cream separator); the giant rock that sat behind the barn—a rock that Mother Nature, eons earlier, had carved into the distinct shape of an armchair.

I recall sheep contained in small paddocks throughout the farm. There were snakes seemingly everywhere—in the garden, in the orchard, under the porch, even in the outhouse. The ever-growing pyramids of stones, painstakingly retrieved from the surrounding fields year after year; The hand pump outside the back door, and a smaller unit adjacent to the kitchen sink, which was replenished from the cistern in the cellar. Then there were the apple trees that we'd climb as kids, or the potato patch that seemed acres in size.

Many years ago, I mentioned to Eldon that I'd like to take a walk back through the fields of the old place and renew some memories from when I was a teenager. The current proprietors were basically just using the house at this juncture, and the barn and land were for the most part neglected.

I had fond memories of walking down that rock-strewn back lane that stretched eastward from the barn, past equally proportioned fields, neatly enclosed within boundaries of rail, wire, and stone. As I strolled along, it wasn't difficult to imagine my ancestors making their way across these very fields, behind a team of matched horses and a single-furrow plow, maybe cutting a thick stand of timothy-alfalfa hay with a Massey-Harris mower—or, with pitchforks in hand, building sheaves under an unrelenting August sun.

My nostalgic re-creation of the past was interrupted when my uncle responded. "I took a walk back there a while ago myself. All I discovered was waist-high grass and weeds. The fences were completely overgrown. Everything appeared so rough, unfamiliar, and uncared for…I wished I'd never gone. My suggestion is don't bother…enjoy your memories."

Aware that over time, memory often trumps reality—painting a more picturesque but less accurate version of the truth—I heeded his advice.

With both my aunt and uncle now in their eighties, a time will eventually come when there will no longer be a Turner living on Turner's Hill.

Wouldn't it be interesting, after all this time, to hear Solomon and Martha's thoughts on this entire matter; to realize that the rocky hill they unofficially adopted so long ago has celebrated an unbroken 125 years of family ownership.

Memories of individual personalities fade with the years, but thanks to a whim by a future great-granddaughter, their name, and the spirit and strong sense of family values they relayed to the generations that followed, will continue indefinitely.

Rural Poetry...Final Glance

I STOPPED BY OUR NEIGHBOURHOOD CEMETERY TODAY. THERE'S something about a cemetery on an autumn afternoon that releases an inner peace that knows no equal. Strolling among the rows of granite and marble is paramount to walking down the rural side roads of yesterday. I paused to inspect the faded name on a weathered monument.

I recall my father talking about Fred Hargrave. Fred and his father had gained local recognition with their wheelbarrow races. Probably for no better reason than to dispel the monotony of cleaning stables, the duo had developed time trials. The object was to run a loaded wheelbarrow of manure from the stable to the manure pile, dump it, and return. He with the shortest time was the winner. Who knows—with a little publicity and a good sponsor it might have become an Olympic event!

Then there was Bob and Sara Smith. As the pantry shelves were often empty at home, they'd drop in at my grandfather's farm on a regular basis—usually at mealtime—on the pretext that their old horse needed a drink. Rural folk being what they are (or were), they were always invited in.

Bob and Sara were about as mismatched a couple as one could find. She was pale, petite, refined, and quiet, while Bob had a very dark complexion and coarse features, and was an incessant talker, whether or not his mouth was full. Although he seldom used a fork, Bob held one in his left hand when he ate. He used the knife clenched in his right to scoop whatever filled his plate directly into his mouth. He'd also, if the need arose, use the utensil to scratch his bald head, clean his fingernails, pick his teeth, or whack the flies that strayed near.

A neat white memorial brought back memories of Waldimar Crossland. When I recall Waldy I'm reminded of a friendly man in short pants. Up until that time, I'd been under the impression that only kids wore short pants. Waldy performed custom baling for us during the 1950s. One day a thunderstorm was brewing, and, knowing that Dad was at work and the hay he'd baled earlier was in danger, Waldy drove over to our place, retrieved the 100 or so bales from the ground, loaded them on his wagon, and placed the load in our barn before it rained. To Waldy, thoughtfulness and kindness were simply second nature.

Shortly after, the Crosslands moved from the neighbourhood. We dropped into their place one afternoon preceding their relocation. Waldy and his wife were packing up their belongings, and on top of one cardboard box lay an army bugle.

"How would you like to have this, son?" asked Waldy, placing the bugle in my hand. I just looked at it, so he took the instrument, placed it to his lips, and played a bit of the army reveille.

"You can use this to wake up your parents," cracked Waldy, handing it back.

By the time I reached home I was quite excited about the prospect of becoming the next "little boy blue." However I couldn't coax a sound from that horn except "pfft...pfft...pfft." I tried for a couple of days, but the result was always the same. Nobody else seemed to have much luck either. We must not have had the correct breathing technique or lip shape or something.

Whatever became of that old bugle I don't know; when no one was able to produce anything resembling music, it was probably tossed. I wonder whether in his final years Waldy ever gave any thought to that old war memento? I wonder if he remembered to whom he gave it? Hopefully not.

The thick granite gravestone of our next door neighbour, Mickey McGivern, mirrored his personality. He was a powerful man with shoulders like cement blocks. Mickey's right arm had been crippled since childhood, but the left more than compensated. Stories about his "good" arm were legendary. In one, Mickey was in the local hotel, and as the whisky took hold, he began bragging about the one-hundred-dollar bill he had in his possession. When he left for the washroom, a couple of punks tried to relieve him of the bill. But they were no match for Mickey drunk or sober, one arm or two. Both in short order found themselves embracing the washroom floor, followed by climactic headfirst shove down the basement stairs.

Mickey's frenzies of displeasure were well-documented. Once he purchased a pull-type John Deere combine for

$450 at a dealer close-out sale. "For that price a fellow can't lose," he commented to me.

However, the machine had been sitting idle for several seasons, exposed to the elements, and now it was completely seized. When a few minutes of aptly chosen four-letter words in conjunction with a long-handled pipe wrench failed to free any of the frozen bearings, Mickey picked up a sledge hammer, venting his frustration against the machine's metal framework. Returning the combine complete with dents, Mickey demanded his money back. Despite the "no return" policy, the dealer obliged...no questions asked!

Mickey had a hired man named Rufus, who was what used to be referred to as "retarded." The County paid Mickey a monthly allowance for his welfare, and in return, Mickey got an extra hand. Rufus wore an interesting wardrobe much of the time...an old tweed suit, topped by a yellow hard hat. Rufus' vocabulary was limited...mostly swear words. That should have come as no surprise, since he was in the regular company of Mickey, who probably held the local record for the longest string of obscenities in a single sentence. Rufus went to town every Saturday night—sometimes in the car with Mickey, and sometimes walking. If you were within earshot, you could hear Rufus muttering to himself as he paraded by. "Shit, goddamn. Shit, goddamn."

I passed by a modest monument and recalled that when we first moved to our Perth County farm, the Hansons were one of the first of our new neighbours to visit. They had a kid who went to our school. Jimmy wasn't in any particular grade, but rather several. He was in grade three arithmetic, grade one reading, and grade two spelling. Jimmy's parents may have lacked finesse in their grasp of events outside their neighbourhood, but they seemed a likable pair. The pinnacle of the Sunday evening visit, as I recall, was Mr. and Mrs. Hanson chatting breezily about some major car accident that had occurred the previous autumn, just a quarter mile away.

"The Mercury went right up the side of that elm tree," declared Bill Hanson, rising from his chair and pointing out the kitchen window. "Skinned the bark off that tree like a banana! You probably noticed...it's still plain as day."

"There was nothing recognizable left of the one guy," interjected his wife. "And the other guy...well..."

"Then there was that '55 Buick that hit the bridge down there," Bill went on. "It must've been going 100 miles an hour!" His eyes were as big as saucers. "The impact split that big V8 in two!"

It's curious the fascination some glean from roadside carnage. One weekend a neighbour of ours was involved in a head-on collision that nearly killed his daughter. The following evening another neighbour rolled in just as we were finishing supper. "Hey Harold," he said. "I was just heading into town up to see what's left of Wesley's car! Do you want to come?" I'm sure there were things Dad would have rather done. However, he went along to survey the mangled Ford.

As a kid I was no better. Anytime a collision occurred at our intersection I'd be on my bike and on the scene usually before the police. There was the time a Texaco fuel truck broadsided that '57 Pontiac. Another time a Fargo pickup pulled out in front of that '56 Dodge, which ultimately landed on its roof in the ditch. The "best" was when that '53 Ford failed to yield for that furniture truck. The Ford was demolished and the 18-wheeler came to rest on its side leaning against a tree, its trailer split wide open. It took a good part of a day to clean that one up!

I don't recall any life-threatening injuries in the above mentioned catastrophes. I never gave any thought there might be human injury...I was interested only in mangled metal. For someone who constantly agonized about their parents' safety when they were away, I'm at a loss to understand my fascination at the time with highway mayhem.

"Easy going" was the phrase that came to mind as I stopped at Emerson Stoltz's monument. Emerson was habitually a season behind everyone else in the neighbourhood. While haying would be in full force, Emerson would still be planting grain. When wheat and oats were being harvested, he was baling hay. He owned a vintage 1930s McCormick-International tractor that rode on steel, and what other machinery he had was a relic of the horse age. Yet strangely enough one spring he purchased a brand-new John Deere manure spreader. Its shiny green and yellow paint appeared so out of place.

One year, Emerson decided to build a new wagon rack for the upcoming haying season. He'd drive over to our place periodically and lay for lengthy periods beneath our wagon, studying the frame, noting the bracing, monitoring not only the thickness of the lumber but the kind and grade as well; all the while observing, measuring, and making mental and written notes to assist with his creation. The haying season came and went, and Emerson was still engrossed in the planning stages of his manufacturing masterpiece. One sultry evening while he was supposedly fabricating the final planning details of his project, I looked under the wagon to see how he was faring...he was fast asleep.

Yesterday's Moments...Today's Memories

In a remote corner of the cemetery, far from real-world distractions, I paused beneath the inviting boughs of a huge maple. The only audible sound was the hushed whisper of drying leaves floating softly onto the colourful and thickening mantle at my feet.

As I stood there, lost in time among the avenues of monuments, it occurred to me that practically every name to whom I had paid tribute this day were farmers—individuals who almost without exception expended their entire life working a 100 acre parcel of land in a seemingly unhurried existence.... but an existence that was now long gone. In this solitude it was easy for my heightened senses to clearly remember these departed friends and neighbours... a smile perhaps, or a laugh, or a distinct temperament or idiosyncrasy that somehow set them apart.

In this slower-paced world of the mid-twentieth century, there was always time to attend a couple of local fall fairs. The one-room community school was still the nucleus of the neighbourhood; where functions celebrating primary school students and grade eight graduates were held, new neighbours were welcomed and old neighbours bid farewell. These gatherings were the ideal venue for neighbours to converse on community news and gossip, and were often integrated with euchre, "Lost Heir," or crokinole tournaments. The annual Christmas concert guaranteed a packed house, and political rallies, school board meetings, and public speaking expositions were all vital components of this close-knit community experience.

But that unique identity recognized as "the 100 acre farm" has now passed on. 1000 acres is now the yardstick by which most agricultural operations are measured. In the 1950s and 60s, only custom operators providing heavy-duty tillage or silage harvesting owned 100 horse-power tractors; this horsepower range is considered a "chore" tractor nowadays. And the 40-60 horsepower machines that we utilized for the everyday assault on heavy clay and steep hills have now become the "lawn" tractors of weekend urbanites.

Change is inevitable, and most of it is positive. The personal connection with communities has perhaps been the biggest loser. I'm not lamenting a way of life passed...nor am I trying to be particularly nostalgic...just call it a reflective mood if you will. There's something very personal but difficult to define about growing up on a small family farm; a feeling of unequalled freedom and wonder that only one born close to the earth can truly appreciate.

In today's world of seemingly endless scientific advancement, perhaps we need a technological time-out, a chance to pause and recall a simpler (not necessarily better or easier) time...just a relaxed rearward glance, if for no other reason than to see how far we have come.

Canadian author H. Gordon Greene, a contributing editor to *Family Herald* magazine for decades, must have been in a reflective mood as well some fifty years ago when commenting on the passing of this important element of our heritage:

> When the last small farmer is forced from our landscape, we will have suffered something far more than irreparable damage to our external strength; nor will it merely mark the passing of a certain kind of pastoral poetry...we will have lost part of our soul.

David and Mary at their Bluevale home (2015)

Epilogue

The expression "it's a small world" is often applied to events that colour our lives...measures that appear suddenly or unexpectedly.

After spending fifty-seven years in Perth County, thirty-four of them married, my wife and I retired to Huron County in 2014; in a sense, our new next door neighbour Diane was already familiar with our family, having recently purchased my first book. Imagine her surprise when reading that my father had worked at B.H. Bull and Sons, a large Brampton Ontario dairy farm.

That was in the 1940s. At the time and for many years after, B.H. Bull had the largest Jersey cattle herd in North America, milking over three hundred cows. My father was one of more than sixty workers that Bull employed.

Diane had grown up in the heart of Brampton, and as a young girl recalled seeing the cattle grazing in the surrounding fields. Her family operated a garage in Brampton, initially selling and servicing Hudson cars and International Harvester trucks and, later, Mack trucks.

Bull's contracted the entirety of their milk and livestock hauling needs to Moore's Trucking, who purchased and serviced their vehicles at Diane's family's dealership.

By the early 1960's, most of the dairy herd had been dispersed. Brampton and a scattering of nearby villages and towns, collectively to become known as Mississauga, slowly but methodically swallowed what was once the dairy farm.

Thanks to a dedicated historical society, the main house on the Bull estate was saved and is now a designated heritage building, while a section of what was once the southwest corner of the farm has evolved into Peel Village Park. Retained as a faint reminder of Brampton's agricultural roots, the street circling the perimeter of this park has been named after the Bull family.

Winding leisurely through this park is Etibicoke Creek, where seventy-five years ago Jersey cattle quenched their thirst. Traversing the narrow waterway and undoubtedly the focal point of this picturesque park is a wooden footbridge; a bridge across which my father often walked in the early morning hours to retrieve the cattle from their pasture for the upcoming milking.

Beginning in the early 1960's, the floral gardens of Peel Village and in particular the quaint charm of the wooden bridge became a popular setting for wedding photos. In 1969, one of the couples who took advantage of this scenic pictorial was my neighbour Diane and her husband. Like I said...small world.

One last thought...the year was 1944, and my grandfather William Carruthers had just presented my two-year-old brother, Bill, a tricycle constructed from odds and ends scrounged from the Massey-Harris reject bin where he worked. A chunk of maple cut from a packing crate served as a seat, while various pieces of strapping and tubing provided the handlebars and frame. Two brass rear wheels were courtesy of a discarded feed cart. The tricycle, although crude, provided transportation for a year or two before being junked. Our father, herdsman for a dairy operation in Simcoe County at the time, observed how one of the brass wheels would make an ideal candidate for a much-needed drain cover in the milk house's concrete floor.

Occasionally over the years I'd re-visited the Simcoe County farm where I was born, noting how little things had changed… the dairy actively producing milk as it had for decades.

The clock moves steadily onward, and in May 2015, Bill and I attended an auction sale in the area and decided to stop in at the farm that held so many memories.

In the interim, major changes had altered the landscape; on the pastured hills where Holsteins once roamed and Oliver tractors laboured, an eighteen-hole golf course resided. Although appearing tired and faded, the 160-year-old barn still projected a presence of strength, but all vestiges of the concrete and steel stabling had been removed. The place where two long rows of Holsteins once patiently waited to be milked was now was crowded with golf carts, lawn mowers, and other indicators of this cultural shift.

The milk house was crowded with what appeared to be leftovers from a garage sale. Plastic toys, clothes, appliances, and cardboard boxes struggled for space on the cracked concrete floor once dominated by milking equipment. Trying to gain some semblance of the massive change surrounding us, we stood lost in thought.

Turning to go, Bill's attention was drawn to something. Taking a couple of steps across the floor, he reached down, retrieved a heavy round metal object from a recess in the concrete, and handed it to me. I stared at the metal wheel; not as an inanimate object but rather what it represented. It was the brass wheel our father had placed there seventy years earlier!

Arguing that he should remain in possession of this link to our family's past, my brother simply answered, "I know you'll take care of it."

With not a person or a metal detector in sight, I carried my little piece of family history to Bill's truck. It was easy to convince myself that this chunk of brass was a part of our heritage and was merely being returned to its rightful owners. Driving slowly out the angled maple and oak-lined laneway, I glanced at the special object on the seat between us. To most, its plain and unobtrusive appearance, dulled by decades of drainage control, would merit not a second look. To me, it was a direct link to the legacy of my grandfather—its value limitless.

No doubt it was with pride and satisfaction my grandfather constructed that tricycle for my brother. Heading home that day seventy years later, I couldn't help but feel the same emotions.